P9-DFW-167

UNDERSTANDING THE NATURE OF POVERTY IN URBAN AMERICA

UNDERSTANDING THE NATURE OF POVERTY IN URBAN AMERICA

James Jennings

Prepared under the auspices of the William Monroe
Trotter Institute, University of Massachusetts at Boston

In cooperation with The Boston Foundation's
Persistent Poverty Project

Westport, Connecticut
London

Library of Congress Cataloging-in-Publication Data

Jennings, James.
  Understanding the nature of poverty in urban America / James
Jennings.
    p.   cm.
  "Prepared under the auspices of the William Monroe Trotter
Institute, the University of Massachusetts at Boston. In cooperation
with the Boston Foundation's Persistent Poverty Project."
  Includes bibliographical references and index.
  ISBN 0–275–94953–2 (alk. paper).—ISBN 0–275–94984–2 (pbk.)
    1. Urban poor—United States.   2. Public welfare—United States.
I. William Monroe Trotter Institute.   II. Boston Foundation's
Persistent Poverty Project.   III. Title.
HV4045.J46   1994
362.5′ 0973—dc20   94–16111

British Library Cataloguing in Publication Data is available.

Library of Congress Catalog Card Number: 94–16111
ISBN: 0–275–94953–2
    0–275–94984–2 (pbk.)

First published in 1994

Praeger Publishers, 88 Post Road West, Westport, CT 06881
An imprint of Greenwood Publishing Group, Inc.

Printed in the United States of America

The paper used in this book complies with the
Permanent Paper Standard issued by the National
Information Standards Organization (Z39.48–1984).

10 9 8 7 6 5 4 3

*Dedicated to the memory of my grandmother
Esperanza Guzman
who taught me that the most heroic examples
of sacrifice, struggle, and sharing are found
among poor people*

CONTENTS

TABLES AND FIGURES ix

PREFACE xi

ACKNOWLEDGMENTS xiii

INTRODUCTION 1

CHAPTER I 9
What Is Poverty, and How Is Poverty
Measured by the Federal Government?

CHAPTER II 19
What Kinds of National Policies
Have Been Utilized to Manage Poverty?
—— From the New Deal to the Clinton Administration

CHAPTER III 55
What Are the Major Characteristics and
Trends Associated with Poverty in the United States,
and How Are Race and Ethnicity Reflected in These Trends?

CHAPTER IV 79
What Are the Major Explanations
for Persistent Poverty in the United States?

CHAPTER V 109
What Are the Major Characteristics
and Themes Reflected in the United States
Welfare System and Anti-Poverty Policies?

CHAPTER VI 123
How Is the "Underclass" Defined and Explained?

CHAPTER VII 133
How Have the Poor Utilized Political
Mobilization to Fight Poverty in the United States?

CHAPTER VIII   147
How Does Social Welfare Policy
Directed at Poverty in the United States
Compare to Social Welfare Systems in Other Countries?

CONCLUSION   157

NOTES   169

INDEX   199

TABLES AND FIGURES

TABLE 1   57
Number of Families Below Poverty Level
and Poverty Rate: 1959-1990

TABLE 2   58
Number and Proportion of Poor Persons
by Race: 1959-1988

TABLE 3   58
Persons Below the Official Poverty Level by
Race and Ethnicity: 1989 and 1990

TABLE 4   59
Poverty Status in 1989 by Regions and States

TABLE 5   61
Number and Proportion of Families in Poverty
by Race and Ethnicity: 1990

TABLE 6   63
Poverty Distribution Percentage by Place of
Residence and Race: 1986

FIGURE 1   65
Poverty Rates of Persons by Race: 1969-1989

FIGURE 2   65
Percent of Families in Poverty by
Type of Family and Race: 1969-1989

TABLE 7   68
Median Income Levels of Households
by Race and Hispanic Origin: 1970-1990

TABLE 8   75
Average AFDC Benefits to a Family of Four
Compared to Official Poverty Level:
1970, 1975, 1980 and 1991

TABLE 9   77
Workers as a Proportion of Poor Persons:
1978-1990

TABLE 10   84
Percent of Household Heads Below Poverty Line
by Education and Race: 1985

TABLE 11   94
Number of Families Below Poverty
Level by Race and Hispanic Origin:
1980-1988

TABLE 12   103
Labor Force Participation Rates of Males,
16 to 34 Years, by Race: 1950-1980

TABLE 13   116
Total Federal Government Anti-Poverty
Expenditures and Per Capita Expenditures: 1968-1987

TABLE 14   118
Federal Expenditures for Major Social Welfare
Programs: 1976 and 1984

TABLE 15   119
Estimated Federal Direct and Tax Expenditures
for Social Welfare: Fiscal Year 1990

PREFACE

In 1991, under the auspices of the Rockefeller Foundation and the Boston Foundation's Persistent Poverty Project, a racially and ethnically diverse group from labor, government, business, and religious and neighborhood organizations was convened in Boston. The forty-member Strategy Development Group, as it is called, represents extensive personal, professional, civic, and political involvement with urban poverty. With the guidance of the Strategy Development Group, the Boston Persistent Poverty Project has been working to develop effective local strategies to build community capacity and a constituency for sustained collaboration, and to provide a framework for the new skills, relationships, and leadership required for the eradication of chronic, intergenerational poverty in Boston.

After several early meetings, the Strategy Development Group expressed a need for familiarizing itself with some aspects of the vast and often contradictory literature on urban poverty. James Jennings, director of the William Monroe Trotter Institute at the University of Massachusetts at Boston and a consultant to the Boston Persistent Poverty Project, was asked to assist us with this endeavor. He suggested that one way to accomplish this would be to develop an overview of some of the major political questions and policy debates about poverty in urban America. Such a summary would provide the members of the Strategy Development Group with both a context for recent literature and a review of major theories to complement and augment their extensive direct experience. Finally, it would help the group to crystalize its thinking and develop more effective strategies.

This study focuses on eight major topics written about and debated by researchers about the nature of poverty in urban America. These topics were selected for their pertinence to questions asked by the Strategy Development Group, but we hope that they will also inform public officials, media professionals, and community-based organizations about the major public policy and research debates related to urban poverty, and narrow the information gap that too often exists between the research community and the general public.

We hope this information is useful to the many people committed to understanding and confronting one of the most difficult and pressing issues of our time: the growth of poverty in our nation's cities. We are grateful to Professor James Jennings for his timely and important contribution.

Ana Faith Jones, President
The Boston Foundation

ACKNOWLEDGMENTS

I want to acknowledge and thank several individuals for their assistance in the development and completion of this study. In 1991, Rukiah Abdul-Malik spent many hot and uncomfortable summer hours in various libraries collecting information for this work. Ilene Carver assisted this project by editing an early draft of the study. The following staff of the Trotter Institute of the University of Massachusetts were very helpful in assisting me to meet various deadlines: Muriel Ridley, Eva Hendricks, and especially Gemima Remy. Ms. Remy provided important editorial assistance throughout the project. She typed, and retyped, several drafts and also pointed out to me errors in the organization of the study. Special and great appreciation by the author is also extended to members of the faculty and staff of Boston University who in 1991 helped to initiate and plan this study. My fellow members of the Boston University team included Professor Melvin Delgado, Ms. Sherdena Cofield, and Ms. JoAnn Edinburg.

The many discussions of the Boston Foundation's Strategy Development Group helped me realize the importance of completing this study in a timely manner. The director of the Persistent Poverty Project at the Boston Foundation, Charlotte Kahn, and her staff, including Ellen Steese and Nancy Roob, were very supportive in guiding this report in its initial stages. Also, Charlotte Kahn and Jenifer Snow's early editing improved significantly the organization and flow of the book. Dr. Leticia Rivera-Torres was retained by the Trotter Institute to edit early drafts and to make suggestions regarding the germane literature. Her insightful eye was crucial to strengthening the arguments presented here. Paul Wright, editor of the University of Massachusetts Press, was also helpful in suggesting the organization of this book. Tobie Weiner, at the Massachusetts Institute of Technology, also helped significantly with editing and typing. Suzanne Baker helped to guide the production of the book in its final stages.

I would also like to thank Martin Kilson, Bette Woody, Jemadari Kamara, Estela M. Carrion, Charles Diggs, Fred Johnson, Reinaldo Rivera, Clinton Jean, and many others for all of the conversations and discussions we had on various aspects of this study. My great and deep appreciation is extended to all of these individuals. And finally, both the Boston Foundation's Persistent Poverty Project and the William Monroe Trotter Institute at the University of Massachusetts at Boston must be thanked for financial support towards initiating and completing this study.

James Jennings
William Monroe Trotter Institute
University of Massachusetts at Boston

INTRODUCTION

Such poverty as we have today in all our great cities degrades the poor, and infects with its degradation the whole neighborhood in which they live. And whatever can degrade a neighborhood can degrade a country and a continent and finally the whole civilized world, which is only a large neighborhood. Its bad effects cannot be escaped by the rich. When poverty produces outbreaks of virulent infectious disease, as it always does sooner or later, the rich catch the disease and see their children die of it. When it produces crime and violence the rich go in fear of both, and are put to a good deal of expense to protect their persons and property. When it produces bad manners and bad language the children of the rich pick them up no matter how carefully they are secluded; and such seclusion as they get does them more harm than good...The old notion that people can "keep themselves to themselves" and not be touched by what is happening to their neighbors, or even to the people who live a hundred miles off, is a most dangerous mistake...though the rich end of the town can avoid living with the poor end, it cannot avoid dying with it when the plague comes.

George Bernard Shaw (1928)

The economist Barry R. Schiller suggests that the American public has neither a complete nor a sophisticated understanding of the nature of poverty. Political scientist Adolph Reed, Jr. states more imaginatively in the title of an article that in this country there is a "poverty in the discourse about poverty." Often current discussions are not well-informed of the history of anti-poverty efforts. As Reed states: "Arguments about policy possibilities for the future need to become better anchored in an understanding of the forces that have previously shaped public social provision in the United States, especially from the New Deal to the present."[1]

In *The Economics of Poverty and Discrimination*, Schiller writes that poverty, and the related topic of welfare, arouses "the attention and interest of students, policymakers, and taxpayers alike. Mention 'welfare,' for example, and almost every taxpayer will have a firm opinion on how to improve the 'welfare mess.'"[2] He continues,

Unfortunately, the popularity of these subjects far exceeds understanding of them. In spite of extended and often heated discussions of poverty and discrimination, very little consideration has been given to the nature and sources of these social ills. As a result, popular discussions, and even public policy, are most often based on very superficial views of what poverty and discrimination are, why these phenomena exist, and what policies will eliminate them. In this context, it is hardly surprising that we often perceive only limited progress in our public efforts to combat these ills.[3]

The American public should begin to increase its level of understanding of the nature of poverty, and change the ways in which it reacts to this growing and persistent social, economic, and political problem. Sociologist, and now U.S. senator (New York), Daniel Patrick Moynihan's concern for this problem in the early 1970s, when it began to have an impact on living conditions for people of color, is still relevant: "The poverty and social isolation of minority groups in central cities is the single most serious problem of the American city today. It must be attacked with urgency, with a greater commitment of resources than has heretofore been the case, and with programs designed especially for this purpose."[4] There are conceptual barriers, however, that continue to limit the public's understanding and commitment to the elimination of poverty.

Many Americans, for instance, approach poverty as if it were only a local problem, generally divorced from major national and international economic and political developments. Related to this is the misconception that poverty is simply an "individual" problem, or the result of cultural inadequacies of certain groups. It is also common to approach poverty within a "zero-sum" political and economic framework where resources devoted to fighting poverty presumably must be detracted from other, more important problems.

Finally, as is suggested by sociologist Nathan Glazer in *The Limits of Social Policy*, the American public seems to think of the problem of poverty and social welfare responses as primarily a "black" or "Latino" problem.[5] This is reiterated by political scientists Lee Sigelman and Susan Welch: "whites view poverty as a black problem. Many whites apparently translate 'assistance to the poor' into assistance to blacks." Thus, according to these two researchers, there is "a link in the minds of whites between being poor and being black. In this sense, poverty and welfare are seen, in part, as black problems."[6] While it is true that significant proportions of black and Latino populations in the United States live in poverty, this problem exists among many racial and ethnic groups. Most Americans who experience poverty, for example, are white. Although this should not serve as an excuse for ignoring or dismissing major differences in how various racial and ethnic groups experience poverty, it does reflect the fact that poverty is not only a "black" or "Latino" problem.

Perhaps one small step in raising the public's consciousness about the growth, complexity, and extent of urban poverty is to make the American public aware of the major ideas and themes that have been generated about this problem over the last several decades. Unfortunately, much of the literature on urban poverty in America is not written for or disseminated to the people, civic organizations, and neighborhood-based groups that are attempting to reduce or eliminate poverty at a local level.

As Reed explains in the previously cited essay, "The Underclass as Myth and Symbol," much of the literature on urban poverty is written primarily for the benefit of an elite sect of the academic industry, the foundation community, or the government.[7] Literature on urban poverty — poverty trends and characteristics, the effectiveness of policies, and comparable anti-poverty efforts in other countries — is generally not written for general audiences, other than researchers or policymakers.

Unnecessary informational and conceptual gaps exist between the work and studies of many poverty researchers, the practitioners, and people who are involved in important civic and community experiences aimed at overcoming poverty. This gap makes it difficult for researchers to tap the insights of people and organizations with "hands-on" expertise in reducing poverty; it also discourages research aimed at assisting the communities being studied.

As civic and community groups around the country consider strategies to fight urban poverty, a familiarity with and an understanding of the germane literature will become increasingly important. Such understanding is crucial for better public policy and for the development by community-based organizations of effective strategies for reducing poverty. Hence, summarizing and disseminating some of the significant findings and major ideas of the massive literature on urban American poverty is the goal of this study.

Methodology of This Study

Determining how to undertake a review of selected topics and literature on urban poverty is difficult when we consider the sheer quantity of materials that has been produced. There are literally hundreds and hundreds of books, articles, and reports on poverty in America. As an indication of the scope of this literature, note the finding of Michael Wiseman, who reports that between 1983 and 1986, the *Christian Science Monitor, Los Angeles Times, New York Times, Wall Street Journal,* and *Washington Post* together published an average of 357 articles per year on welfare.[8]

Most of the studies cited in this review focus on black and Latino urban communities. This focus is not to negate the existence of white poverty. Instead, it is adopted because poverty among blacks and Latinos is more widespread and concentrated than it is among whites, as is indicated in the chapter on trends and characteristics of the poverty population. There is also less attention paid to poverty in the Asian communities of urban America, or to rural poverty. Compared to the vast literature on black poverty, and even the growing literature on Latino poverty, there is a dearth of research on Asian poverty. This is partly due to the much smaller size of this population nationally, and in part to the perception of Asians as a "model minority group."[9] As Asian communities continue to grow rapidly in urban America, however, in all likelihood there will be an increasing amount of research focusing on this community's profile and the misperceptions that have been presented about the Asian population.[10]

As already noted very little information is provided here regarding rural poverty. This should not suggest in any way that rural poverty is less significant or important than poverty in the American city. During the late 1980s there were more than 9 million poor persons in rural America. As stated by researchers Cynthia M. Duncan and Stephen Sweet, "the poverty rate among the rural population in 1987 was 17 percent, close to the 19 percent poverty rate in central cities and higher than the poverty rate for the urban population overall."[11] But the focus of this study is the American city.

The purpose of this review is not to summarize every significant piece of literature published on poverty. Such a task would be virtually impossible. Instead, this study attempts to capture the essence of the germane literature published during the last 30 or 40 years on the major ideas and questions regarding the nature of poverty in urban America. With this goal in mind, the study is organized on the basis of eight major queries that have been raised in various ways in the urban poverty literature.

These questions have been chosen for their significance for public policy, planning, and civic and neighborhood activism directed towards reducing or eliminating poverty. Each chapter is devoted to one of these queries. These queries have been raised in scholarly, government, and civic arenas over the last several decades; many have not yet been resolved definitively.

These queries are:

WHAT IS POVERTY, AND HOW IS POVERTY MEASURED BY THE FEDERAL GOVERNMENT?

WHAT KINDS OF NATIONAL POLICIES HAVE BEEN UTILIZED TO MANAGE POVERTY? — FROM THE NEW DEAL TO THE CLINTON ADMINISTRATION

WHAT ARE THE MAJOR CHARACTERISTICS AND TRENDS ASSOCI-
ATED WITH POVERTY IN THE UNITED STATES, AND HOW ARE RACE
AND ETHNICITY REFLECTED IN THESE TRENDS?

WHAT ARE THE MAJOR EXPLANATIONS FOR PERSISTENT POVERTY
IN THE UNITED STATES?

WHAT ARE THE MAJOR CHARACTERISTICS AND THEMES RE-
FLECTED IN THE UNITED STATES WELFARE SYSTEM AND ANTI-
POVERTY POLICIES?

HOW IS THE "UNDERCLASS" DEFINED AND EXPLAINED?

HOW HAVE THE POOR UTILIZED POLITICAL MOBILIZATION TO
FIGHT POVERTY IN THE UNITED STATES?

HOW DOES SOCIAL WELFARE POLICY DIRECTED AT POVERTY IN
THE UNITED STATES COMPARE TO SOCIAL WELFARE SYSTEMS IN
OTHER COUNTRIES?

For each query covered, the relevant literature has been reviewed to
determine the major ideas or debates associated with the topic. The books,
articles, and reports highlighted here represent a broad range of opinion
and analysis that crosses ideological boundaries. Each section attempts to
respect the diverse philosophical undercurrents surrounding the query in
order to allow the reader an opportunity to consider which ideas or
approaches may be most effective or feasible in reducing urban poverty.

U.S. Poverty Data Sources

Many sources of data and information can be utilized in composing a
profile of poverty and major characteristics associated with poverty in
America. The United States Bureau of the Census publishes various
reports focusing on poverty, one of the most recent being "Poverty in the
United States: 1990," issued in August 1991. The following reports issued
by the U.S. Bureau of the Census in the "Series P-60" also focus on poverty
in the United States:

"The Extent of Poverty in the United States, 1959 to 1966"
"Socioeconomic Trends in Poverty Areas: 1960 to 1968"
"Poverty in the United States: 1959 to 1968"
"24 Million Americans: Poverty in the United States: 1969"
"Characteristics of Low Income Population" (1970 to 1973)

"Characteristics of the Population Below the Poverty Level" (1974 to
   1984)
"Poverty in the United States" (1985 to 1989)
"The Hispanic Population in the United States: March 1991"

Two other references that help to establish a foundation for this literature
review are the "Statistical Abstract of the United States: 1992" and the
"Historical Abstracts of the United States."

An additional and concise source of information about poverty includes Leatha Jamison-White's, "Income, Poverty, and Wealth in the
United States: A Chart Book." This is a report published by the U.S. Bureau
of the Census under its Current Population Reports series.

The Social Science Research Council established a computerized data
base on "underclass" data for the one hundred largest metropolitan areas,
which was directed by John D. Kasarda at the University of North Carolina
at Chapel Hill. As described in the preface of the manual for the data,
"Urban Underclass Database," this database includes "5,800 economic,
social demographic, and health indicators." Since 1981, the U.S. House of
Representatives has published an annual report of social welfare data.
This massive report is known as "The Green Book" and is compiled by the
House Ways and Means Committee. The General Accounting Office also
published a report in 1992 which focused on changes in the family
composition of the poor, *Poverty Trends, 1980-1988*. Another recent source
for a profile and a list of characteristics is the excellent report by demographer William P. O'Hare entitled *Poverty in America: Trends and New
Patterns*. In addition to reporting various kinds of poverty data, O'Hare
discusses some of the major explanations for changes in American poverty. He also examines selected social welfare programs that have been
instituted to fight poverty in this nation, and has compiled many useful
tables illustrating trends in poverty.

There are at least three publications through which the reader can
obtain basic and concise information about the characteristics of poverty
in the United States. *Programs in Aid of the Poor*, by Sar A. Levitan, director
of the Center for Social Policy Studies at George Washington University,
has recently been published in its sixth edition. This continues to be a
useful introduction to the characteristics of the American poor. While this
book focuses on programs designed to help the poor, its introduction
provides the demographic context of American poverty. Another important source on poverty, race, and related topics in both the United States
and abroad is the reference work of the Institute of Race Relations in
London, England. Edited by Louis V. Kushnick, *Sage Race Relations
Abstracts* is published quarterly and is one of the most concise and useful

publications reviewing the international literature on race. Another important work, *The State of Working America* by Lawrence Mischel and David M. Frankel, focuses on economic trends for all Americans, examining how families change in relation to shifts in incomes, taxes, wages, employment, and housing. This study has a separate chapter on poverty, and provides some comparison with European nations. There are, of course, many other publications that one could turn to in order to obtain information about American poverty. However, I found these studies particularly useful in initiating and completing this review of major questions related to poverty in urban America.

CHAPTER I
What Is Poverty, and How Is Poverty Measured by the Federal Government?

[Let us not] allow statistical quibbling to obscure the huge, enormous, and intolerable fact of poverty in America.

Michael Harrington
The Other America (1962)

In modern society defining poverty has been an exercise involving much debate. It has been defined differently in various historical periods and has reflected a range of ideological orientations. Today, even the quantitative approaches to defining poverty have been debated widely. Five areas have been identified by Daniel H. Weinberg, chief of the Census Bureau's Housing and Household Economic Statistics Division, as needing further attention in order to develop a better model for determining poverty. These are: "the evaluation of non-cash benefits, developing a new measure of spending needs, finding ways to account for tax burdens, reducing the underreporting of income and changing the adjustments for family size."[1] Defining poverty is difficult because the very definition one uses has immediate ideological and public policy implications. How one defines poverty reflects something about what one feels is the nature of poverty, and what one believes should be the government's response to it. How poverty is defined can also predetermine the public policies that will be chosen to eliminate, reduce, or alleviate poverty in urban America.

According to Peter Townsend's *Poverty in the United Kingdom,* one of the first modern researchers to attempt to determine an empirically-based definition of poverty was B. Seebohm Rowntree.[2] In *Poverty: A Study of Town Life,* a work published in Britain around the turn of the century, Rowntree attempted to establish a definition of poverty by determining how much an individual needed to obtain food.[3] Rowntree's work was partially based on that of philosopher Friedrich Engels in 1857. Engels noted that there was an inverse relationship between income and the percentage of total expenditure spent on food; this is referred to as "Engels' Coefficient."[4] Rowntree moved from this point and reasoned that poor families are those where "total earnings are insufficient to obtain the minimum necessaries for the maintenance of merely physical efficiency."[5]

Social welfare analyst Michael Sherraden writes that Robert Hunter provided the "first statistical view of poverty in the United States...He concluded that, in a total population of 80 million, 10 million lived in poverty."[6]

Economist Robert J. Lampman reports in *Ends and Means of Reducing Income Poverty* that,

> In 1892 Jacob Riis estimated that from 20 to 30 percent of New York City's population lived in penury. Robert Hunter guessed that 12 to 24 percent of all Americans lived in poverty in 1904. In making his rough calculations, Hunter suggested a guideline of $460 in annual income for a family of five in an urban setting, and $300 for the South. But in 1906 Father John A. Ryan set a poverty line of $600. The fact that this was above the median wage for adult males suggests that he thought about half of all families had incomes below what was required for "health and self-respect."[7]

In 1935 the Works Progress Administration (WPA),U.S.Department of Agriculture, and National Resources Committee developed a "maintenance" standard of living level used by the Bureau of Labor Statistics in the post-World War II period.[8] The WPA also developed an "emergency" budget that was 70 percent of the maintenance budget. Gabriel Kolko describes how poverty was defined during this period in *Wealth and Power*: "Below this line, it is clear, the family or individual lives in poverty, and expenditures are guided, not by social norms of well-being, but by the demands of survival."[9] In the same year that Kolko published this book, by the way, Michael Harrington claimed that between 40 million and 50 million Americans were impoverished.[10]

The matter of determining the appropriate measure of poverty is very important today; and it has significant political and public policy implications. A recent *New York Times* article queried: "In Rising Debate on Poverty, The Question: Who Is Poor?" The reporter, Jason DeParle, wrote:

> While the debate about how much of the nation is poor might seem esoteric, it has important consequences. The poverty line helps govern eligibility for billions of dollars in benefit programs. It also helps guide assumptions about the nation's economic soundness and social fairness, which are particularly important as the country is heading into a recession.[11]

DeParle reiterated the query of Joyce E. Allen and Margaret C. Simms in their earlier article, "Is a New Yardstick Needed to Measure Poverty?" Allen and Simms wrote: "Measuring poverty is important because eligibility for many federal programs...is based in part on the official poverty level. A change in how poverty is measured could affect the amount of money Congress budgets for programs essential to the well-being of millions of Americans."[12]

.

The Official Poverty Line

The United States federal government did not start to use an officially determined measure of poverty based on annual income until the mid-1960s. This measure of poverty income was based on an approach and assumptions developed by an official of the Department of Agriculture in 1963, Mollie Orshansky. The Council of Economic Advisors adopted her model in 1964, and has used it since that year. The official poverty income level is adjusted annually for inflation. In 1964, the poverty threshold for a family of four was $3,169; in 1990 it was $13,359 for the same size family.

Three steps were utilized by Orshansky to develop her model.

1) Based on a survey of American consumption patterns, the Department of Agriculture assumed that a four-person, non-farm family consumed approximately *one third* of its annual income on food.
2) The Department of Agriculture determined the income required to purchase food, under an "Economy Food Plan."
3) The income required to purchase food under the Economy Food Plan was simply multiplied by a factor of three.[13]

With several modifications, this is still the basic model utilized by the Council of Economic Advisors to define and measure the poverty status of individuals and families in the United States. A few technical changes to the model were adopted in 1980; these changes were summarized in the *Statistical Abstract of the United States: 1992* as follows: "(1) distinctions based on sex of householder have been eliminated; (2) separate thresholds for farm families have been dropped; and (3) the matrix has been expanded to families of nine or more persons from the old cut off of seven or more persons."[14]

Criticisms of the Official Poverty Line

There are several problems with the official model for measuring poverty in the United States. First, the assumption that a four-person, non-farm family spends one-third of its budget on food is considered arbitrary by many scholars. This criticism was, in fact, supported by Orshansky in a paper presented to the American Statistical Association in 1979.[15] Thus, the very author of the model argues that the application of the methodology is now erroneous because it is based on a *1955* Department of Agriculture survey of American food consumption. By 1965 the proportion of family income spent on food consumption was much less than one third. In her paper Orshansky recommends multiplying the Economy Food Plan by a factor of 3.4 rather than three. According to Michael Harrington, who reports this information in his book, *The New American Poverty*, this change would have resulted in an additional 25 million Americans being officially defined as living in poverty in 1977.[16] Researchers also believe that regional differences in the cost of living should be taken into account. Sociologist Reynolds Farley writes that "a family of four might be able to get by on $9,900 [1982] in Dothan, Alabama, but would find it impossible to survive on such a meager amount in New York or San Francisco."[17]

Some researchers believe the model currently utilized by the federal government produces an official level of poverty that is unrealistically low; and, many Americans seem to agree. In a national Gallup poll conducted in 1989, Americans were asked what they felt was a necessary minimum annual income to keep a family of four out of poverty. The response was $15,017; but the official poverty threshold that same year was only $12,674.[18] And in 1990 the official poverty threshold for a family of four was determined to be $13,359. An implicit acknowledgment that the official way of determining poverty is inadequate is the decision on the part of the U.S. Bureau of the Census, as well as many researchers, to utilize an index of 124 percent of the official poverty level (referred to as "near poverty" level) in determining a more realistic poverty income threshold. Some public agencies have found it necessary to distribute benefits to the poor based on income levels that are higher than the officially determined poverty threshold. For instance, current family eligibility for food stamps is based on income of less than 130 percent of the poverty line, and Medicaid family eligibility is based on earned income of less than 133 percent of the official poverty line.

If 124 percent of the official poverty level is used, then the problem of poverty in America is much greater than official data indicate. For example, in 1986 the black poverty rate was 32 percent based on the official definition of poverty income, according to U.S. Bureau of Census reports. But at 124 percent of the poverty income level, the black poverty rate in 1986 would have been 39 percent. In 1990 the number of all Americans below the official poverty level was 33.6 million, or 13.5 percent of the total population. If a figure of below 125 percent of the poverty level had been utilized, then 44.8 million Americans (or 18 percent of the total population) would have been classified as poverty stricken.

Another problem with the income-based model used by the federal government is the assumption that the problem of poverty stems merely from the lack of money; this criticism is offered by the economist John Kenneth Galbraith who argues for a relative, rather than absolute measure of impoverishment. As he writes:

People are poverty-striken when their income, even if adequate for survival, falls markedly behind that of the community. Then they cannot have what the larger community regards as the minimum necessary for decency; and they cannot wholly escape, therefore, the judgement of the larger community that they are indecent. They are degraded for, in the literal sense, they live outside the grades or categories which the community regards as acceptable.[19]

Thus, according to Galbraith, poverty is much more complex than simply not having a certain level of income.

The official poverty line model is also criticized by social psychologist Lawrence E. Gary in his article "Poverty, Stress and Mental Health":

Another approach to defining poverty is looking at relative deprivation—that is, the failure to attain living standards that are customary in the society. This approach views poverty not only in terms of material goods, but also in terms of the psychological effects on an individual of not having certain resources that people around him or her have...The basic principle underlying this approach is that poor people see affluence all around them and assess their situation or position in relation to both their basic needs and the wealth in society as a whole.[20]

Barry R. Schiller explains in *The Economics of Poverty and Discrimination* that "the contrast between relative and absolute measures of poverty highlights a basic policy issue. Is our primary policy concern with the misery of those who command low incomes, or are we more concerned with the unequal distribution of incomes?"[21] But in answering this query, the income criteria used to measure the amount of resources provided to poor people are biased in favor of the interests of middle- and upper-class sectors in the United States.

In order to compensate for this bias, Victor Fuchs proposes a definition of income tied to a measure of equality. In his 1967 essay, "Redefining Poverty and Redistributing Income," he argues for defining poverty as income which is less than half of the national median level of income.[22] This relative measure is known as "Fuchs' Point," and is similar to Townsend's approach in defining poverty: "Poverty can be defined objectively and applied consistently only in terms of the concept of relative deprivation...Individuals, families and groups in the population can be said to be in poverty when they lack the resources to obtain the types of diet, participate in the activities and have the living conditions and amenities which are customarily, or at least widely encouraged or approved, in the societies to which they belong."[23]

There are other non-income criteria that could be used by the government for measuring and responding to poverty in relative terms. Sociologist Louis A. Ferman describes three other kinds of criteria: "community resource criteria," individual inadequacies (negative risk criteria), and "behavior or attitudinal criteria."[24] This, by the way, is similar to the classical approach used by Adam Smith in 1776 when he discussed the basic necessities that are required to remain above poverty status. In his famous work, *The Wealth of Nations*, Smith wrote: "By necessaries I understand not only the commodities which are indispensably necessary for the support of life, but whatever the custom of the country renders it indecent for creditable people, even of the lowest order, to be without."[25] Again, this suggests a relative, rather than absolute, definition of poverty.

Social and Political Dimensions of Poverty

Historically, poor people have been perceived as lazy, immoral, or, to use a term historian Michael B. Katz utilizes in one of his books, "undeserving."[26] Notwithstanding intervening protest events on the part of poor people, like "Coxey's Army" march on Washington D.C. in 1894, impoverishment has in this country been generally associated with lack of morals, sin, and vice. For short periods of time and during periods of protest, however, the nation often reconsiders the causes and persistence of poverty. After 1894, this kind of reevaluation was again forced upon the nation during the Great Depression, when millions of Americans became unemployed and impoverished. But hostility toward poor people, especially toward those on welfare, seems to remain steadfast among the general public today.

One way in which a negative image of people living in poverty is manifested and perpetuated is the automatic association of "welfare" with the poor. It is inaccurate, however, to associate public welfare policies solely with poverty. Mimi Abramovitz argues in her article "Everyone Is on Welfare" that many people, including the poor, are on one form or another of "welfare."[27] As Abramovitz explains, "welfare," can be defined not only as subsidies for the impoverished, like AFDC benefits and Medicaid, but also as "fiscal welfare" which provides income support and subsidies through taxation benefits such as interest deductions. She expands this concept further to include "occupational welfare," which provides additional income and support to people through fringe benefits. Abramovitz refers to fiscal and occupational welfare as the "shadow welfare state" that strongly, but perhaps quietly, provides many benefits to the middle and upper classes.

People living in poverty are also characterized by the inability to make certain choices available to other Americans. And it is generally true that poor people do not have access to political power. This is a point made by Bertram M. Beck in his essay, "How Do We Involve the Poor?"[28] He writes that poverty basically reflects a lack of power on the part of the poor: "I say to you that more important than money is what money buys. And what money buys is freedom to choose, freedom to do, freedom to get out of a tight spot. This is power, and the people we are discussing are relatively powerless. They are not a political bloc. There is no group of poor which votes as poor."[29]

In response to the political and social dimension of poverty, S. M. Miller and Pamela Roby propose comprehensive public policies that should be pursued by the federal government in order to eliminate poverty and inequality. They argue that a public welfare policy program must include means to improve the well-being of the poor. They propose six basic areas for consideration:

income, including income mobility and non-monetary benefits from pensions and stock options;
assets, such as savings and property;
basic services: access to health, protection, neighborhood amenities, social services and transportation;
self-respect: what discriminatory barriers have to be overcome;
opportunities for education; [and]
participation in many forms of decision making.[30]

Public welfare policies have been criticized by both the left and the right for not providing services oriented towards the empowerment of the poor. Public assistance bureaucracies have been accused of stultifying the aspirations of some poor people, or politically and socially oppressing them and maintaining a sense of powerlessness on the part of the recipients. Frances Fox Piven and Richard A. Cloward in *Regulating the Poor* on the ideological left, and Milton Friedman in his classic work *Capitalism and Freedom* on the right, all argue that poor people are kept politically weak by public assistance bureaucracies.[31] Yet this kind of political dimension of poverty is not revealed by relying exclusively on annual income to determine and gauge poverty.

Some researchers and observers suggest that the model used for determining poverty exaggerates the problem and extent of poverty in the United States. According to a study published in 1990 by the Heritage Foundation, "How 'Poor' Are America's Poor?"

A key reason that the Census undercounts the financial resources of the "poor" is that, remarkably, it ignores nearly all welfare spending when calculating the incomes of persons in poverty. Thus, as far as the Bureau is concerned, billions of dollars of in-kind benefits to poor Americans have no effect on their incomes. Out of $184 billion in welfare spending, the Census counts only $27 billion as income for poor persons. The bulk of the welfare system, including entire programs that provide non-cash aid to the poor, like food stamps, public housing, and Medicaid, is completely ignored in the Census Bureau's calculations of the living standards of the "poor" U.S. household.[32]

It has been proposed that if benefits such as food stamps, Medicare and Medicaid, and subsidized housing were counted, the proportion of Americans living in poverty would be significantly reduced.

Director Robert Greenstein, writing for the Center on Budget and Policy Priorities, has issued a detailed critique of both the methodology and conclusions utilized by the Heritage Foundation in making this kind of claim. As is pointed out by Greenstein, "The $184 billion in government 'welfare spending' that Heritage cites includes billions in expenditures for programs that were never intended to be poverty programs exclusively or even primarily and that serve millions of Americans with incomes well above the poverty line."[33]

Examples of such benefits to the non-poor include reduced-price school lunches, job training programs, legal services programs, compensatory education programs, programs to provide in-home services to disabled people, and other programs.

Robert D. Plotnick and Felicity Skidmore review the changes in the poverty population, and also analyze the impact of cash transfer programs on the number and percentage of poor persons between 1965 and 1972 in their study *Progress Against Poverty*. They conclude that, despite the doubling of social welfare expenditures during this period, the amount actually going to the poor did not change significantly.[34] Much of social welfare expenditures, as a matter of fact, goes primarily to the nonpoor and to the elderly.

One sociologist reported a significant decrease in the poverty rate for blacks and whites during the 1970s on the basis of counting the market value of in-kind food and housing programs. As Reynolds Farley reports, "attributing monetary value to in-kind benefits substantially reduces the estimated extent of poverty. The change in the estimated proportion below the poverty line in 1979 was from 30 to 24 percent for blacks and from 9 to 7 percent for whites. The adjustment for noncash benefits increases the proportion who are near poor as well as above the poverty line."[35] Farley adds, however, that "even taking such assistance programs into account, about one black in four and one white in fourteen were impoverished in 1979; the poverty rate of blacks was still more than three times that of whites."[36]

A comprehensive examination of poverty-rate changes resulting from 15 income-related factors, before and after taxes, was conducted by the U.S. Bureau of the Census and published in "Measuring the Effect of Benefits and Taxes on Income and Poverty, 1990." This study concludes that, while adding benefits and factoring in pre- and post-tax income did produce some fluctuation in the poverty rates, it did not significantly reduce poverty rates for the nation.[37] Furthermore, as Lawrence Mischel and David M. Frankel point out, the increase in the poverty rate since 1979 grew faster using this model than using the official model because of cutbacks in benefits to the poor![38] These researchers report that the official poverty rate increased by 1.7 percentage points between 1979 and 1987, but would have increased by 2.3 points if changing levels of food and housing benefits had been calculated.[39]

According to the 1985 report of the Center on Budget and Policy Priorities, "Smaller Slices of the Pie," the claim that poverty levels would be reduced if all resources received by the poor were counted is valid only if one also considers factors that "result in an understatement of the number of those considered to be poor." The report reads:

> In determining whether households are poor, households' gross incomes before taxes are counted. This means that the portion of a household's earnings that is withheld for taxes, and that never even passes through the household's hands, is counted in full as though it were available to be spent...This matter is of no small significance. If the poverty definition were based (as it should be) on after-tax incomes, the number of persons considered to be poor would increase by two and one half to three million. A substantial number of families whose gross incomes place them above the poverty line — and who currently are not counted as poor — would be considered to be below the poverty line if after-tax incomes were used as the basis for the poverty determination.[40]

Attempting to place a market value on noncash benefits for purposes of counting it as income also can create an illogical scenario where someone who might be elderly and without income, for instance, but receives Medicaid, would be considered to be above the poverty line based on the value assigned to these kinds of benefits. "In other words," the above report states, "for some elderly persons, a Medicaid card is considered to have a monetary value greater than the poverty line — so that some elderly persons with Medicaid coverage are considered not to be poor, even if they are destitute and have no funds to purchase basic necessities. Such a definition of poverty seems to defy common sense."[41]

Jane Axinn and Mark J. Stern attempt to factor in noncash benefits in determining an accurate indication of poverty in their 1988 work *Dependency and Poverty*, but conclude that such an approach is unwieldy and, furthermore, does not significantly reduce the level of poverty.[42]

As pointed out in the previously cited report by Mischel and Frankel, "Poverty has been getting worse since 1979, no matter how you measure it."[43] The debate about how to define poverty in the United States will persist for two basic reasons. First, as this chapter shows, there are a variety of ways to define poverty and to count the number of poor persons. A range of different quantitative models has been proposed for measuring poverty, each of which has implications for the kinds and costs of public policies needed to reduce or eliminate poverty. Second, there are ideological stakes in the definition of poverty. The particular approach one takes generally reflects a certain ideological orientation about the nature and cause of poverty.

Despite the debate about how to define poverty, however, Greenstein believes that three major conclusions about the measure of poverty can be asserted: 1) "No matter what measure of poverty is used, the poverty rate has risen sharply since 1989 after declining much less than would have been expected during the recovery of the 1980s"; 2) "...poverty is now high by historical standards" and, 3) "The poverty rate in the United States is well above that of other western, industrialized nations, and the sharp disparity between our rate and that of other countries is not affected much by non-cash benefits."[44]

Data illustrating and supporting Greenstein's conclusions are provided in chapter 3, which focuses on the contours of urban poverty in the United States. But first, chapter 2 provides a brief overview of major anti-poverty policies pursued by national administrations between the New Deal and the current period.

What Kinds of National Policies Have Been Utilized to Manage Poverty? — From the New Deal to the Clinton Administration

When the object is to raise the permanent condition of a people, small means do not merely produce small effects; they produce no effect at all.

John Stuart Mill

National policies directed at the reduction or elimination of poverty have a mixed record in achieving desired goals. For instance, while white elderly poverty as well as poverty for the total population has been reduced considerably in the United States over the last 50 years, there are still instances of abject poverty for millions of Americans. One-third of all blacks and more than half of all black children remain impoverished regardless of different policies and strategies pursued by national administrations. These rates are far surpassed by Latinos in some parts of urban America and there are indications that poverty rates for some Asian groups are increasing.

In considering the last 50 to 60 years, two general approaches to poverty can be discerned. One approach has been directed at stimulating economic development and growth in generating jobs. The other has involved specific efforts aimed at reducing or eliminating poverty. National anti-poverty policy over this period of time has moved from a concentration on the structural basis of this problem to greater focus on presumed pathological aspects of poor people. A current perception of the existence of an undeserving poor, compared to a deserving poor under the New Deal, reflects this change. It can be stated that to a limited degree the New Deal attempted to *fix the system* in response to poverty, while the Reagan and Bush and, now, Clinton administrations have attempted to *fix the poor*. The following section will highlight major characteristics, themes, and programs associated with the anti-poverty policies of each national administration between the New Deal period and the current administration.

The New Deal Administration (1933-1945)

Franklin Delano Roosevelt's New Deal administration ushered an era of government activism in the area of poverty and social welfare. The New Deal offered a contrasting approach to other national policies developed in earlier administrations. Charles V. Hamilton and Dona C. Hamilton write in "The Dual Agenda" that:

> The New Deal is the proper beginning for this discussion, because then this country launched its modern-day version of the American "welfare state." With the Social Security Act of 1935, the country established a *two-tier social welfare system*. The first tier (Social Insurance) was contributory, funded from payroll taxes levied on employers and employees. Covering retirement pensions, and unemployment compensation, it has expanded over the years to include survivors, spouses, disability provisions, Medicare. This was indeed a landmark piece of legislation coming out of the crisis of the Great Depression...The second tier (Public Assistance) was for those unable and generally not expected to work. This included dependent children (Aid to Dependent Children), later AFDC; the elderly poor and disabled who had not contributed to the Social Security fund. This category of assistance was *means-tested*...But it was also perceived to provide help on a temporary basis, because the "recipients" were expected to be able in time to go into the labor market and become self-supporting.[1]

The New Deal social welfare policies became the policy reference map for national anti-poverty efforts in subsequent administrations as is illustrated by political scientist David McKay in *Domestic Policy and Ideology*.[2] Similarly, historian Edward D. Berkowitz writes in *America's Welfare State*, that the New Deal gave birth to several new kinds of social welfare policies directed against poverty: "We tend to forget that the 1935 Act also marks the beginnings of national unemployment compensation and welfare."[3] And political scientist Robert X. Browning points out that only one major program involving payment to individuals was enacted in the United States during the first two decades of the twentieth century: the Veterans-Non-Service Pensions.[4]

An immediate challenge for the New Deal administration was massive unemployment resulting in millions of American families becoming impoverished. Unemployment was a major concern of the Roosevelt administration; in 1933 slightly more than 25 percent of Americans over the age of 14 were out of work. (After 1947 unemployment rates included individuals 16 years of age and over.) In response to this crisis Roosevelt established the Federal Emergency Relief Administration in 1933. This program provided relief payments to states and funds for creating jobs. In 1935 the Works Progress Administration (WPA) was founded; under this program three million persons were employed in public works projects across the country. The WPA was a massive public works program for the unemployed. (The name of this agency was changed to the Works Projects Administration in 1939.) It had provided eight million jobs by 1943. The cost of the effort was $11 billion between 1935 and 1943, when the agency was disbanded. Harold Hopkins, the first director of the WPA until 1939, believed that the agency should seek to preserve the self-respect of the poor and the unemployed through public employment. The WPA provided a broad range of jobs, including construction of hundreds of public buildings and facilities throughout the United States.

The New Deal administrators also established a minimum wage (25 cents per hour) under the Fair Labor Standards Act passed in June 1938. The minimum wage was considered important as a means of guaranteeing a basic standard of living for workers. But the passage of a minimum wage probably also had much to do with the growing political power of unions; between 1935 and 1940 union membership more than doubled, from 3.7 million to almost 9 million persons.[5]

A major anti-poverty effort arising in the latter stages of the New Deal was "Urban Renewal." When enacted this program was described as necessary for the reduction of poverty in America.[6] Martin Anderson argues in his book, *The Federal Bulldozer*, however, that although Title I (i.e., urban renewal) of the 1949 Housing Act was marketed as an effort to eliminate slums and urban blight, it in fact benefited real estate speculators while depriving poor people, especially blacks and Latinos, of affordable housing.[7]

The New Deal approach to poverty was different in some ways from earlier local and federal government approaches. Berkowitz writes that some aspects of New Deal social welfare policies represented a major departure from the traditional "poor laws" used earlier by states:

Beyond the sheer factors of scope and size, social insurance differed from the traditional poor laws...Where poor laws were administered by the localities, social insurance laws became the concerns of federal and state governments. Where poor laws concentrated their aid on people who could demonstrate that they were poor, social insurance limited benefits to families headed by someone who had once worked. Where towns funded poor laws from revenues gathered through such means as property taxes, workers or their employers paid for social insurance themselves. Where the poor laws provided aid in many different forms, including lodging, food, and money, social insurance programs nearly always supplied beneficiaries with a check, the commodity they most wanted.[8]

By examining some of the historical antecedents of various New Deal social welfare initiatives, Mimi Abramovitz discredits the claim regarding the "newness" of New Deal social welfare policies directed at the poor. She suggests in her book, *Regulating the Lives of Women*, that, while many of the specific programmatic initiatives could be described as new, the philosophical and political assumptions and goals of the New Deal did not really represent a break with traditional anti-poverty approaches regarding the response to poverty, as many scholars have proposed.[9]

The New Deal was quite *American* in tradition, in other words. The New Deal did not represent a radical departure of previous policy within the framework of American capitalism. As argued by political scientist Dorothy B. James in her book, *Poverty, Politics and Change*: "Despite public rhetoric antagonistic to their alleged 'socialist' or 'collectivist' tendencies, these programs were fully in accord with the tenets of organic liberalism. The American social and economic systems were assumed to be basically sound, merely needing to open greater employment opportunities in order for the poor to enter the work force without further help."[10] The tradition and continuity of national anti-poverty policy in the United States is also discussed by Michael B. Katz in his work, *In the Shadow of the Poorhouse*.[11] Here he argues, as he does in another work, *The Undeserving Poor*, that anti-poverty policies were attempts to maintain the economic status quo rather than focusing on the problems of the poor.[12]

The emergence and growth of social welfare programs during the New Deal period cannot be deemphasized, however, as a critical development. In 1929 social welfare expenditures represented 3.9 percent of the nation's GNP (3.9 billion); by 1940, this figure jumped to 9.2 percent (8.8 billion).[13] Much of the philosophical underpinning for utilizing government and fiscal policy as a tool for generating economic expansion was provided in the classic 1936 work by John Maynard Keynes, *General Theory of Employment, Interest and Money*.[14]

Presumably, a major characteristic of the social welfare and poverty policies of the New Deal is "universalism." This idea suggests that broad demographic groups, such as the elderly, should be the recipients of a national policy, rather than targeted groups that must pass a means test to qualify for the benefit. As is explained by sociologist William J. Wilson:

> In 1932 Franklin D. Roosevelt received a popular mandate to attack the catastrophic economic problems created by the Great Depression. He then launched a series of programs — such as Social Security and unemployment compensation — designed to protect all citizens against sudden impoverishment...Jobs for able individuals, Social Security, and unemployment compensation for the unemployed were to provide a modicum of security for all.[15]

In fact, however, even the universalism of the New Deal was not so "universal." This is explained by Hamilton and Hamilton in their previously cited work; as these two authors remind us: "The initial legislation did not cover agricultural workers and domestic servants, and this meant that a good two-thirds of black workers were initially not covered...Of 5,500,000 black workers in the country, 2 million worked at that time in agriculture, and 1 1/2 million in domestic service. These were 'left out'...Thus, what was perceived by some as a 'universal' program was not that at all."[16] This is also verified by historian Nancy L. Grant who points out in *TVA and Black Americans* that, despite public pronouncements regarding full access and fair treatment for all, within the Tennessee Valley Authority, which was established under the New Deal, black workers were confined to the most menial labor and second-class status compared to white workers.[17]

One contemporary social welfare debate involves scholars calling for an expansion of universal strategies to fight poverty versus the call for targeted approaches in helping to reduce poverty. Professor of sociology Theda Skocpol has argued that "The lesson is clear. Those who would do more now to help the poor through public social policies...should work toward replacing welfare with new policies along with those of the middle class and the stable working class." She writes that the poor could be most effectively helped by strategies that are broadly accepted and "rooted in deeply and broadly held values" like Social Security.[18] But Skocpol also reminds her readers that some situations still may require targeted efforts within universal strategies.

"Universalism" may not be universal in its effects according to professor of social welfare and social services Neil Gilbert in his work, *Capitalism and the Welfare State*. In one chapter, "Contradictions of Universal Entitlement," Gilbert describes how "universalism" tends to serve the interests of middle-class clients over those of poverty-stricken groups. He writes: "The theoretical case for heightening social integration, however, fails in practice to take into account the inclinations of social service providers and client behavior...Less troublesome clients will be served before more troublesome ones. Those who can pay will be served before those who cannot. Higher status clients will be served before lower status clients."[19]

An example of this may be the finding that "only 70 percent of the Hispanic elderly population receive Social Security benefits compared to 92 percent of the rest of the population"; as reported by the National Puerto Rican Coalition, Inc., "the lack of bilingual services at the Social Security Administration (SSA) prevents limited-English proficient (LEP) minorities from receiving eligible benefits such as Supplemental Security Income (SSI), Medicaid, and Medicare."[20] Additionally, two other researchers have discerned that even universal programs may not enjoy the widespread public support that is sometimes intimated. Fay L. Cook and Edith J. Barrett found that support for three universal social insurance programs — Social Security, Medicare, and Unemployment Insurance — did not receive the uniform and consistent support on the part of the American public or the U.S. House of Representatives as seems to be suggested by proponents of universal social welfare approaches.[21] As a matter of fact, the Center on Budget and Policy Priorities' Robert Greenstein points out that some targeted programs have fared better in the late 1980s than did some universally-based programs. As he reminds us,

> the cuts in the early Reagan years did hit targeted programs hardest. But most of these programs were subsequently expanded. The principal Medicaid cuts enacted in 1981 expired after 1984. Since then Medicaid coverage has been substantially enlarged and will ultimately include all poor children under age 19 and most elderly and disabled poor people. Moreover, some of these Medicaid expansions were financed through reductions in Medicare, a universal program...Also, while the universal Social Security program was cut modestly in 1981 and 1983, the targeted welfare program for the elderly poor — Supplementary Security Income — was expanded.[22]

The issue regarding universal versus targeted approaches, spawned during the New Deal, is still unresolved and will continue to be debated.

The Truman/Eisenhower Administrations (1945-1961)

Although, as Mark J. Stern writes, "Scholars are apt to ignore the quiet welfare state of the 1950s," there were significant social welfare developments related to poverty during this period.[23] Notably, for instance, Social Security provisions and eligibility were liberalized. President Harry S. Truman's domestic social welfare policies were known collectively as the "Fair Deal" and, as was the case with President Dwight D. Eisenhower's administration, represented a continuation of New Deal strategies and initiatives. Federal contributions increased considerably under the Truman administration, despite the president's veto of legislation in 1948 extending eligibility and expanding welfare benefits. The expansion of benefits to the poor and Social Security recipients, while welcomed by the states, also meant that the federal government would be more involved in monitoring states. During this period "the principle that states must follow procedural rules to be eligible for matching funds was more strongly established."[24] Under the Eisenhower administration, the 1954

Housing Act basically repeated the thrust of earlier urban renewal legislation. Partially due to some of the successes of the New Deal, the somewhat activist government model was used by these administrations to continue generating jobs and thereby reduce poverty. In 1958 President Eisenhower approved an Anti-Recession Act which provided $1.85 billion to generate 500,000 jobs through the construction of 200,000 housing units.

This approach to reducing poverty was also reflected at the state level. A summary of public assistance spending patterns at the state level for the period of the 1940s and for 1961 is provided in "The Politics of Welfare," by political scientists Richard E. Dawson and James A. Robinson.[25]

The Kennedy Administration (1961-1963)

Poverty as a national issue gained momentum in the mid-1960s, partially as a result of the publication of Michael Harrington's book *The Other America* and the review of this work by Dwight McDonald in *The New Yorker*.[26] Under John F. Kennedy's administration the Public Welfare Amendments of 1962 called for professional activities targeted at coordinating services to the poor. It is interesting to note that the goals of this legislation included:

1) Services — services to help families become self-supporting and independent.

2) Prevention — prevention of dependency in dealing with the problems causing dependency.

3) Incentives — incentives to recipients of public assistance to improve their condition so as to make public assistance unnecessary; and incentives to states to improve their welfare programs.

4) Rehabilitation — services to rehabilitate recipients or those likely to become recipients of public assistance.

5) Independence — useful community work and training programs and other measures to assist recipients to become self-supporting and able to care for themselves.

6) Training — assistance in the provision of training in order to increase the supply of adequately trained public welfare professionals, this being necessary for achieving the foregoing objectives.[27]

These are goals that are still relevant in the current period.

A major reason for the initiatives of President Kennedy in responding to national attention about poverty was the civil rights movement. This mass social movement provided a political foundation for making the existence of poverty a national issue. The linkage between civil rights and poverty was highlighted by Martin Luther King, Jr.'s mobilization of a multiracial coalition for a Poor People's March on Washington, D.C. in 1967 and 1968.

There were other important anti-poverty initiatives undertaken during the Kennedy administration in addition to the Public Welfare Amendment of 1962. One sociologist, Lillian B. Rubin, writes that the administration "took a major step toward moving the federal government into the domestic community development and action programs" through the president's appointment of the Committee on Juvenile Delinquency and Crime, on May 11, 1961.[28] This executive initiative led to the Mobilization for Youth (MFY) program, which was also funded with monies from the Ford Foundation and its "Gray Areas Project."

Rubin describes the goal of Mobilization for Youth as follows:

to uproot poverty by engaging the total local community in self-help, assisting residents to teach and to help one another instead of relying on professional social workers...MFY workers counseled and advised on issues of concern to the area, stimulating community awareness of available remedies. Lawyers and community action workers helped to organize a rent strike; supported the civil rights boycott of the NY City schools in February 1964; and acted to protect citizens from capricious police and welfare decisions. Militant social action was to be the vehicle through which the community would learn to help itself.[29]

Other initiatives under this national administration included the Area Redevelopment Act in 1961, the Accelerated Public Works Act, and the Manpower Development and Training Act (MDTA) in 1962.

Under the Kennedy administration states were encouraged to expand services to the poor. Federal welfare grants were also increased under the Public Welfare Amendments of 1962. This act increased the federal share of rehabilitative services provided to the poor from half of the total costs to seventy-five percent. Additionally, this legislation allowed states to provide assistance under the Aid to Families with Dependent Children (AFDC) program to families with an unemployed father at home.

President Kennedy also emphasized tax cuts, including corporate and personal income tax cuts, to generate jobs, which was considered as one approach to reducing poverty in the United States. A 1962 Kennedy proposal to grant a seven percent tax credit on industrial equipment was part of this strategy.

Education and training was a popular approach used to fight poverty under the Kennedy administration, as well as subsequent administrations. This approach responds to the "human capital" proposition that the poor are such because they do not have the educational skills or training to be able to take advantage of the economic opportunities and jobs available in the system. The Kennedy administration instituted two national efforts in the area of education and training. As mentioned above, one was the Area Redevelopment Act of 1961, and the other was the Manpower Development and Training Act of 1962; both of these acts focused on providing occupational training to economically disadvantaged individuals. A long-time Boston-based activist, Henry Allen, described these kinds of approaches by stating that "The thrust of government unemployment programs...has been the continuing assumption that the existing economic system needs no fundamental alterations. The 'theory of human capital' which in essence blames the unemployed worker for his low level of skills and unemployability has been the guideline of government policy."[30] This criticism is cited because it may be germane to policy debates about the effectiveness of human capital approaches in the current period.

The Johnson Administration (1963-1969)

Initiatives developed during the Kennedy administration were followed by President Johnson's Great Society, which reflected similarities with the earlier Roosevelt administration, despite important differences. President Johnson declared the "War on Poverty" in his State of the Union speech on January 8, 1964. Incidentally, as Lampman points out, the terminology of "war" in the context of fighting poverty was actually first used by a member of Parliament in England, David Lloyd George, in 1909 while requesting from Parliament funds to wage "warfare against poverty."[31]

In 1965, 11 percent of the nation's gross national product was accounted for by social welfare expenditures ($77.1 billion). Within five years this figure increased to 15.2 percent of the GNP or $145 billion. This signaled a major expansion of governmental activism in specific social welfare arenas. As reported by Gilbert, "every category of social welfare expenditure increased significantly during this period."[32] In terms of real dollars, social welfare expenditures increased by 10.1 percent during the Eisenhower presidential years, 11.4 percent during the Johnson years, and 8.8 percent and 7.0 percent during the Nixon and Ford years respectively.[33]

One of the longer-lasting education and training programs established under Johnson was the Job Corps, established in 1964 under the Economic Opportunity Act. While the program is still in effect, since 1982 it has been administered as part of the Job Training Partnership Act (JTPA) enacted by the Reagan administration. Despite its continuing popularity as an approach to reducing poverty, however, education and training has never been adequately funded. Sheldon H. Danziger and Daniel H. Weinberg write that despite being the "cornerstone of the War on Poverty," federal spending for education and training programs has been small: "federal spending on them has never been large relative to that on transfers, rising from almost nothing to 0.85 percent of GNP in 1978, but accounting for less than 0.45 percent of GNP in 1984."[34]

Other major legislative and governmental social welfare initiatives established in the early part of the 1960s included the Food Stamp Act of 1964; the Older Americans Act of 1965; the Medicare and Medicaid programs in 1965; and the Demonstration Cities and Metropolitan Development Act of 1966. The food stamp program was actually established in 1939, but was terminated in 1943. President Johnson renewed it during his administration. Up until 1977 eligible recipients had to pay for food stamps. In 1988 approximately 18.8 million Americans received food stamps at a total cost of 12.6 billion dollars.

Medicaid and Medicare represented the first, but limited, forms of federal health insurance programs. While Medicare was designed (as was Social Security) for the elderly and was administered nationally, Medicaid was designed as a means-tested program funded jointly by states and the federal government and administered by states. In 1967 the Johnson administration also recommended to Congress that it pass the Work Incentive Program (WIN), requiring employable welfare recipients to apply and participate in job training programs. The purpose of the WIN program was to reduce the AFDC rolls, thereby reducing spending on this program.

Other programs that were a part of the "War on Poverty" included VISTA, Neighborhood Youth Corps, Job Corps, Head Start, and the Community Action Programs. In *The Great Society's Poor Law*, Sar A. Levitan traces the development of the Economic Opportunity Act, which was enacted on August 20, 1964.[35] This legislation allowed the federal government to directly fund a range of community-based organizations servicing the poor. This act was initially funded at a level of $315 million in order to cover a range of services including job training, counseling, day care, education and health programs. The legislation also called for the "maximum feasible participation" of the poor in determining how funds for these services should be spent. Although the national economy was relatively healthy in the mid-1960s, Johnson was responding, in part, to continuing problems of poverty and unemployment in the black community with this legislation.

Levitan believes that the Economic Opportunity Act represented a refreshing and creative approach to poverty because it was characterized by a new focus on the part of the national administration — the concept and goal of maximum feasible participation, a system of administrative coordination, and institutional rearrangement at the local level. Louis A. Ferman, writing the foreword for *The Annals'* special issue on the War on Poverty in the late 1960s agrees with Levitan, stating that "The War on Poverty embodied a number of new intellectual propositions" such as "creative federalism," "maximum feasible participation," and "the need for a central community action agent to coordinate, and to centralize, resources at the local community level."[36] Despite much fanfare about this act's focus on community groups, the proportion of public dollars going into the coffers of community action organizations was relatively small during this period. Even in 1965 the proportion of "War on Poverty" funds going to community action groups was limited and started to decline quickly from initial allocations; furthermore, the implementation of a comprehensive "War on Poverty" was becoming increasingly problematical in terms of a range of political questions.[37] One major political issue involved the adverse reaction of urban mayors to the organization and mobilization of poor and working-class blacks and Latinos on the basis of anti-poverty resources.

Daniel P. Moynihan and others have critiqued some of the ideas encouraged by social science and the professional community in response to poverty during this period. He suggests in one of his books, *Maximum Feasible Misunderstanding*, that the concept of "maximum feasible participation" is flawed.[38] He suggests that not only was the moral and fiscal commitment of the nation unrealistically overestimated by zealous reformers, but political obstacles to various community action initiatives were unjustifiably minimized during the planning and implementation stages of various anti-poverty programs of the 1960s.

Many have similarly proposed that these kinds of anti-poverty efforts failed. But according to other observers this conclusion is erroneous because it reflects a misunderstanding of the limited nature of these efforts. The former executive director of the Southern Regional Council (1961-1965), Leslie W. Dunbar, argues that

> From numerous sources the public hears that past governmental anti-poverty programs have "failed," and that therefore, none should again be tried. Besides being flawed logic, the conclusion has few analogues in other areas of policy. What ever does work, once and for all? Our foreign policies...have not reduced the USSR's influence

or power...Our former policies...have failed miserably...Our policies to reduce use of narcotics have not worked."[39]

Dunbar is suggesting that to hold higher expectations for anti-poverty policies than for policies in other areas, especially when the former have not been adequately funded, is unrealistic.

Professors of planning Peter Marris and Martin Rein provide a description and critique of this effort at empowering communities to fight poverty in their book *Dilemmas of Social Reform*.[40] They note that the national government did not really prioritize its anti-poverty strategies, as its rhetoric and symbolism may have implied at that time. Marris and Rein state that the lack of a strong and consistent national commitment to fighting poverty forced a model of local assistance on poor people they were not equipped to handle:

> Forced to apply their remedies without the backing of complementary national reforms on which any widespread success depended, the projects could only act as pioneers — exploring the means to implement a policy that had to be undertaken. And even as pioneers, they were handicapped by the lack of any foreseeable funds adequate to the need. The competition for scarce resources accentuated institutional rivalries; unemployment and the impoverishment of social services embittered relations between poor neighborhoods and any official source of help. Thus the search for an enlightened, rational plan to promote change, endorsed by the whole community, set out to confront problems aggravated by a vacuum of national policy it could do nothing to fill.[41]

It was this situation, the authors propose, that actually led the staff and advocates of community-based efforts to become frustrated, apathetic, and angry. Thus, it is important to note two qualifications to the above statement.

The first is that according to Marris and Rein it was not poor people who were apathetic, but rather governmental officials: "Indeed, it was not amongst the poor, but amongst the staff of the institutions which served them, that apathy and indifference more often frustrated progress."[42] The second qualification is that some of President Johnson's national initiatives known as the Great Society did open significant political doors, even if unintentionally, for the poor to begin mobilizing on their own behalf. This is proposed by professor of history Roger Wilkins, who served in President Johnson's administration: "My recollection is that community action (along with Head Start) nurtured a level of leadership in the black community that enriched the next two decades of our national life...Community action also brought more life and self-help activity to the black ghettos than I've ever seen before or since. Since the thrust of the current conservative complaints about the programs of the 1960s and 1970s is that they left people debilitated and dependent, community action can't be the target. As a matter of fact, in the 1960s the knock on the program was that it made the people in the ghettos too active, too noisy, too demanding."[43] According to Susan H. Hertz in *The Welfare Mothers' Movement* this was done by putting "real pressure on local governments through: 1) the dissemination of information to the poor about the availability of welfare; 2) litigation which challenged a host of local laws and policies; and 3) indirect support of grass-roots organizations of the poor."[44]

After several years of racial conflict in urban America, including major racial riots, President Johnson appointed the Kerner Commission (i.e., the National Advisory Commission on Civil Disorders) in July 1967. On March 1, 1968 the Kerner Commission issued its report. In addition to reporting a continuing and widening racial divide in the United States, it also documented widespread racial discrimination and black poverty in major cities.[45] The Kerner Commission Report made several important anti-poverty recommendations including 1) "a commitment by the federal government to provide 'more adequate levels of assistance, on the basis of uniform national standards,' 2) the extension of welfare payments to a far broader range of potential recipients — at a minimum, two-parent families with children, and 3) the development of job training, day care centers, and other programs to enhance the self-reliance of welfare recipients."[46]

These recommendations and others were basically ignored or only half-heartedly supported by subsequent national administrations over the next twenty-five years.

The New Deal and the Great Society Compared

There were some important differences between the New Deal and the Great Society. In a comparison of the philosophical and strategic approaches to poverty by both the New Deal and the Great Society programs, Thomas Gladwin discusses several differences in *Poverty USA*.[47] He claims that under the policy framework of the New Deal, poverty was considered a structural weakness in the economy, rather than a matter of individual pathology. He points out that the Roosevelt administration put less emphasis on education and training, and more on economic opportunity.

Poverty under the New Deal was assumed to be a temporary national economic mishap with implications for all citizens; this allowed poverty to be approached in a way that did not undermine a sense of dignity among the poor. But under the Great Society, poor persons were approached as an unfortunate, unlucky, or uneducated sector of the population that simply did not have the tools to join the train of American economic abundance and opportunity. While Johnson tried to figure out how to get the poor to participate in the American dream of economic security, Roosevelt understood that the system had to be reformed and restructured if the working class was ever going to be able to partake of the fruits of capitalism.

Another difference between these two periods involves race. Under the Great Society umbrella, poverty became a "black" problem, as James A. Morone points out in *The Democratic Wish: Popular Participation and Limits of American Government*:

> [T]he Kennedy and Johnson administrations negotiated the black threat to New Deal politics (and American liberalism) in a remarkable fashion: they converted the racial crisis into a class crisis. Complaints about racial oppression were answered with programs designed to ameliorate poverty...As the urban riots pressed the complex problems of Northern black people on to the political agenda, existing poverty policies were hastily converted into racial ones...For the next decade, *poverty* became an ironic political euphemism for *black*. In public documents and political rhetoric, *poor* meant *black*, regardless of income.[48]

Some have also presented the New Deal as much broader, expansive and aggressive than the Great Society. S. M. Miller and Pamela Roby, in "The War on Poverty Reconsidered," criticize the Great Society as being too limited:

> [T]he difficulties of the Office of Economic Opportunity are to be found in the enabling legislation of the Economic Opportunity Act of 1964. This law, which provided the War on Poverty with very narrow boundaries, rested on a set of compromises among competing government bureaus, Congressional sentiments, and budgetary restraints. The Act had no job provisions. Housing was untouched...There was no effort to deal with the sizable number of the poor who were dependent upon cash transfer allowances, welfare, and Social Security...Only limited gains could be expected from OEO, given the limited activities it was permitted to pursue.[49]

Essays in a reader edited by Chaim Isaac Waxman in a 1968 publication, *Poverty: Power and Politics*, are also strident in describing the weaknesses of the Great Society's War on Poverty.[50] In one essay, entitled "The War on

Poverty: Political Pornography," activist Saul Alinsky claims that poverty funds were essentially being "used to suffocate militant independent leadership and action organizations which have been arising to arm the poor with their share of power."[51]

Political scientist Theodore J. Lowi devotes a major chapter in his book published during this period, *The End of Liberalism*, to a comparison of public policy and poverty under different national administrations. In his chapter "Interest Group Liberalism and Poverty," Lowi distinguishes between the "old" and "new" welfare, summarizing the differences in how national administrations responded to the problem of poverty. Regarding the New Deal, he writes: "Old welfare was a creation of old liberalism, which took capitalism for what it was and sought to treat the poor as the inevitable, least fortunate among the proletariat...New welfare is the creation of new liberalism, interest-group liberalism. While new welfare defines poverty in simple economic terms, it rejects the notion of poverty as a natural and inevitable sector of economic life."[52] The old welfare approach was more effective in reducing poverty than the new welfare according to the author.

Political scientist Hugh Heclo also compares the New Deal and the Great Society approaches to poverty in his essay, "The Political Foundations of Anti-poverty Policy."[53] He sees the former as more politically acceptable to the American public than the latter. The Great Society, he argues, highlighted certain political obstacles regarding the extent and limits of anti-poverty policies: "weak linkages between the policy community and political backers; weakness of president-centered reform; vulnerability of a black-dominated coalition; and program effectiveness as the price of passage."[54] According to Heclo, these remain potential political obstacles to expanded anti-poverty strategies and policies in the current period.

The Nixon Administration (1969-1974)

Although some differences emerged between the Nixon and Johnson administrations, the two were not radically different in terms of their anti-poverty and urban programs. As was suggested by Lowi: "The Nixon approach involved a contrast from Democratic policies only in terms of scale; there was a reduction in the rate of increase of federal appropriations for urban programs."[55] Grants to the states for social services grew at a rapid rate during the Nixon administration. Total grants to states for social services were 346 million dollars in 1968, but more than one and one-half billion dollars by 1972.[56] Very importantly, the following major social welfare programs were indexed for inflation during this period: food stamps (1971), child nutrition programs (1971), Social Security (1975), railroad retirement (1975), and Supplemental Security Income (1975).[57] Despite the rhetoric of President Nixon, there was much support for social welfare and anti-poverty programs during his administration. As reported by Marc L. Miringoff of the Fordham Institute for Innovation in Social Policy:

> During this period, many of the social programs of the 1960s began to have their full impact, which alleviated some problems. But it is also true that the Nixon administration was more supportive of social programs in practice than in rhetoric. Few social programs were significantly cut back during those years. In fact, programs such as food stamps and health insurance reached more of those eligible for benefits than was the case in the latter years of the Carter administration or during the Reagan and Bush administrations.[58]

The Nixon era's social welfarism was identified legislatively by the call for the Family Assistance Plan (FAP) in August 1969 and the State and Local Fiscal Assistance Act in 1972. The Family Assistance Plan represented an unsuccessful attempt to replace AFDC with a more nationalized income maintenance program. The FAP would have been different from AFDC because it called for national uniform benefits and would have also provided income supports for the working poor. In other words, eligible recipients would have received the same amounts of income regardless of the state in which they resided; but additionally, families of four persons would have received up to $1,600 annually. In order to encourage the work ethic, recipients would also have been allowed to keep fifty cents of their FAP income for each dollar earned on a job.

The State and Local Fiscal Assistance Act of 1972 was founded on the basis of less government activism in the area of social welfare and on a call for fewer resources to be devoted to the arena of anti-poverty policies. It is important to note, however, that governmental cutbacks during this period were sought not on the basis of affordability but rather for ideological reasons. Although he advocated free food stamps for the poor President Nixon believed, for instance, that the government dole would encourage Americans to become overly dependent.[59] The goal of less federal governmental activism in the area of anti-poverty efforts was also reflected in the adoption of the Comprehensive Employment and Training Act in 1973. According to Henry Allen, this federal program channelled funds that had been going to community and neighborhood groups to state and city bureaucracies instead, thus tending to weaken the political base of poor people being served under earlier employment and training programs.[60]

A lessening of governmental activism and social welfare directed at poverty was a goal of the Nixon administration. It was hoped that this could be achieved by providing non-earmarked funds to states rather than the traditional categorical grants for specific federal government objectives. Concomitantly, the State and Local Fiscal Assistance Act also resulted in less federal support and resources for the kind of neighborhood initiatives that had been used by poor blacks and Latinos to challenge traditional local power structures. This is pointed out and discussed by David Greenstone and Paul Peterson in *Race and Authority in Urban America*.[61] This book focuses on the effects of these national policies in five cities: New York, Detroit, Philadelphia, Chicago and Los Angeles.

One intellectual justification for less government activism in the area of reducing poverty was provided by Moynihan. He called for a policy strategy of "benign neglect," suggesting that the problem of blacks in poverty could not be resolved through social engineering and that poverty might eventually be reduced as the black family became more stable. During the Johnson and Nixon administrations, many accepted Moynihan's proposition that a major part of the problem of black poverty reflected the deterioration of family structure. Moynihan suggested, furthermore, that the effects of slavery helped to explain this family deterioration.[62]

The Ford Administration (1974-1977)

As part of his anti-poverty initiative, in 1975 President Ford signed a $4.5 billion economic stimulus program that included $2.5 billion for hiring unemployed workers at the state and local levels. President Ford also continued to support another federal jobs program initially aimed at poor people: the Comprehensive Employment and Training Act (CETA) passed in 1973.

The earned income tax credit, also passed in 1975 under the Ford administration, resembles a negative income tax, but it is instead a way to relieve the poor with children of payroll taxation. This law provides a refundable tax credit to low-income families with children. In 1975 it was funded at $1.250 billion; by 1991 funding had increased to $8.806 billion. While the concept of the earned income tax credit is progressive, Harrell R. Rodgers, Jr. has recently stated in *Poor Women, Poor Families* that it is "flawed in major ways." He writes:

First, a low-income parent does not qualify for the credit unless he or she earns enough income to provide at least 50 percent of the support of the children in the family. A single mother receiving 50 percent or more of her income from AFDC would not qualify for the credit. Second, the credit does not vary by number of children in the family. Third, even those families that qualify for the credit receive it only at the end of the year in a lump sum.[63]

While the law was amended under the Tax Reform Act of 1986, there have been several attempts in recent years, including the current Clinton administration, to increase the credit allowed under this program. The projected increase for 1993 was $11.914 billion. Such increases still pose a problem, however, as suggested by Rodgers. In an article by Ellen Teninty, "Tax Credits Divide and Conquer," she points out that many low-income people may not even file for the earned income tax credit because they do not file for taxes.[64] Thus, this benefit may not be reaching as many people who might be eligible for it.

The Carter Administration (1977-1981)

In 1977 President Carter expanded considerably the CETA program to cover 725,000 persons. At the same time he changed the program's focus in part by emphasizing public service jobs, rather than public works. This change made it possible to reach many unemployed workers who, due to lack of skills or discrimination by unions, would not have been hired for public works jobs.

A major legislative effort of the Carter administration in the area of poverty and public policy included attempts to institute an income maintenance program, or negative income tax, in lieu of public assistance as it had been then structured. On August 6, 1977, Carter presented to the U.S. Congress the Program for Better Jobs and Income (PBJI), a proposal that resembled Nixon's Family Assistance Plan. As described by Professor K. Sue Jewell:

[T]his program, while exempting the aged, blind, disabled, and single parents with children under seven, required the principal wage earner in each family seeking public assistance to participate in a five-week program to secure a job. If a job could not be found, then a public sector job would be made available. Ultimately the wage earner was to obtain a private-sector job. In addition, this proposal contained a provision that individuals who did not generate sufficient incomes could receive a direct cash benefit or an expanded earned-income tax credit.[65]

A summary of the Carter income maintenance proposal can also be found in a study for the Urban Institute by James R. Storey, Robert Harris, and Frank Levy, *The Better Jobs and Income Plan: A Guide to President Carter's Welfare Reform Proposal*.[66] The major arguments favoring Carter's measure were that this initiative was an alternative to a welfare bureaucracy that had become too self-serving and demeaning to the poor. Furthermore, it was argued that this income maintenance proposal would allow standardization and uniformity of services and reduce welfare costs and fraud in the long run. Related to this, a minimum income maintenance program, it was hoped, would counter the presumed socialization in inferiority and low expectations of poor persons by the bureaucratic welfare system.

The Carter income maintenance initiative was defeated, as the earlier Family Assistance Plan during the Nixon administration had been because a coalition supporting the initiative did not materialize in the Congress. David McKay analyzes the failure of Carter's welfare reform initiative and proposes that interdepartmental warfare at the federal level, as well as "policy confusion" regarding the inconsistent goals of both simplification and reduced costs, doomed the initiative.[67]

Robert H. Haveman is critical of an exclusive income floor approach and argues in "The Changed Face of Poverty" that poverty policy should focus on increasing opportunities rather than solely on providing an income floor.[68] Parcel to this provision of opportunities is universal child care, employment subsidies for low wage workers, universal personal capital allowance for youth to pay for education, and health care. Only the provision of these services, the author proposes, will guarantee that the poor will escape poverty and not merely be shifted back and forth between non-working, and working poor status.

Arguments against this kind of public policy include the claim that such an approach is an indirect way of reducing the public funding available to assist the poor, and that this approach responds only to the economic dimension of poverty in urban America.

Theresa Funiciello revives the debate about income maintenance in an essay titled, "The Poverty Industry."[69] This author proposes that the income security approach could be more successful and less costly in reducing poverty. Because the current system has a vested interest in maintaining large numbers of poor people, she argues, income maintenance could directly equip poor individuals to escape from poverty.

One idea that emerged during the Nixon and Carter administrations in response to the problem of urban poverty was embraced in various ways by some in the academic community. This was the proposition that the poor should be geographically dispersed. Anthony Downs, writing in 1968 as part of a group of political scientists and economists identifying the concentration of blacks in urban ghettos as a social and economic problem in the late 1060s, suggested that poor blacks be dispersed in white suburban communities. Blacks would be dispersed on the basis of his "Law of Cultural Dominance" which meant that they would not be put into places where a possible preponderance of black culture would threaten the cultural attributes or tastes of suburban whites.[70] Other economists, such as John F. Kain and Joseph J. Persky, argued that "the impact of the ghetto on the processes of metropolitan development has created or aggravated many of our most critical urban problems."[71] These two writers advocated dispersing ghetto residents via low-income housing outside the ghetto.

Another poverty dispersion plan was advocated by Roger Starr while he served as administrator for housing in New York City. Starr called for "planned shrinkage" as a way of eliminating social and economic problems associated with significant numbers of poor persons.[72] This meant that blocks of land in the black community would be abandoned by government until there were no services available in these areas. Presumably, this would discourage the concentration of poor people, and concomitantly make the area available for highly profitable land speculation and development. This plan had a common ring with some of the policy recommendations made by Edward C. Banfield in his work *The Unheavenly City* in the early 1970s.[73] While these kinds of suggestions have never been officially adopted by national administrations, support for such ideas arises periodically in academic and government circles.

The Reagan Administration's "New Federalism" (1981-1989)

Despite the conservative rhetoric and policies of the Nixon administration, federal involvement and activism in the area of social welfare and poverty grew considerably during his presidency. Both Presidents Ford and Carter called for a decrease in federal government involvement in social welfare, but it was not until the election of President Ronald Reagan that the nation began to understand what it really meant for the federal government to cut back in the area of anti-poverty social welfare policy. This change is reflected in the stark contrast between Reagan's call to "get government off our backs" and President Kennedy's call for "basic soul searching" on the part of the Council of Economic Advisers (CEA) for new anti-poverty programs.[74] In 1981 President Reagan used tax cuts to stimulate economic development and the generation of jobs. This was the largest tax cut in American history, resulting in a tax reduction of $280 billion over three years and a 25 percent cut in individual income tax rates. The 1981 Omnibus Budget Reconciliation Act (OBRA) as well as the

Economic Recovery Tax Act signalled the elimination and/or consolidation of many grants enacted in previous national administrations. Under OBRA "408,000 families lost [AFDC] eligibility altogether, and another 299,000 had their benefits reduced. Federal and state governments realized savings of $1.1 billion in 1983.[75] While President Reagan's lopsided reelection victory was interpreted as a mandate for strengthening initiatives and actions under the "New Federalism," the U.S. Congress provided some resistance to certain cuts. Some of the impact of the tax cuts was countered, however, by the Tax Equity and Fiscal Responsibility Act, passed in August 1982.[76]

The "New Federalism" under President Reagan meant massive cutbacks in anti-poverty programs of federal assistance to states and localities. For example, a 1987 study authored by William P. O'Hare, *Poverty in America*, reports that budget cuts in 1981 and 1982 resulted in a combined cut of $2 billion in the Food Stamp Program and termination of AFDC payments and Medicaid coverage for 500,000 low-income working families.[77] This same study reveals that, according to the Congressional Budget Office, "funding for programs targeted mainly for the poor was cut $57 billion in the four years from fiscal year 1982 through fiscal year 1985, after adjustment for inflation and employment."[78]

In the area of housing assistance, the cutback on spending shrunk the budget from $33 billion in 1981 to $10 billion in 1988. In the first term of President Reagan the domestic budget was cut between $30 and $40 billion while the military budget was increased significantly and corporate tax breaks and credits were expanded considerably.[79] Rodgers explains in a previously cited work that "President Ronald Reagan's idea of reform consisted of three principles: 1) compulsory work programs for the poor; 2) reducing or abolishing as many welfare programs as possible; and 3) convincing the states to assume a larger share of the costs and administrative burdens of those programs that survived."[80] K. Sue Jewell argues similarly that the "radical shift in social policy from liberal to conservative did far more than reduce moneys to social and economic programs." She adds that this shift was also decidedly anti-black and anti-poor; the shift

> established a new social climate with a growing intolerance for conditions facing black and poor families in the United States. In making monumental changes in social policy, the federal government insisted that middle-class families had been ignored and had become the caretakers of black and poor families for twenty years.[81]

Robert X. Browning suggests that President Reagan's action should not be perceived simply as his disagreement with anti-poverty efforts, but rather reflecting his view of the limited nature of the federal government:

"The Reagan administration priorities were not targeted primarily at the War on Poverty programs, but at the expansion of the welfare state realized in the post-Johnson years. Most of these eligibility changes and new programs were enacted during the Nixon and Ford presidencies."[82]

In 1982 President Reagan signed legislation creating the Job Training Partnership Act (JTPA). According to political scientist John Donahue in *The Privatization Decision*, this represented a philosophical and programmatic repudiation of the Comprehensive Employment and Training Act (CETA) established in 1973 under the Nixon administration.[83] Some black leaders and activists had had suspicions about the impact of CETA from the very beginning of this legislation. Charles S. Bullock points out in a 1975 essay, "Expanding Black Economic Rights,"that "black leaders view the shift in policy authority from federal to state and local officials with misgivings...The CETA seems designed to weaken not only federal control but also the influence of local poverty groups who have run some programs in the past."[84] In some cities, the elimination or weakening of CETA and related regulation strengthened the political hand of mayors and city halls at odds with local poverty groups as a matter of fact.

This suspicion was partially borne by the groups who benefited from employment under the CETA Program. In 1975 about 300,000 workers were on city and country payrolls under the CETA program; by 1978 this number grew to 750,000 workers. But these employees were not necessarily economically disadvantaged, and in many cases included skilled and unionized workers who were temporarily unemployed. While CETA focused on training and public employment, Reagan's legislation relied on privatization of training for the economically disadvantaged.

An improvement over the CETA program is that JTPA regulations require that 40 percent of all funds be expended on youth 16 to 21 years of age, and that 70 percent of all funds be exclusively expended on training. It should be noted, however, that training is not conducted by JTPA administrative offices, but instead is contracted to other sectors. According to Donahue there are three major weaknesses in this act's approach. One is that the typical JTPA graduate is provided with a job paying little more than half of the average wage. As Donahue observed, "most of the working poor move in and out of such jobs with dismal regularity, with or without government help."[85] Second, there is an incentive to "cream"candidates, or select those with the greatest chances of success, rather than serve the most economically disadvantaged. And finally, the JTPA programs serve only between 2 and 3 percent of the eligible poor each year. This figure is very low and not impressive when it is noted that about 10 percent of the poor escape poverty each year regardless of the work of JTPA. Donahue believes that the Job Corps approach is superior to JTPA because *recruitment* and *placement* of enrollees is controlled not by those who are providing training, but instead by social agencies, schools, and local employment agencies.[86]

Just as the philosophical and economic guiding light of the New Deal was represented by the work of John Maynard Keynes, another economist, Alfred Laffer, provided the philosophical rationalization and justification for President Reagan's "supply side economics." Laffer's work, however, was based on a 1924 publication by Andrew W. Mellon, *Taxation, the People's Business*.[87] "Laffer's Curve" was used to illustrate a hypothesis regarding the relationship of tax and government revenue. The hypothesis is that beyond a certain tax rate, tax revenues will begin to fall.

As pointed out by economist Frank Ackerman, "Laffer's argument begins with a question. At what percentage tax rate will the government receive the maximum tax revenue?"[88] Simply explained, Laffer's Curve illustrates that while relatively low tax rates initially increase government revenue, beyond a certain point higher tax rates will begin to reduce revenues because savings is discouraged by this higher taxation.

Economist Anthony S. Campagna summarizes and explains this proposition in his work, *U.S. National Economic Policy, 1917-1985*:

> The route by which revenues would rise follows the path from an increase in saving, and thus investment, which would increase economic activity, to an increase in economic growth, which would bring in greater tax revenues. Along the way private incentives would be restored, since high tax rates discourage risk taking and investment and divert investment into unproductive investment in the attempt to minimize taxation; productivity would rise, as people feel they could retain more of their hard-earned income, and of course, more jobs would be created by the economic growth bringing in more revenue, and so on.[89]

Under the Reagan administration massive cutbacks in domestic social welfare were accompanied by a strong ideological orientation that called for greater public policy deference to laissez-faire and supply-side economics. Thus, the federal government would utilize its resources to primarily assist the corporate sector, and replace traditional social welfare mechanisms to help the poor with market-driven models such as urban enterprise zones, privatization, and greater utilization of vouchers for delivering a range of services.

A senior staff economist for tax policy in President Reagan's Council of Economic Advisors argues in *The Growth Experiment* that the supply side policies of Reagan did, in fact, work to spur unprecedented economic growth. In this way, according to this analysis, Reagan's tax polices reduced poverty for Americans. Economist Lawrence B. Lindsay argues in this study that the rise in poverty rates in the first Reagan administration was due to policies pursued by President Carter. By the time the Reagan policies started to take effect, " the poverty rate was back down to the level it was at when Reagan took office. It dropped even further during his last three years in office."[90]

There is a presumption inherent in Reagan's "New Federalism" that poverty was not a flaw of the system, as had been reflected in some of the programs started in the New Deal administration, nor a flaw in how the poor are prepared to partake of economic opportunity, as proposed in the Great Society. Rather, the assumption in the Reagan administration's approach to poverty is that persistent poverty involves cultural and human flaws such as dependency and the lack of motivation. Some current writers such as Charles Murray suggest, as did President Nixon earlier, that a significant number of people are poor because they have become overly dependent and lazy as a result of liberal governmental programs.[91] This was a theme supported by Senator Barry Goldwater during the Eisenhower years as is pointed out by political scientists David B. Robertson and Dennis R. Judd in *The Development of American Public Policy*. They describe the Senator's reaction when a city manager of Newbury, New York, instituted draconian measures to reduce welfare costs. This city manager "stipulated that all able-bodied men who refused to do city work would forfeit benefits, that unwed mothers would lose benefits if they had an additional child, and that all recipients, except the aged and disabled, were entitled to only three months of aid per calendar year. Senator Barry Goldwater applauded. "I don't like to see my taxes paid for children out of wedlock...I am tired of professional chiselers wailing up and down the streets who don't work and have no intention of working. I would like to see every city in the country adopt the plan."[92]

Both the Reagan and Bush administrations were ardent supporters of free market approaches, volunteerism, and "workfare" as solutions to the problem of poverty in the American city. Workfare requires recipients of public assistance to accept employment assignments in return for welfare benefits. These employment assignments are determined by the agency dispensing benefits and usually involve labor for community service projects. Workfare requirements were first established for food stamp recipients in 1977 and were expanded by the 1981 Omnibus Budget Reconciliation Act, which permitted states to require AFDC and AFDC/UP recipients to earn their welfare benefits through labor for public service projects. This approach was continued with the Family Support Act signed by President Reagan in late 1988. Since this legislation was implemented under President Bush's administration, it will be explained further in the next section.

Economist Lawrence M. Mead has hailed workfare as a response to poverty because, according to him, able-bodied males receiving welfare assistance have refused to work, even when jobs have been available. Mead goes so far as to forewarn that this "dependency" means "the end of the *Western Tradition*."[93] Political scientist M. E. Hawkesworth contends, on the other hand, that the policy presuppositions of workfare are seriously flawed. As Hawkesworth writes in *Theoretical Issues in Policy Analysis*:

An examination of the demographic characteristics of the poor suggests that the pathological theory is fundamentally flawed. More than two-thirds of the poor in the contemporary United States are unable to work because of age, disability, or caretaking responsibilities for pre-school children. Forty-eight percent of the households with pretransfer incomes below the poverty level are headed by individuals age sixty-five or older; another twelve percent are headed by disabled individuals; seven percent are headed by women with children younger than six. Of the remaining households below the poverty line, seven and a half percent are headed by persons who work full-time year round, but whose incomes do not meet family subsistence needs; 20.4% are headed by part-time workers, and five percent are headed by students...Only a small proportion of households receiving public benefits remain on welfare for longer periods of time. The vast majority resort to welfare to upgrade their total income because their earnings from work are inadequate or because they are temporarily unemployed.[94]

Workfare is based on a pathological view of poverty that is erroneous and presumes incorrectly, according to Hawkesworth, that young male or female heads of families are poor because they refuse to work, and that generous governmental assistance allows these individuals to continue to avoid work. This criticism is supported by Richard A. Cloward and Frances Fox Piven, who point out that "14.4 million year-round, full-time workers 16 years of age or older (18 percent of total) had annual earnings below the poverty level in 1990, up from 10.3 million (14.6 percent) in 1984 and 6.6 million (12.3 percent) in 1974."[95]

The British idea of establishing "free enterprise zones" to revitalize decaying urban areas also became prominent during the Reagan administration.[96] Opponents to this kind of market-driven approach point out, however, that the history of the private sector in terms of assisting with social welfare is not sanguine. Furthermore, efficiency is not an automatic or inherent hallmark of the private sector as indicated by the number of business failures and bankruptcies, as well as corruption.

It has also been argued that some of the significant social and economic advances of the poor have not been based on the activities of the private sector, but rather on government activism and employment. This is especially the case for blacks and Latinos in the United States. The public sector has been a critical foundation of black and Latino economic well-being. In 1976, for instance, 27 percent of all blacks worked in the public sector; the comparable figure for whites was 16 percent. According to Sheldon Danziger in "Poverty and Inequality Under Reaganomics," between 1960 and 1976 more than half of all the employment increase for blacks occurred in the public sector.[97] A shrinking of the government sector, therefore, would in all likelihood mean greater economic distress for blacks, and probably Latinos as well.

The Bush Administration (1989-1993)

The social welfare and anti-poverty initiatives of the Bush administration are summarized, in part, in a fact sheet issued by the Office of the Press Secretary for the White House on February 27, 1991. The memo states that the Bush administration "seeks to use numerous administrative, regulatory, and budgetary means to expand economic opportunity for low-income individuals." Program initiatives under this strategy include: educational choice, educational flexibility, homeownership for low-income persons, enterprise zones, anti-discrimination laws, community-opportunity areas, the Social Security earnings test, and anti-crime efforts.[98]

In addition to making "proper and effective use of the incentives on which private enterprise relies to reward work and achievement," another major initiative in the Bush administration regarding the issue of poverty was continuation of the education and training approach under the Job Training Partnership Act (JTPA).[99] As have others, this administration reflected a strong belief that poverty can be reduced or eliminated for individuals if they have an adequate level of training and education. This approach is supported in various ways by studies like the one published by the Ford Foundation in 1988, *Toward a More Perfect Union*.[100] It is reported in this study that of the lowest-scoring fifth of those persons taking the Air Force Qualifying Test, and those between the ages of 19 and 23, 46 percent were poor, 40 percent were jobless, 53 percent were public assistance recipients, 59 percent were unwed mothers and 52 percent were dropouts from school before the twelfth year.[101] These kinds of statistics encourage the creditability of the idea that expanding educational and training opportunities will significantly improve the job marketability of poor people.

There is, of course, some relationship between education and training, and the marketability of the individual. But for several reasons, the former does not always lead to the latter. First of all, education and training programs are not as simple to administer as it may initially appear. Michael Morris and John B. Williamson write in "Workfare: The Poverty/Dependence Tradeoff," that, unlike a transfer program like Social Security which is relatively straightforward in how it gets benefits to clients, education and training policies must be able to ensure at least six conditions. These are:

Participants must possess or develop the motivation and ability necessary to learn the skills being taught;

The model of skill training that is used must be educationally sound;

Training must be at a sufficiently high level to qualify program graduates, in either the short or the long run, for jobs paying nonpoverty wages;

These jobs must actually be available in the communities where program graduates reside, or in communities they can move to;

Graduates must have the ability and motivation to hold onto these jobs once they obtain them;

The local, regional, and/or national economy must be vigorous enough to support the continued existence of these jobs.[102]

In addition to these concerns, political economist Bette Woody adds that the benefits of employment training programs have not addressed fully the needs of black women. Job training must be reformed, she argues, by targeting black women and "acknowledging the need to address a population currently in the workplace, but employed in very low skilled, low paid jobs. This would reverse current policy directions which are aimed more at AFDC recipients, or at unemployed men."[103] This finding is also interesting in light of the earlier discussion regarding universal vs. targeted social welfare approaches.

The Bush administration inherited and supported the legislative enactment of a major welfare reform initiative which reflected an education and training approach. The Family Support Act (FSA) was signed into law as P.L. 100-485 on October 13, 1988 by President Reagan. The purpose of this law has been to reform the Aid to Families with Dependent Children program (AFDC) by emphasizing training, education, and employment as a way of reducing the number of persons receiving assistance. In an article for the *Trotter Review*, Bette Woody provides a concise summary of the legislation, as well as some of the pro and con arguments raised during congressional testimony.[104] A report by Linda McCart for the National Governor's Association, "A Governor's Guide to the Family Support Act: Challenges and Opportunities," is also useful in providing basic information about this legislative initiative, as is a chapter, "Reforming the American Welfare System," in Rodgers's, *Poor Women, Poor Families*.[105]

The Family Support Act has several components, including the following:

Child Support: The law requires that courts force absent fathers to pay support for children through income withholding, and to establish procedures for establishing paternity in contested cases.

Job Opportunities and Basic Skills (JOBS) Program: Most AFDC recipients are required to participate in a JOBS program. Parents with children over age 3 are required to participate in this jobs program. States must make available to recipients training, basic and remedial education, job readiness activities, and job placement. The JOBS program is aimed at the following groups: a) parents under age 24 who are high school dropouts, and not enrolled in an equivalency diploma program; b) parents under age 24 with little or no work experience; c) individuals who have received public assistance for at least 36 of the last 60 months; and d) those targeted to lose AFDC benefits within two years as a result of youngest child losing eligibility as a dependent child.

Child Care: Recipients participating in training and education activities are eligible for child care. States must ensure that child care is available for families with dependent children as is necessary for an individual to accept employment.

Transitional Services: If, as a result of employment families are no longer eligible for AFDC, then the law provides a limited amount of extended medical coverage. Former recipients will receive 6 months of medical assistance free of charge; after this period states may impose a premium for an additional six months of coverage.

Benefits for Minor Parents: Unmarried individuals under 18 years of age with dependent children can only receive support if residing with parents, legal guardians, foster home, or maternity home.

Benefits for Two-Parent Families: Coverage is available for two-parent families who are unemployed.

Despite these kinds of programmatic initiatives, however, researcher José E. Cruz reports in a 1991 study for the National Puerto Rican Coalition, Inc., *Implementing the Family Support Act*, that the JOBS program may, in fact, only transform the welfare poor into the working poor: "findings suggest that employment will be less likely for Puerto Rican AFDC mothers with little or no employment history, that as long as they have to take care of their children they will prefer not to work, and that employment training programs will not fare well in the context of economic restructuring and population decline in the Northeast, where Puerto Ricans concentrate."[106]

In a recent evaluation of the Family Support Act by the Manpower Development Research Corporation it was noted that poor program attendance in the education and training programs identified by the act is a major problem in moving welfare recipients off welfare. Barriers to greater program attendance include child care issues, transportation, health, and family crisis, as well as earlier negative school experiences of the recipient. Perhaps some of these weaknesses explain why the number of AFDC caseloads increased between 1988 and 1991, along with an increase in costs, and 1.9 million additional children falling into poverty.[107]

Several other weaknesses have been ascribed to this law. For instance, the Family Support Act initially called for spending an average of $745 per participant on training and education programs. The U.S. Government Accounting Office, however, has determined that the amount needed for quality training leading to employment is closer to $2,500 per participant. Rodgers writes in a previously noted work that "The provisions of the bill will be phased in over fiscal years 1989-1993. With a five-year cost of $3.3 billion, it will be too modest to impact poverty greatly."[108] Concerns about available resources for welfare reform are also expressed in a review of the Family Support Act's impact on states in a recent article published in *Governing*, where reporter Kathleen Sylvester writes that the economic recession is not allowing states to obtain their share of matching federal dollars to institute welfare reform.[109] Many states must limit their efforts in this area due to a host of budget problems. Tennessee, for example, will collect only 1.5 million dollars of the total 17 million dollars it could collect, as a consequence of this state's economic downturn. Many other states are in similar straits.

Attaining decent living wages is not an explicit goal of the Family Support Act; rather, its goal is to reduce the welfare rolls. This is related to the claim by journalist Laurie Udesky, of the Center for Investigative

Reporting in San Francisco, that the purpose of this legislation is not to end poverty, but rather to end "dependency."[110] As Udesky suggests, this initiative could even be viewed as a benefits program for employers in that its indirect effect is to depress the demands for higher and decent living wages. There is a difference between the goal of reducing poverty and the goal of reducing what some might refer to as "dependency," as is explained by Morris and Williamson in their work.[111] These two researchers point out that, while conservative anti-poverty approaches seek to reduce dependency rather than poverty, the preoccupation with workfare, ironically, will "divert attention from and ultimately undermine support for the much more important goal of poverty reduction." These two authors add, furthermore, that "even high quality training does not appear to have the potential to reduce poverty to the extent that can be achieved through generous benefit levels."[112]

The Joint Center for Political and Economic Studies points to a similar conclusion regarding its analysis of the Family Support Act in a recent study titled, *The Declining Economic Status of Black Children*:

> FSA is unlikely to have much impact on the large number of working poor families in the South. Nor will it lift children from poverty if their parents are merely shifted from the dependent poor to the working poor column and in the long run, even a Family Support Act that is appropriately implemented and adequately funded cannot stand alone as the sole means for improving the well-being of children. Rather, the situation calls for comprehensive strategies and programs to improve the quality of education, provide skills training for the jobs of the future, and ensure equal access to employment opportunities.[113]

These criticisms are similar to those reported by Marcia Bok, professor of social research and social work at the University of Connecticut:

> The Family Support Act of 1988, "welfare reform" has been touted as a major change and improvement in social policy. In fact, the new legislation incorporates myths about the poor that uphold traditional beliefs about the work ethic, the family ethic, and the so-called culture of society. As far back as history records welfare practices, there has been an emphasis on the work ethic, almost always defined in righteous terms, usually without reference to labor market conditions.[114]

Bok adds:

> At the present time, means-tested, mandated education and employment training, without job creation, and without an increase in the minimum wage, will not lift AFDC recipients out of poverty conditions...In order for women of all ages to achieve economic self-sufficiency, there is the need for adequate income, universal national health insurance, subsidized child care, transportation, and scattered-site, low-income housing.[115]

In sum, these and other observers and researchers are suggesting that the Family Support Act of 1988 is limited conceptually, programmatically, and fiscally in terms of reducing poverty in this country.

There is yet another problem with this act, and it has implications regarding the earlier discussion of "universalism" and social welfare. According to researcher Katherine McFate, those states where the majority of AFDC clients are white have much greater funding for employment and training than those states where a majority of AFDC clients are black. For example, in Massachusetts and Rhode Island, the 1988 funding level per recipient for welfare-to-work programs was $1,379 and $1,120, respectively. In both of these states between 80 and 85 percent of AFDC participants are white. But in Alabama and Tennessee, where the majority of recipients are black, the 1988 funding level provided $33 and $24, respectively, per recipient for the same program.[116]

President Bush's national initiatives and policies related to anti-poverty efforts included a number of other components. Some of these initiatives, cited earlier, are summarized and outlined briefly in a White House memo describing the appointment of an "Economic Empowerment Task Force."[117] For instance, homeownership for poor persons was to be promoted under the "Homeownership and Opportunity for People Everywhere" (HOPE): "By offering residents greater control and access to property, the HOPE program will instill pride of ownership and enhance incentives for maintenance and improvement."[118] In the area of free enterprise zones, the administration announced that: "Enterprise zones will attack poverty by promoting investment in economically distressed neighborhoods. Enterprise zones will attract new seed capital for small business start-ups, create new incentives for entrepreneurial risk-taking, and reduce high effective tax rates on those moving to work from welfare."[119]

Overcoming overly-specialized and disconnected approaches to service delivery in poor communities was another feature of the Bush initiatives. Acccording to a September 1990 White House memo this problem was to be tackled through the Community Opportunity Act of

1991: "Programs providing social, welfare, health, education, and nutritional services are often delivered in fragmented ways. Allowing services to be integrated will better serve the recipients of these programs and promote self-sufficiency and opportunity...The Community Opportunity Act of 1991 will enable local communities to develop 'community opportunity systems' and allow them to restructure Federal programs to provide services and benefits in the way the community deems best to meet the needs of the individuals and families served."[120] Finally, President Bush also approved a major transportation bill mandating the expenditure of $151 billion for roads and mass transit over six years, in order to generate economic growth. Included in this program was highway construction, which remains the largest of federal jobs programs.

In addition to these broad sweeps at the generation of jobs and economic development, national administrations have also sponsored specific programs and actions aimed at reducing or eliminating poverty. Despite the symbolic attempts to reduce poverty in America, a review of efforts on the part of national administrations shows that poverty reduction has not ever been a sustained, high priority of federal policy. Robert J. Lampman reminds us that the size and impact of the poverty problem was becoming less predominant nationally during the 1960s and 1970s. In his 1971 publication *Ends and Means of Reducing Income Poverty*, Lampman writes that the poverty gap between 1959 and 1968 had actually shrunk.[121] Since that time, however, the total "poverty gap" — or the actual number of dollars required "to bring all poor households up to the poverty line" — has increased from $31.8 billion in 1965, to $45.6 billion in 1983 (1982 dollars) regardless of various attempts by national administrations to manage and reduce poverty.[122]

The Clinton Administration (1993-)

Unfortunately, President Clinton's administration does not seem intent on offering any major new strategies to reduce poverty. Nor, to use Clinton's own term, does it seem as though the current administration will "end welfare as we know it." As was the case with previous administrations, the current one also suggests that there exists an "undeserving" poor who should be forced to work and whose behavior should be monitored closely by government. President Clinton's call for "personal responsibility" and an end to "dependency" is similar to the calls of Presidents Reagan and Bush, as is pointed out by journalist David Futrelle: "some liberals (and a few vaguely on the left) have attempted to recapture the language of morality — and, in particular, the language of responsibility — from the right."[123] This similarity should not be surprising given President Clinton's support of and role in the enactment of the Family Support Act of 1988 while he served as governor of Arkansas.

The apparent failure or ineffectiveness of this legislation has now heralded yet another call by both Republicans and Democrats to clean up the "welfare mess." The suggested proposals emanating from the Clinton administration include draconian and punitive legislative and executive orders at the federal and state levels aimed presumably at reducing "dependency" by forcing poor people into low-wage jobs, discouraging poor, single women from giving birth to more than one child, and generally developing huge governmental bureaucracies to monitor the activities and behavior of poor people. Due to the fact that blacks and Puerto Ricans tend to be more persistently poor than whites, invariably the Clinton administration's punitive proposals will have the effect of targeting these groups to a greater extent than others. According to economist Randy Abelda, welfare reform aimed at forcing poor women to work is particularly aimed at single mothers and diverts attention from issues like child-care reform, wage reform, and job reform.[124]

The Clinton administration's movement regarding welfare reforms reflects the decisions of many state governments who are finding that attacking "dependency" (a behavioral condition) rather than actual poverty (an economic condition) is electorally and politically popular. States like California, New Jersey, Michigan, and others are preparing a range of actions that include cuts in benefits, freezing benefits to mothers on AFDC if they give birth to additional children, requiring single teen mothers receiving AFDC to live with their parents, forcing mandatory school attendance on high school youth on government rolls, and even fingerprinting recipients of welfare assistance as a response to welfare fraud. In California, Governor Pete Wilson has called for drastic reductions in AFDC benefits aimed towards a transitional process where welfare would be eliminated for any family with an "able-bodied adult" (including mothers with young children). It is admitted that the purpose of these draconian measures is not simply fiscal; according to Russell Gould, secretary of Health and Welfare for California: "This is not just about reducing the grant...It is far more about trying to encourage personal responsibility."[125]

A strategy aimed at generating personal responsibility, whether at the federal or state levels, diverts attention from economic factors that may cause poverty and near-poverty status for millions of Americans. As the next chapter illustrates, furthermore, focusing on presumed behavioral aspects of poverty status overlooks some fundamental characteristics and trends associated with poverty. Particularly, this kind of approach overlooks the fact that the poverty population is diverse; it also ignores certain kinds of characteristics that manifestly are not related to the behavior or attitudes of poor people. At least two such characteristics include a continuing racial gap in how the poor experience poverty and lesser public revenues being directed at poverty over the last several decades.

There are other conceptual problems with the welfare reform strategy that the Clinton administration is pursuing. One is that welfare reform that targets the behavior of poor people has most political saliency when the economy is shrinking and state budgets are tight; yet to change the welfare system does involve, inevitably, public resources. The attempt to reduce so-called dependency arises when taxpayers and workers feel that they have less to afford their more needy fellow citizens. But, ironically, the attempt to reduce welfare dependency as a way of cutting costs, does require up-front start-up costs for new initiatives and administrative changes. Thus, despite its electoral popularity, welfare reformers' calls to end dependency are usually not affordable.

Another contradiction with a focus on dependency as a way to reform welfare has to do with the actual availability of jobs. Getting, or being forced into a job — any job — is being touted as a solution to welfare dependency during a period when the private sector continues to lose jobs nationally, and the federal government has decided to scale back its commitments as a result of the national deficit and debt.

Journalist Penelope Lemov points out that in this economic period, if welfare time limits are adopted and implemented, it will give rise to some "troubling questions" for which there are no answers presently. She asks, "Will there be enough jobs in the private sector to accommodate all the people forced off welfare who will be looking for employment?...Will the states create subsidized work in return for welfare benefits, or will they just kick a family off the rolls? If the only job available doesn't pay the rent, food and clothing bills, will the state step in and subsidize incomes? In the end, might it actually be more expensive than 'welfare as we know it'?"[126] It is certainly much easier for President Clinton and a host of state governors to talk about personal responsibility and ending welfare dependency than it is to answer these kinds of questions about welfare reform.

In addition to welfare reform, the Clinton administration has also embarked on a strategy of generating enterprise, and empowerment, zones, as did the preceding Bush administration. The Clinton administration argues, however, that its approach to enterprise zones is different than earlier Republican versions. President Clinton requested $4.1 billion for one hundred enterprise communities and ten empowerment zones that would receive the major share of tax incentives under the program. Most of the $4.1 billion is represented by wage tax credits that would benefit residents of these zones. Another major feature of Clinton's approach is an insistence on developing a coordinated proposal and strategy for each zone that would reflect partnership and linkage between government, non-profits, and the private sector. In return, the president has promised the elimination of red tape and federal bureaucracy; as claimed by President Clinton's staff: "We'll give you one check, we'll break down the walls between the programs, and that money therefore will be more valuable...If we can combine the programs, reduce the regulations, reduce the bureaucracy that one must traverse between the need and funding, you will indirectly be getting more out of the levels of bureaucracy, all of which charge an administrative fee."[127]

Two initiatives that should impact favorably on Americans who are poor or near-poor and, interestingly, do not rely on the presumed behavior of poor people, are the earned income tax credit and national health insurance. The adoption of national health insurance should mean that all Americans, regardless of income level, will have access to at least a minimum level of health care. As stated earlier, the earned income tax credit is not a new idea. However, this is one program that seems to be effective in getting income into the hands of poor and near-poor families — without, importantly, the stigmatization typically associated with assisting the impoverished population.

What Are the Major Characteristics and Trends Associated with Poverty in the United States, and How Are Race and Ethnicity Reflected in These Trends?

To be a poor man is hard, but to be a poor race in a land of dollars is the very bottom of hardships.

W.E.B. Du Bois
The Souls of Black Folk (1903)

Now I am perfectly aware that there are other slums in which white men are fighting for their lives, and mainly losing. I know that blood is also flowing through those streets and that the human damage there is incalculable. People are continually pointing out to me the wretchedness of white people in order to console me for the wretchedness of blacks. But an itemized account of the American failure does not console me and it should not console anyone else.

James Baldwin
Nobody Knows My Name (1960)

In city after city and in many suburbs and rural sections of the nation, the face of poverty is visible in the lives of millions of Americans, and continues to grow larger and more pronounced. This can be illustrated in descriptions of poverty characteristics compiled from numerous reports and studies. These documents suggest, as economist John Kenneth Galbraith stated in his classic work, *The Affluent Society*, that while poverty in America is no longer as widespread as it was in earlier periods, it should not be treated as an "afterthought."[1] Along the same line of argument, Mollie Orshansky's claim in 1965 that poverty was not a "random affliction" has a truer ring a quarter of a century later.[2] The poor in this nation can no longer be hidden in a corner of society or ignored as a passing problem or an economic aberration. The Center on Budget and Policy Priorities reported that between 1989 and 1991 about 4.2 million more people became poverty-stricken in the United States. Slightly more than half (51 percent) were whites.[3] In 1991 the United States counted among its poverty population 17.7 million whites, 10.2 million blacks, and 6.3 million Latinos. Since the Second World War, poverty rates within the United States have been consistently different for men and women, and for children and the elderly. Generally, men have fared better than women in the reduction of poverty, and the elderly have fared better than children.[4] Additionally, as will be illustrated later in this chapter, blacks and Latinos have consistently fared worse than whites.

Despite a range of policies aimed at reducing its length and impact, poverty among Americans persists as a major economic problem, with far-ranging social, health, and educational implications. The term "persistent poverty" was utilized by George L. Beckford to describe extensive poverty and inequality in "underdeveloped" and "plantation" economies in the international arena.[5] Today, it is utilized by American researchers to differentiate poverty that is short term and episodic, from long term, sustained poverty. Sar A. Levitan and Isaac Shapiro suggest that poverty is "persistent" when a person or group are poor for more than three to four years. This should not obscure the fact that there is "considerable movement of persons into and out of poverty" according to Levitan and Shapiro in *Working but Poor*.[6] These authors conclude that "for most households, poverty is not a long-term affliction. Three-fifths of the nonelderly subject to a spell of poverty from 1970 to 1982 were poor for no more than two years."[7] The problem of persistent poverty, however, is significant: "...nearly a fourth of all poverty spells last five or more years, and 12 percent endure for a decade or more."[8] There are also major differences among racial groups regarding the persistence of poverty: "Whites and two-parent families experience primarily transitory poverty, but blacks and children born into poor families often face lengthy destitution."[9] And, while "childhood deprivation is widespread...long-term poverty is highly concentrated among blacks."[10]

In addition to the persistence of poverty, the actual size of the U.S. population living in poverty has grown since 1970. Although in 1965 there were approximately 33.2 million persons living in households below the officially determined poverty line (representing 17 percent of the total population at that time), by 1973 both the absolute number of persons living in poverty (23 million) and the proportion of poverty-stricken persons (11 percent) had declined significantly. By 1983, however, the number of persons in poverty had increased significantly, to 35.3 million persons or 15.2 percent of the population.[11] The Census reports that the rate of poverty increased again in 1991, with 2.1 million more Americans living below the poverty threshold than in 1990.

The growth and persistence of poverty in the United States is alarming in contrast with other industrialized nations. Researcher Isabel V. Sawhill reported that "Poverty has been surprisingly persistent in the United States. Despite considerable efforts to reduce it, the incidence of poverty in 1986 was as high as it had been in the late 1960s. It was also higher than the rate in most other industrial countries for which comparable data are available. This much poverty in one of the world's wealthiest democracies invites notice."[12] In 1986, the Luxembourg Income Study reported that the poverty rate among whites was 9.1 percent, a much higher rate than for Canada, France, Germany, the Netherlands, Sweden, and England. And the 13.2 percent poverty rate for white children in the United States in 1986 was more than twice the rate in these same countries.[13]

Trends in Poverty

Table 1 shows that the number of poor families in the United States declined between 1959 and 1979. As is noted in this table, since 1979 the number of poor families increased, from 5,461,000 to 7,098,000 by 1990, or by 3.9 percent. As is explained in chapter 1, a family is considered "poor" by the federal government if its annual income falls below a designated level considered necessary to meet "basic" living needs. In 1990, this amount was determined to be $13, 359 for a family of four.

TABLE 1
Number of Families Below Poverty Level
and Poverty Rate: 1959-1990

Year	Number of Poor Families (Thousands)	Poverty Rate (Percent)
1959	8,320	18.5
1964	7,160	15.0
1969	5,008	9.7
1974	4,922	8.8
1979	5,461	9.2
1984	7,277	11.6
1989	6,784	10.3
1990	7,098	10.7

SOURCE: U.S. Bureau of the Census, *Current Population Reports*, "Poverty in the United States: 1990," Series P-60, No. 175, (Washington, DC, 1991), table 16.

Table 2 shows the number of poor persons and poverty rates by race between 1959 and 1988. These statistics reflect the significant and continuing racial and ethnic differences in poverty rates among all families in the United States. Based on this table and table 3, poverty rates among blacks are the highest, followed by Latinos, Asians, and then whites. For example, in 1959, 55.1 percent of blacks were poor, compared with 18.1 percent of whites. In 1988, 31.6 percent of blacks were poor, whereas 10.1 percent of whites were poor.

Table 3 illustrates the increase in the number and proportion of poor persons between 1989 and 1990, by both race and selected ethnicity.

TABLE 2
Number and Proportion of Poor Persons
by Race: 1959-1988

Year	Number of Poor (Millions)			Proportion of Poor (Percent)		
	Black	White	Total	Black	White	Total
1959	9.9	28.5	39.5	55.1	18.1	22.4
1970	7.5	17.5	25.4	33.5	9.9	12.6
1980	8.6	19.7	29.3	32.5	10.2	13.0
1988	9.4	20.8	31.9	31.6	10.1	13.1

SOURCE: Derived from "Demographic Characteristics of the Poverty Population Over the Last Generation," in Sar A. Levitan, *Programs in Aid of the Poor* (Baltimore, MD: The Johns Hopkins University, 1990), table 5.

TABLE 3
Persons Below the Official Poverty Level
by Race and Ethnicity: 1989 and 1990
Number of Persons (Thousands) and Percent

	1989		1990	
White*	15,599	8.3%	16,622	8.8%
Black	9,302	30.7	9,837	31.9
Hispanic	5,430	26.2	6,006	28.1
Asian and Pacific Islander	939	14.1	858	12.2
Total	31,528	12.8%	33,585	13.5%

SOURCE: Derived from U.S. Bureau of the Census, *Current Population Reports*, "Poverty in the United States: 1990," Series P-60, No. 175·(Washington, DC, 1991), table A.
* Not of Hispanic origin

In addition to the existence of a diverse poverty population in terms of race, ethnicity and demographic category, there is also much variation across states in the nation. As table 4 shows, New Hampshire had the least proportion of persons below the poverty level in 1989 (6.4 percent), while Mississippi ranked first, with 25.2 percent of all persons living below the poverty level.

TABLE 4
Poverty Status in 1989 by Regions and States
Percent Below Poverty Level and Rank

Region and State	Persons		Related Children		Families	
	Percent	*Rank*	*Percent*	*Rank*	*Percent*	*Rank*
United States	13.1	(x)	17.9	(x)	10.0	(x)
Northeast	(NA)	(x)	(NA)	(x)	(NA)	(x)
Maine	10.8	35	13.2	37	8.0	34
New Hampshire	6.4	50	7.0	50	4.4	50
Vermont	9.9	41	11.5	44	6.9	41
Massachusetts	8.9	44	12.9	39	6.7	44
Rhode Island	9.6	42	13.5	35	6.8	42
Connecticut	6.8	49	10.4	49	5.0	49
New York	13.0	20	18.8	16	10.0	19
New Jersey	7.6	48	11.0	46	5.6	48
Pennsylvania	11.1	33	15.4	26	8.2	32
Midwest	(NA)	(x)	(NA)	(x)	(NA)	(x)
Ohio	12.5	23	17.6	20	9.7	21
Indiana	10.7	37	13.9	34	7.9	35
Illinois	11.9	26	16.8	24	9.0	26
Michigan	13.1	19	18.2	18	10.2	17
Wisconsin	10.7	36	14.6	29	7.6	38
Minnesota	10.2	39	12.4	41	7.3	39
Iowa	11.5	29	14.0	32	8.4	30
Missouri	13.3	17	17.4	21	10.1	18
North Dakota	14.4	16	16.9	23	10.9	16
South Dakota	15.9	11	20.1	13	11.6	13
Nebraska	11.1	32	13.5	36	8.0	33
Kansas	11.5	30	13.9	33	8.3	31

TABLE 4
(Continued)

	Percent	Rank	Percent	Rank	Percent	Rank
South	(NA)	(x)	(NA)	(x)	(NA)	(x)
Delaware	8.7	45	11.7	43	6.1	45
Maryland	8.3	46	10.9	47	6.0	47
District of Columbia	16.9	(x)	25.0	(x)	13.3	(x)
Virginia	10.2	38	13.0	38	7.7	37
West Virginia	19.7	4	25.9	4	16.0	4
North Carolina	13.0	21	16.9	22	9.9	20
South Carolina	15.4	14	20.8	11	11.9	12
Georgia	14.7	15	19.8	15	11.5	14
Florida	12.7	22	18.3	17	9.0	25
Kentucky	19.0	6	24.5	6	16.0	5
Tennessee	15.7	13	20.7	12	12.4	10
Alabama	18.3	7	24.0	8	14.3	7
Mississippi	25.2	1	33.5	1	20.2	1
Arkansas	19.1	5	25.0	5	14.8	6
Louisiana	23.6	2	31.2	2	19.4	2
Oklahoma	16.7	9	21.4	10	13.0	9
Texas	18.1	8	24.0	7	14.1	8
West	(NA)	(x)	(NA)	(x)	(NA)	(x)
Montana	16.1	10	19.9	14	12.0	11
Idaho	13.3	18	15.8	25	9.7	22
Wyoming	11.9	27	14.1	30	9.3	23
Colorado	11.7	28	15.0	28	8.6	29
New Mexico	20.6	3	27.5	3	16.5	3
Arizona	15.7	12	21.7	9	11.4	15
Utah	11.4	31	12.2	42	8.6	28
Nevada	10.2	40	12.8	40	7.3	40
Washington	10.9	34	14.0	31	7.8	36
Oregon	12.4	25	15.2	27	8.7	27
California	12.5	24	17.8	19	9.3	24
Alaska	9.0	43	10.9	48	6.8	43
Hawaii	8.3	47	11.1	45	6.0	46

SOURCE: Derived from U.S. Bureau of the Census, *Statistical Abstract of the United States*, 1992 (Washington, DC, 1992), table 90-6.

Table 5 illustrates major differences for individuals and families in the incidence of poverty among racial and ethnic groups in 1990.

TABLE 5
Number and Proportion of Families in Poverty
by Race and Ethnicity: 1990

Characteristic	Total No.	No. Below Poverty Level	Poverty Rate (Percent)
All families	66,322	7,098	10.7
Married couple fam.	52,147	2,981	5.7
Male householder, no wife present	2,907	349	12.0
Female householder, no husband present	11,268	3,768	33.4
White families	56,803	4,622	8.1
Married couple fam.	47,014	2,386	5.1
Male householder, no wife present	2,276	226	9.9
Female householder, no husband present	7,512	2,010	26.8
Black families	7,471	2,193	29.3
Married couple fam.	3,567	448	12.6
Male householder, no wife present	472	96	20.4
Female householder, no husband present	3,430	1,648	48.1
Hispanic origin fam.	4,981	1,244	25.0
Married couple fam.	3,454	605	17.5
Male householder, no wife present	342	66	19.4
Female householder, no husband present	1,186	573	48.3

SOURCE: Derived from U.S. Bureau of the Census, *Current Population Reports*, "Poverty in the United States: 1990," Series P-60, No. 175, (Washington, DC, 1991), table 1.

Table 5 also illustrates that the poverty rate is different depending on the type of family structure; however, as will be discussed later in this chapter, a racial gap among poor persons, even controlling for family structures, remains.

Sawhill illustrates how diverse the poor are in the United States by pointing out that this group is composed of "five mutually exclusive groups, which are divided according to the major reason for the low income of the head of the household in which these people live." These groups and their proportion of the total poverty population in 1987 include: a) elderly and disabled (33 percent); b) single parents (22 percent); c) underemployed poor (16.7 percent); d) full-time employed poor (12.4 percent); and e) a residual group that includes students, early retirees, and homemakers (15 percent). Interestingly, single parents comprise slightly more than one fifth of the poverty population, but the underemployed poor and full-time employed poor comprise a higher proportion of the poverty population at 29.1 percent.[14]

According to a study by the General Accounting Office, elderly-headed families made up 21 percent of all poor families in 1988, disabled-headed families and single-parent families with children under 18 stood at 22.8 percent, married-couple families with children under 18 at 11.1 percent, unrelated individuals (single) at 25.8 percent of all poor families, and families without children under 18 were 5.0 percent of all poor families in 1988.[15]

To better understand the magnitude of urban poverty, it is important to at least discuss briefly the literature on comparisons between the urban, rural, suburban, and aged poor. Such comparisons serve to examine differences among these populations, including racial and ethnic groups. In her 1972 publication, *Poverty, Politics and Change*, political scientist Dorothy B. James, compares different sectors of the poverty population.[16] Beyond finding differences among urban, rural, and elderly poverty, she also found distinctions in terms of how these urban and rural environments impacted racial and ethnic groups. The central point she made — a point which is still relevant today — is that poverty in America is not solely an urban problem.

Unfortunately, as one recent writer has pointed out, "insufficient attention has been given to the severe problems of the rural poor...[W]hile rural areas contain only one-fifth of the population, they contain one-third of the poor...Hidden in the hollows of Appalachia, in makeshift villages along the Rio Grande, in shriveled industrial towns in Pennsylvania, on the back roads of Maine, and at the edge of cotton fields in Mississippi, the world of rural poverty endures...not to mention migrant workers, share-croppers, and Native Americans on reservations. For most Americans, rural poverty is more remote and invisible."[17] Supporting this claim, one study by the Population Reference Bureau in Washington, D.C., reports that less than 30 percent of the total national poverty population lives in the largest central cities. Approximately 80 percent of non-Latino white poor live in the suburbs of these metropolitan areas and in rural or non-metropolitan America.[18] The Population Reference Bureau also reported that the rural poor tend to be white and more persistently poor than urban poor individuals.[19]

Table 6 illustrates the extent to which the location of the poor in America varied by race and ethnicity in the mid-1980s.

TABLE 6
Poverty Distribution Percentage by Place of Residence and Race: 1986

	Central City Area[a]	Other Central City Area	Suburban Poverty Area	Other Area	Suburban Metro-politan Area
Black[b]	42.8%	14.4%	7.7%	10.1%	25.0%
White[b]	14.7%	19.3%	4.7%	29.2%	32.1%

SOURCE: Derived from "Poverty Distribution, by Race and Place of Residence, 1986," Gerald D. Jaynes and Robin M. Williams, Jr. *A Common Destiny: Blacks and American Society* (Washington, DC: National Academy Press, 1989), figure 6-4.
[a]Such areas include census tracts in which poverty rate is greater than 20%.
[b]The total black poverty population was 8,953,000, and the total white poverty population was 22,183,000.

An overview of poverty's national profile also shows that poverty is becoming more geographically concentrated; because of this development, the poor are becoming increasingly "socially isolated." This is a major finding of sociologist William J. Wilson in his work, *The Truly Disadvantaged.*[20] By examining the incidence of individuals and families living in poverty in various Chicago census tracts, Wilson shows that the poverty population has increased recently and significantly in certain areas. Researchers have reported similar findings for several other cities. While this is generally true of suburban and rural areas, the central cities did have a greater concentration of poverty according to Wilson.[21] Another researcher, Peter Dreier, reports similarly that "the poor are increasingly concentrated in America's cities. Using the official poverty standards, the percentage of poor people living in cities increased from 30% in 1968 to 43.1% in 1989."[22]

Persistent Racial and Ethnic Gaps in Poverty

As has already been suggested, there are persisting gaps between blacks, whites, and Latinos in how they experience poverty and, in many instances, in how society treats the poor in these different communities. Racial differences in how the poor are treated by society date back to the American colonial period, as is implied in the "Act of 1726," in Pennsylvania. This act declared, "Whereas free Negroes are an idle and slothful people and often prove burdensome to the neighborhood and offered in examples to other Negroes, therefore be it enacted...that if any master or mistress shall discharge or set free any Negro, he or she shall enter into recognizance with sufficient securities in the sum of £30 to indemnify the county for any charge or incumbrance they may bring upon the same, in case such Negro through rendered incapable of self-support." Many similar laws for blacks were passed across the country for decades.[23]

Partially due to social welfare policies of the New Deal, poverty for all groups in the United States has been drastically reduced since the late 1930s. Other factors that have contributed to the reduction of poverty over the last 50 years have included periods of sustained economic growth and wage increases, greater labor force participation by women and migration from the South to higher wage sectors of the economy, and the achieving of higher levels of education for a significant proportion of the population. Despite these changes, a gap between the poverty experienced by black and white families and persons has remained over this 50-year period. While there has been some fluctuation in the ratio of the poverty to the nonpoverty population for blacks and whites, and some differences in this ratio by regions, the odds for black impoverishment have been consistently higher through this 50-year period. According to U.S. Census reports, the proportion of black families in poverty, compared to the proportion of white families in poverty has remained at a ratio of at least 3:1 over the last 50 years. In other words, in 1939 the black poverty rate was 3.6 times higher than the white poverty rate; in 1970 this ratio was 3 times; and in 1988 the black poverty rate was still at least 3 times the white poverty rate.

The persistent gap in the proportion of black persons experiencing poverty compared to white persons during the last quarter of a century is illustrated in a graph composed by the U.S. Bureau of the Census, which shows that between 1969 and 1989 a consistent gap between blacks and whites in the percent of population below poverty level has been steadfast even during recessionary periods (see figure 1).[24] Although smaller for black and white full-time, year-round workers, the black/white poverty gap has been steadfast despite changes in the economy, family structure, and the educational levels of both groups.

FIGURE 1
Poverty Rates of Persons by Race: 1969-1989

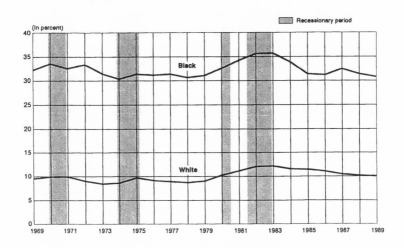

FIGURE 2
Percent of Families in Poverty
by Type of Family and Race: 1969-1989

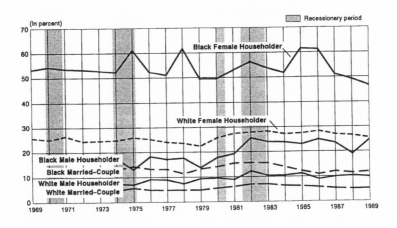

SOURCE: U.S. Bureau of the Census, *Current Population Reports*, "The Black Population in the United States: March 1990 and 1989," Series P-20, No. 448, (Washington, DC, 1991), figures 9 and 10.

Figure 2 illustrates that, while the racial gap for impoverished families does change depending on family structure, it nevertheless remains even for married-couple, or male-headed households.

The Joint Center for Political and Economic Studies documented the racial gap in the poverty experiences of Americans in its 1988 report, "Statistical Portrait of Blacks and Whites." It was reported that "Although black Americans have made enormous strides economically and educationally in the last two decades, in terms of economic well being they still lag far behind whites." This report showed blacks lagging whites in the areas of employment, earnings, education, and homeownership.[25]

In 1988 54.3 percent of all black children under 3 years of age were poor, compared to 41.3 percent of all Latino children, and 17.6 percent of all white children of this age. Similarly, only 9.6 percent of all whites 65 years of age and over were poor in that year, compared to 30.8 percent of all blacks, and 20.6 percent of all Latinos of the same age. Among those 12 to 17 years old, 36.5 percent of all blacks, 31.8 percent of all Latinos, and 11.9 percent of all whites were poor in 1988.[26] More information about the impoverization of children is presented in the next section.

The problem of poverty among Latinos is overwhelming. As reported in one study for the National Council of La Raza in Washington, D.C.: "In 1989, more than a quarter of all Hispanics lived in poverty (26.7%), including 37.6% of Hispanic children, 16.2% of Hispanic married-couple families, and 16.4% of Hispanic families with a working head of household. Poverty has been a factor in virtually every Hispanic issue, from education to community development, from housing to civil rights."[27] A summary of several important studies about the experiences of Latinos in the United States economy, as well as poverty related studies, is provided in a bibliographic report edited by Harriet Romo, *New Directions for Latino Public Policy Research*.[28]

The poverty rate for Latinos has been increasing at a rapid rate in recent years. According to Marta Van Haitsma, the Latino poverty rate has increased by one-third between 1978 and 1987. In her 1989 study, "The Underclass, Labor Force Attachment and Social Context," the author points out that Mexican-born Latinos are experiencing increasing rates of crime, high school drop-out rates, joblessness, teen pregnancies, and welfare dependency.[29] This view is confirmed in another article by Jennifer Juarez Robles, "Hispanic Poverty: Hispanics Emerging as Nation's Poorest Minority Group." While Latinos represented about 7.9 percent of the population in 1986, they comprised 15.8 percent of all the poor in the nation. In that year, the poverty rate for all Latinos was lower (27.3 percent) than for blacks (31.1 percent). As do many studies, this one illustrates that there are different rates of poverty among the various groups making up the Latino population in the United States. In 1986, for example, 39.9 percent of all Puerto Ricans were poverty-stricken, while 28 percent of all Mexicans and 18.7 percent of all Cubans and Central and South Americans were impoverished.[30]

One earlier essay reporting statistical differences among racial and ethnic groups regarding the experience of poverty is Raymond F. Clapp's, "Spanish Americans of the Southwest."[31] This essay describes the different social, economic, and poverty characteristics of blacks, Latinos, and whites more than three decades ago. More recently, economist Jeremiah Cotton points out major differences in how various racial and ethnic groups experience poverty in an essay, "Toward a Theory and Strategy for Black Economic Development."[32] The long continuing gap among poverty rates for blacks, Latinos, and whites was also reported in the earlier cited work by Gerald D. Jaynes and Robin M. Williams, Jr., A Common Destiny.[33]

Reynolds Farley and Walter Allen's The Color Line and the Quality of Life in America utilizes 1980 census data and compares black and white poverty rates.[34] They found that a continuing racial and ethnic poverty gap seems to persist despite improvement and increased productivity in the economy. Theodore Cross, in his monumental work The Black Power Imperative, states, for example, that between 1970 and 1980 the gross national product increased by 33 percent; as a result of this, 181,000 white families escaped poverty, but during this same period 141,000 black families actually became impoverished.[35] This contention seems to be supported by political scientist Andrew Hacker who points out that the last twenty years were not very good in economic terms for any Americans — but that they were worse for blacks. As he states, "Between 1970 and 1990, the median income for white families, computed in constant dollars, rose from $34,481 to $36,915, an increase of 8.7 percent. During these decades, black family income barely changed at all — increasing from $21,151 to $21,423."[36]

The racial and ethnic poverty gap is seen in major cities and metropolitan areas across the United States. In a study by Katherine McFate cited earlier it was reported in 1988 that the 48 metropolitan areas with a black population of at least 100,000 had black poverty rates in the range of 29 to 39 percent. The survey also reveals that in only three of these metropolitan areas did the white poverty rate even slightly exceed ten percent.[37]

As discussed earlier, a major difference in the way that various racial and ethnic groups experience poverty is in the concentration of poverty. William R. Prosser reported in 1991, for instance, that "Approximately 40 to 45 percent of blacks and Hispanics lived in areas of high welfare concentration. For whites it was about 5 percent."[38]

Poor blacks are also "poorer than poor whites" according to researchers William P. O'Hare and his colleagues. They write that in 1989 "the average poor black family had an income $5,100 below the poverty line, while the average poor white family had an income only $4,000 below the poverty line."[39]

As suggested earlier, income differences remain between blacks and whites, regardless of family structure. In 1990 the median income of black married couple families was $33,893, while for white married couple families it was $40,433, producing a gap of $6,540. There is also a gap in median income between black single female households and white single female households.[40] The gap in median income for all black and white families increased between 1970 and 1983 according to political scientist Lucius J. Barker.[41]

As can be seen in table 7, the black/white ratio of median income for households has stagnated since 1970. This general indicator of economic well-being for blacks has not fluctuated significantly despite changes in national administrations or in family structure within the black community over a twenty-year period. In 1970, the median income level for all white households was $30,644; for blacks it was $18,652 (both figures are in constant 1990 dollars). Thus, the black median income level was 60.8 percent of the white median income level. By 1990, the black median income level had actually declined slightly, to 59.8 percent of the white median income level, as is illustrated in the following table.

TABLE 7
Median Income Levels of Households by
Race and Hispanic Origin: 1970-1990
In Constant (1990) Dollars

	All Households	*White*	*Black*	*(B/W Ratio)*	*Hispanic*	*(H/W Ratio)*
1970	$29,421	$ 30,644	$18,652	60.8%	NA[a]	NA
1980	28,091	29,636	17,073	68.0%	22,653	76.4%
1990	29,943	31,233	18,676	59.8%	22,330	71.4%

SOURCE: Derived from U.S. Bureau of the Census, *Statistical Abstract of the United States 1992*, "Money Income of Households — Median Household Income in Current and Constant (1990) Dollars by Race and Hispanic Origin of Households; 1970 to 1990," table 696.
[a] = 1970 figures for Hispanics not available

Poverty and Family Structure

Clearly a relationship exists between poverty status and family structure, as is indicated earlier in this chapter. While almost half (47 percent) of all poor families were married-couple or male-headed families in 1990, the number and proportion of individuals living in poverty in female-headed families is still large relative to two-parent families. Many studies show that female-headed households have a greater chance of being poor than married-couple families. According to Gertrude Goldberg and Eleanor Kremin in *The Feminization of Poverty*, "In 1960, families with a female householder and no husband present constituted less than one-fourth of poor families; in little more than fifteen years this proportion has doubled."[42] This development is also discussed by Harrell R. Rodgers, Jr., who reports in *Poor Women, Poor Families* that the rise of female-headed households in poverty statistics has been significant.[43]

Despite this trend it should be emphasized that the actual nature of the relationship between family structure and poverty has not benefited from definitive or conclusive research, and it has yet to be established whether the relationship should be approached as an isolated factor and consistently causal. For example, demographer Mary Jo Bane reports in "Politics and Policies of the Feminization of Poverty" that "An analysis of the reasons for the increased feminization of poverty suggests that about 40 percent of the increase is accounted for by changes in relative poverty rates and about 60 percent by changes in population composition. Changes in relative poverty rates were considerably more important for blacks than for whites."[44] Bane's research suggests, in other words, that in some cases poverty status is the cause of female-headed household, rather than vice versa! Higher poverty rates do produce changes in family composition. Bane reports similarly in another article that "Family composition changes contributed almost nothing to the increase in poverty between 1979 and 1983." And further, "less than half of the poverty of female-headed and single person households and therefore only about a quarter to a fifth of all poverty appears to have come about *simultaneously with* changes in household composition. Family composition changes in the early 1980s made only a trivial contribution to the increase in poverty."[45]

There are also significant differences among female-headed families and poverty status when approached in terms of race and ethnicity. Bane claims that such differences obscure the relationship between poverty and family structure. A racial and ethnic poverty gap can be seen even when we look at female-headed families separately. In recent times the poverty rate for black female-headed households (controlling for age, education, and region) has been approximately two times the rate for comparable white female-headed households. In 1980, poverty rates for white and black female-headed families were 25.7 percent and 49.4 percent, respectively. The poverty rate for Latino female-headed families in this same year was 51.3 percent.[46]

These differences are also reflected in data for 1990. Policy analyst for the National Council of La Raza, Sonia M. Perez, reported that "Almost two-thirds (64.4%) of Puerto Rican female-headed families were poor in 1990, compared to more than half of black female-headed families (56.1%) and less than half of white female-headed families (44.5%)."[47] By the late 1980s, the poverty rate for all white female-headed families had increased to 25.4 percent; it had decreased slightly for black female-headed families to 46.5 percent; and for Latinos, it had declined somewhat to 47.5 percent, according to Mischel and Frankel.[48]

This racial gap is increasing even between black and white female heads of households who work full-time, year-round. In 1973, the "Black-White Female Head Income Ratio" was .64; that is, black females heading households and working year-round, full-time earned only this percentage of the income earned by white females heading households and working year-round, full-time. By 1987, this ratio declined to .57.[49]

The Joint Center for Political and Economic Studies in Washington, D.C., reported that the rate of impoverization and the "deepening" of poverty among blacks may not be totally related to changes in family structure. The increase in poverty rates has occurred much faster than expected given the rate of changes in black family composition.[50] This finding reiterates an earlier one by the National Academy of Science's Commission on the Status of Blacks in America: family structure changes are "not an arithmetically important factor in the overall increase in black poverty since the early 1970s...rather than family structure, it is low earnings that have led to increased poverty since the 1970s."[51]

Findings in a 1988 report, "Children's Well-Being: An International Comparison" by Frank Hobbs and Laura Lippman, also cast some doubt on the proposition that family structure, particularly female-headed families, is an inevitable cause of poverty. In some European nations, the authors point out, there does not seem to be a strong relationship between poverty status and family structure. It is apparent that in the United States, however, there is some kind of correlation between female-headed family structure and poverty. In 1979, according to this study, 17.1 percent of all American children under the age of 18 lived in poverty, while 51 percent of this group lived in single-parent families. But in other countries the correlation is not as strong as it is in the United States. In West Germany, only 35.1 percent of all children who are poor live in single-parent families, while only 8.6 percent of poor Swedish children live in single-parent families.[52]

Another argument similar to Bane's is that of Barry Schiller, who reports in the *Economics of Poverty and Discrimination* that many women, in fact, were poor *before* they became the female head of family. As Schiller explains:

> Large families and broken families are among the most salient characteristics of the poor. Over 30% of all the poor are in families with at least 5 members, while 1/4 of the poor are in broken families; many of the latter are also from large families...For most of the families in question poverty prevailed before the family either grew larger or broke up. Moreover, economic insecurity itself may have contributed to the dissolution of the family or to excessive reproduction. Hence, stronger causality appears to flow from poverty to family size and status than in the opposite direction.[53]

Interestingly, despite much focus on the impoverishment of female-headed families, a considerable number of married-couple families in the United States are also poor, and the rates of such families experiencing poverty increased between 1973 and 1989. Regarding a point that will be developed later, according to Mischel and Frankel, many married-couple families become impoverished as a result of low hourly earnings as full-time, full-year workers.[54]

Increasing Impoverization of Children

Children, particularly black and Latino children, are experiencing soaring poverty rates. There are at least ten states in the United States where the proportion of children in poverty is more than one fifth of all children. In 1989, the top ten cities with the highest child poverty rates ranged from 40.9 percent in Dayton, Ohio, to 46.6 percent in Detroit, Michigan. In the following cities, more than 60 percent of all Latino children were living in poverty: Erie, Pennsylvania (68.5 percent), Springfield, Massachusetts (66.9 percent), Buffalo, New York (67.6 percent), Lowell, Massachusetts (62.2 percent), and Hartford, Connecticut (61.6 percent).[55]

Indeed, the poverty rate and general well-being of children worsened during the 1980s according to several studies, one of which was a joint study by the Center for the Study of Social Policy and the Annie E. Casey Foundation in 1992.[56] In fact, the poverty rate for children has been increasing since 1969 and has done so at a faster rate than for other age groups in the total population. In 1970, 14.9 percent of all children in families lived below the poverty line; by 1990 this figure had increased to

19.9 percent. During this same period the poverty rate for black children increased from 41.5 percent to 44.2 percent; for white children the figures were 10.5 percent in 1970 and 15.1 percent in 1990. In 1973 the poverty rate for Latino children was 27.8 percent; by 1990, this figure had increased to 39.7 percent.[57]

One previously noted study by Mischel and Frankel points out that: "Child poverty increased from 14.2% in 1973 to 16.2% in 1979, and then to 19.6% in 1988. Moreover, child poverty has grown considerably within each of the three main racial/ethnic groups."[58]

According to David Eggebeen and Daniel Lichter in a 1991 article, "Race, Family Structure, and Changing Poverty Among American Children," in the current period, "Roughly one in five American children lives in a poor family, a level exceeding that of virtually every other Western developed nation."[59] The younger the child, the greater the likelihood that he or she will experience poverty. In 1984, one out of every four American children under six years of age was poor, according to the report. Despite this general trend, however, there were important differences in poverty rates by race and ethnicity. According to the United States Bureau of the Census, 14.1 percent of all white children in America were poor in 1989, while 35.5 percent of all Latino children were poor. Among black children the poverty rate was 43.2 percent nationally. In 1990 the poverty rate for white children increased slightly to 15.1 percent, as it did for black children (44.2 percent) and Latino children (37.7 percent). Another important difference in the impoverization of children by race and ethnicity is that, while a majority of white and Latino children lived in married-couple families in 1990, this was not true for black children in poverty, who overwhelmingly lived in single-parent families.[60]

Data reported in *The State of Working America*, by Mischel and Frankel, furthermore, shows that poverty rates for Latino children increased much faster than the rate for black or white children between 1979 and 1989: "Hispanic children suffered a particularly large increase, from 27.8 percent in 1979 to 35.5 percent in 1989."[61]

The national rate for Latino children in poverty is lower than that for black children; however, this is probably due, in part, to the fact that a larger proportion of Latino children live in male-headed and married-couple parent families.

The study also shows that the incidence of children living in poverty varied widely among the various Latino groups. The rate for Puerto Rican children was 52.2 percent; for Mexican Americans it was 37.0 percent; and Cubans had the lowest rate of child poverty for Latinos at 26.0 percent. Thus, the poverty rate of Puerto Rican children is especially striking. Among blacks, whites, and Latinos, Puerto Rican children have consistently suffered from higher rates. As is pointed out by Sonia Pérez, "The poverty rate for all Puerto Rican children continues to climb, making Puerto Rican children the poorest of any major racial/ethnic group in the United States. More than half of all Puerto Rican children under 18 (56.7 percent) were poor in 1990, compared to almost two-fifths of all black children (44.8 percent) and about one-sixth of white children (15.9 percent)."[62]

Poverty and the Elderly

While the significant decline in the poverty rate for elderly persons (65 years and over) in the United States is well documented and represents a major social welfare achievement, there are still pockets of severe poverty in this group. As will be discussed in a later chapter the decline in elderly poverty was due to the increase in the over-65 population, as well as the development of their organized political power. Yet, despite these developments, many of the elderly remain mired in poverty — this is especially the case for black and Latino elderly persons.

Today, the elderly have a slightly lower poverty rate than the nation as a whole; in 1960, however, one quarter (25.0 percent) of all elderly persons were poor, compared to a national poverty rate of 12.6 percent. In 1970 the poverty rate for elderly persons stood at 24.6 percent; in 1979 the figure was 15.2 percent, and by 1990 it stood at 12.2 percent.[63] But, again, a macro view of elderly poverty hides pockets of deep poverty for many in this group, especially among women and people of color. Scott Bass, director of the Gerontology Institute at the University of Massachusetts in Boston, writes that:

> Elder poverty is far more likely to affect certain identifiable groups than others. Older women who live alone, particularly older women of color, are far more likely to fall into poverty than any other group. In fact, more than 60 percent of elderly black women who live alone exist below the poverty level — and the percentages increase as they age.[64]

In 1990, 2.8 million women over the age of 65 had incomes below the poverty level, while another 1.5 million older women had incomes just slightly above the poverty level; thus 4.3 million older women, out of a total of 17.8 million older women, were in or near poverty.[65] Another report states that,

> It is widely believed that poverty among the elderly has been largely conquered. While it is true that the percentage of older Americans

who are poor is slightly lower than in the rest of the population, major problems remain. A sizable group of elderly people have been excluded from the gains that have been made...The size of the aging population is increasing, and savings are typically inadequate.[66]

Even among the elderly, however, persistent racial gaps can be noted in how this group experiences poverty. In 1990, the elderly poverty rate for whites was 10.1 percent, while it was 33.8 percent for elderly blacks and 22.5 percent for Latino elderly. It is interesting and important to note, furthermore, that during periods when the white elderly poverty rate has declined, the poverty rate for black elderly has actually increased significantly. For example, between 1985 and 1990 the white elderly poverty rate declined from 11 percent to 10.1 percent, but the black elderly poverty rate increased during this same period from 31.5 percent to 33.8 percent.[67]

Increasing Gap Between the Poor and the Non-Poor

Due, in part, to national economic policies inimical to the interests of the poor, such as reductions in certain kinds of social welfare programs, the poor are getting poorer. In addition, there is an increasing economic distance between those persons who experience poverty and those who do not. In 1983 the poorest two-fifths of all families, for example, received approximately 15.8 percent of the total national income. This was the lowest percentage for these families since 1947. To the contrary, during that same year the wealthiest two-fifths of all American families received 67.1 percent of the total national income, the highest proportion for this strata since 1947. Between 1980 and 1984, the bottom two-fifths of all families lost 9.3 percent of their disposable income, but the top one-fifth of all American families gained an additional 8.7 percent of disposable income.[68]

According to information provided by the Center on Budget and Policy Priorities, the poverty rate in 1984 for all Americans was 14.4 percent, or one out of every seven Americans. This was the highest poverty rate since 1966. In this study researchers concluded that "The poverty rate is now the highest for any non-recession year in nearly two decades and higher even than during the major recession of 1975."[69] This finding is reiterated by the Urban Institute in their 1984 study, *The Reagan Record*, which reports that between 1980 and 1984 there was a transfer of 25 billion dollars in disposable income from poor and middle-income families to the richest fifth of all American families.[70] Another illustration of this point is the finding reported in the 1991 report *The State of Working America*:

Another measure of the depth of poverty is the percentage of the poor who have incomes below half of the poverty line. In 1989, 38% of the poor had incomes below half of poverty, compared to 32.9% in 1979. A smaller proportion of the poverty population have incomes close to the poverty line: the percentage with incomes between 75% and 100% of the poverty line fell from 37.4% in 1979 to 34.3% in 1989.[71]

During the last 20 to 25 years the resources available to the poor have declined significantly. The average annual level of benefits for a family of four persons under Aid to Families with Dependent Children (AFDC), for example, was 66 percent of the official poverty level in 1970 (see table 8). The average benefit payment for AFDC in 1970 was $2,652, and the official poverty level was $3,968. In 1975, this ratio declined to 57.6 percent; the average annual AFDC benefit level was $3,168, while the official poverty level this same year was $5,500. In 1980, the average annual AFDC benefit level was $4,200, or 49.9 percent of the official poverty level ($8,414); and in 1985 the ratio declined further, to 41.3 percent. In 1991 the average benefit AFDC level was $4,548, and remained at 41.3 percent of the official poverty level for a family of four ($11,003), as table 8 illustrates.

TABLE 8

Average AFDC Benefits to a Family of Four Compared to Official Poverty Level: 1970, 1975, 1980, and 1991

	Average Benefit Payment	*Official Poverty Income Level*	*Percent of Poverty Income Level*
1970	$ 2,652	$ 3,968	66.0%
1975	3,168	5,500	57.6
1980	4,200	8,414	49.9
1991	4,548	11,003	41.3

SOURCE: Derived from Lawrence Mischel and David Frankel, *The State of Working America* (Armonk, NY: M. E. Sharpe, 1991); also see John Charles Boger, "Race and the American City: The Kerner Commission in Retrospect — An Introduction," *North Carolina Law Review* vol. 71, no. 5, June 1993, p. 1341.

The decline of AFDC benefits compared to the official poverty line remains even when food stamps are added to the AFDC benefit payments.

David Ellwood illustrates this relationship for the years 1960 to 1984 in his book, *Poor Support* .[72]

Another way of showing that the poor are receiving fewer resources than in previous periods is to examine the level of federal income taxes paid by poor families over the last several years. In 1978, a two-parent family of four persons earning no more than the official poverty level of income paid $269 in federal taxes. In 1980, the tax bite for these families increased to $460; in 1984 this figure increased to $1,075, and a year later it increased to $1,147, or to four times what it had been in 1978.[73]

Finally, it should be reiterated that, as we saw in chapter 2, federal funding for some social welfare programs aimed at alleviating poverty was drastically reduced during the 1980s. According to Ellwood, between 1976 and 1984 funding for AFDC was reduced by 17.7 percent, from 20.8 billion dollars to 17.1 billion dollars. Funding for employment training and social services for the poor was reduced by more than a quarter (25.6 percent) during this same period. In 1976, 12.5 billion dollars were spent in this area, but by 1984 this figure had dropped to 9.3 billion dollars.[74] These particular reductions have kept more people and families impoverished.

It is reported by Mischel and Frankel in *The State of Working America*, furthermore, that "Government taxes and benefits removed 39.7% of persons in female-headed families with children from poverty in 1979, but only 22.8% in 1988. Among married-couple families with children, government tax policies removed 33% of poor persons in such families from poverty in 1979, but only 24.4% in 1988."[75] This same report shows that a mother of two children receiving no wages during 1990 received a value of $6,611 worth of food stamps and AFDC grants. But this figure represents a decline of 6.5 percent from the $7,071 received in 1980 (without adjusting for inflation).

The Increasing Number of "Working Poor"

Recently the U.S. Bureau of the Census reported that the number of Americans working in low-wage jobs is actually increasing. In 1979, 13 percent of all workers with a high school degree held a low-wage job ($6.10 per hour or less). By 1990, one fifth (21.0 percent) of all workers with a high school degree were in low-wage jobs. The increase in low-wage jobs also was noted for those with 13 years or more of schooling: from 6.2 percent to 10.5 percent between 1979 and 1990. Consistent with the earlier findings reported in this chapter, the likelihood of low-wage jobs being held by blacks and Latinos, with comparable education to whites, was much greater than for whites.[76]

The number of Americans who work full-time or part-time but are also poor has increased sharply. This is illustrated in the following table, which shows that slightly more than forty percent of all poor individuals aged 15 years and over worked full- or part-time in 1990.

TABLE 9
Workers as a Proportion of Poor Persons: 1978-1990

Year	Number of Poor 15 Years and Over (Thousands)	Worked Full-time or Part-time (Thousands)	Percent
1990	21,783	8,770	40.3
1989	20,474	8,419	41.1
1988	20,857	8,415	40.3
1987	21,316	8,440	39.6
1986	21,352	8,864	41.5
1985	21,954	9,112	41.5
1984	22,246	9,104	40.9
1983	23,465	9,440	40.2
1982	22,812	9,119	40.0
1981	21,260	8,631	40.6
1980	19,517	7,792	39.9
1979	16,907	6,545	38.8
1978	16,194	6,599	39.0

SOURCE: U.S. Bureau of the Census, *Current Population Reports*, "Poverty in the United States: 1990," Series P-60, No. 175 (Washington, DC, 1991).

Researchers Sar A. Levitan and Isaac Shapiro in *Working but Poor: America's Contradiction* write that "Most poor adults who are able to work and find jobs do so, but the number of working poor was sharply higher in the first half of the 1980s than in the 1970s...From, 1978 to 1985, the number of full-time year-round working poor rose by 50 percent and the number of partially working poor rose 35 percent. In contrast, the number and percentage of working poor fell sharply during the 1960s before the number essentially stabilized in the 1970s while the percentage dropped."[77] Similarly, Michael Harrington reports in his book *Who Are the Poor* that "In recent years, the fastest growing group among the poor has been the working poor, not the welfare poor, whose ranks have remained level during the period."[78] Harrington reported that almost 9 million persons were working and poverty-stricken. This represents a substantial increase from the 6.5 million persons in this category in 1979.

The minimum wage level and growth of low-wage occupations may explain this trend of working and being poor. When factoring inflation, the minimum wage has actually eroded since the late 1960s. In 1967 the minimum wage was $1.40 per hour, but this translated to a real value (factoring inflation) of $4.67 in terms of 1989 dollars; but in 1991, while the minimum wage increased to $4.25 per hour, in terms of 1989 dollars, this had a real value of only $3.92 per hour![79] Mischel and Frankel found that "while a full-time, year-round job at the minimum wage kept a family of 3 above the poverty line in 1979, the same job would have placed such a family $2,922 *below* the poverty line in 1989...Even a two-person family dependent on a minimum wage worker would have been $1,373 below the poverty line in 1989."[80]

Levitan and Shapiro reported similarly that in 1987 the "Minimum wage earning in 1986 for a full-time year-round worker provided income equivalent to only four-fifths of the poverty level for a family of three."[81] Despite inflation and a loss of purchasing power, the minimum wage remained the same between 1980 and 1990. In 1990 the minimum wage was set at $4.25 per hour, or $170 per 40-hour week. On an annual basis the minimum wage translates into $8,840 per year, well below the official poverty income line of $13,359 for a family of four in 1990. Even two workers earning the minimum wage would bring in an annual income (pre-taxes) only slightly higher than the poverty level.

This all seems to suggest that poor people are not lazy or lacking in work ethic but, rather, are underpaid. In *The New Politics of Poverty*, however, Lawrence M. Mead states his belief that a significant proportion of poor persons are in such condition simply because they refuse to work.[82] This argument will be revisited in chapter 4, which focuses on major explanations for persistent poverty in the United States.

CHAPTER IV

What Are the Major Explanations for Persistent Poverty in the United States?

This association of poverty with progress is the great enigma of our times. It is the central fact from which spring industrial, social, and political difficulties that perplex the world, and with which statesmanship and philanthropy and education grapple in vain. From it come the clouds that overhang the future of the most progressive and self-reliant nations. It is the riddle which the Sphinx of Fate puts to our civilization and which not to answer is to be destroyed.

Henry George
Progress and Poverty (1879)

The enigma of poverty was foretold as a major philosophical and political question of our times during the Second World War by Karl Polanyi, who stated that the question, "Where do the poor come from was raised by a bevy of pamphlets which grew thicker with the advancing century."[1] He wrote in his 1944 publication, *The Great Transformation*: "This apparent contradiction was destined to become to the next generation of Western humanity the most perplexing of all the recurrent phenomena in social life."[2] Polanyi's prescience was predated by W. E. B. Du Bois's a few years earlier when he delivered the commencement address to graduates of Fisk University in 1938. Du Bois stated, in part, that the

> most distressing fact in the present world is poverty; not absolute poverty, because some folks are rich and many are well-to-do; not poverty as great as some lands and other historical ages have known; but poverty more poignant and discouraging because it comes after a dream of wealth; of riotous, wasteful and even vulgar accumulation of individual riches, which suddenly leaves the majority of mankind today without enough to eat; without proper shelter; without sufficient clothing.[3]

Thus, the enigma of Henry George in 1879 seems to have been unresolved during the period of Du Bois and Polanyi in the Western world of 1938 and 1944, and continues to be unresolved today.

There are many explanations for the existence of poverty that have been offered in the literature. Two professors of city and regional planning, William W. Goldsmith and Edward J. Blakely, categorize theories and explanations of poverty into "poverty as pathology," "poverty as incident or accident," and "poverty as structure."[4] These explanations can be reduced further under two perspectives generally held regarding people who are poor. One is what Barry R. Schiller refers to as the "restricted opportunity" argument, and the second is the "flawed character" argument. Explaining this point, Schiller writes in the *Economics of Poverty and Discrimination* that the "flawed character" perspective:

> perceives the incidence of poverty to be the natural concomitant of individual defects in aspiration or ability. In colonial times this perspective was aptly summarized by the puritanical Humane Society, which concluded that "by a just and inflexible law of Providence, misery is ordained to be the companion and punishment of vice." In more modern times theories of sin and immorality have not fared well...Instead we speak in terms of "work ethic" and attribute individual impoverishment to a lack thereof.[5]

There is still much support for this point of view today in the United States. As political scientists Lee Sigelman and Susan Welch write,

> national surveys of the adult population...during the 1970s and 1980s, bears testimony to the prevailing American faith that in economic affairs "God helps those who help themselves."...This strong strain of individualism is evident in the widespread tendency to blame the poor for their poverty. Most Americans consider insufficient effort, lack of ability, weak motivation, and immoderation to be among the most important reasons for poverty in this country, and a sizeable minority would include "loose morals and drunkenness" as well.[6]

The other major perspective described by Schiller, "restricted opportunity," proposes that "the poor are poor because they do not have adequate access to good schools, jobs, and income, because they are discriminated against on the basis of color, sex, income or class, and because they are not furnished with a fair share of government protection, subsidy, or services."[7]

Characterizing explanations of poverty into these two kinds of schools of thought is common in the writings of many social welfare researchers. Michael Sherraden writes, for example, that "There are many elaborate theories, and variations of themes, on poverty. These can be simplistically lumped into two groups — theories that focus on individual behaviors and theories that focus on social structures."[8] Yet another writer utilizing the conceptual dichotomy reflected in Schiller's work is professor of social welfare Chaim I. Waxman: "There are among American sociologists and policymakers two major conceptualizations and explanations of poverty, one is known as the cultural perspective and the other as the situational perspective."[9]

One historical explanation for black poverty offered by historian Jay R. Mandel in *The Roots of Black Poverty* is a variation of the "restricted opportunity" thesis proposed by Schiller.[10] Mandel correctly points out that black poverty has existed, certainly during slavery, and continually since emancipation. Family structure, group attitudes or attributes may have changed over generations, but poverty in the black community has been consistently more widespread and persistent than it has been for white Americans. Mandel explains continuing black poverty as a reflection and continuation of the effects of the plantation economy in the South that persisted for decades after the Civil War. This echoes the analysis by W. E. B. Du Bois of Southern politics and economy in his classic work, *Black Reconstruction in America 1860-1880*: "It was the policy of the state to keep the Negro laborer poor, to confine him as far as possible to menial occupation, to make him a surplus labor reservoir and to force him into peonage and unpaid foil.[11] Blacks were, in large part, confined to the plantation economy in the last four decades of the nineteenth century even while the industrialized North received 14 million immigrants from Europe.

As Mandel posits, the long duration of the plantation economy in the South has had the effect of placing the "black working class in a difficult half-way position. Only one generation or so removed from the plantation economy, nothing like full occupational integration has occurred and the black working class remains disproportionately in low-wage jobs."[12] He also argues that the effects of a plantation economy have prevented millions of blacks from developing the political tools and economic position they need to obtain control of parts of the emerging industrialized order. This situation prevents effective black community-based responses to continual poverty for large sectors of the community.

Due to their migratory experiences this argument can be extended to the case of Puerto Ricans, another group where significant numbers of individuals and families are impoverished in the United States. Many Puerto Ricans migrating to the United States since the early 1900s have been hampered in building political tools for group advancement in the occupational structure of Northeastern cities. As is noted in a work co-edited by this author, *Puerto Rican Politics in Urban America*, the continual back and forward migration movement between Puerto Rico and Northeastern cities has partially inhibited opportunities for the building of a political base that could be used by this community to realize social and economic mobility.[13]

Historian Elizabeth H. Pleck examines black poverty and its causes in earlier periods in *Black Migration and Poverty, Boston 1865-1900*. This study provides an analysis of how blacks experienced poverty between 1865 and 1900, and concludes that there are two major explanations for black poverty during this period in places like Boston, Chicago, Cleveland, and Philadelphia. The explanation does not have to do with cultural or educational deficiencies on the part of blacks. Instead, Pleck states,

> the handicaps of black workers arose from the operation of two distinct racial barriers to be found within Boston, exclusion and unsuccessful competition. Exclusion, the first of these, involved entry-level racial barriers in hiring and the recruitment of new black arrivals into service jobs. As a consequence, most black newcomers entered menial work and stayed in it, becoming drifters between low-wage jobs and moving incessantly from one city to the next...Aspiring entrepreneurs, professionals, clerks, and craftsmen confronted a second barrier, unsuccessful competition, not because of some unique cultural deficiency but because race was used as a means of firing them or forcing them out.[14]

These kinds of explanations for black urban poverty in earlier periods have appeared in a range of literature focusing on the emergence of black communities in the American city and can be placed under the "restricted opportunity" rather than the "flawed character" framework. Such studies include Harold X. Connally's *A Ghetto Grows in Brooklyn*; Gilbert Osofsky's *Harlem: The Making of a Ghetto*; and Kenneth Kusmer's *Black Cleveland*.[15] One similar type of study that focuses on the emergence and social life of the Puerto Rican community in New York City is *Memorias de Bernardo Vega*, edited by Cesar A. Iglesias.[16]

One work published in the mid-nineteenth century states that poverty is created as a result of broad economic and social forces and the concomitant absence of a political base for impacted groups. In 1879, Henry George asserted in *Progress and Poverty* that the existence of a poverty-stricken population is related to the rise in land values and the fact that poor people do not own land.[17] He observed:

> The ownership of land is the great fundamental fact which ultimately determines the social, the political, and consequently the intellectual and moral condition of a people. And it must be so. For land is the habitation of man, the storehouse upon which he must draw for all his needs, the material to which his labor must be applied for the supply of all his desires; for even the products of the sea cannot be taken, the light of the sun enjoyed, or any of the forces of

nature utilized, without the use of land or its products. On the land we are born, from it we live, to it we return again — children of the soil as truly as is the blade of grass or the flower of the field.[18]

George points out that land values usually rise with an increase in population density and urbanization, but that the increase in the value is hardly ever distributed to the population whose growth produced the rise in value. The "unearned increment" is almost always assigned to those lucky enough to have owned the land that is impacted by the growth in population.

Stephen Thernstrom's *Poverty and Progress: Social Mobility in a Nineteenth Century City*, published in the mid-1960s, also suggests broad economic developments as the major explanation for poverty in nineteenth century America. As he wrote in his case study of poverty in Newburyport, Massachusetts: "Few students of nineteenth century American communities have experienced much optimism about the economic situation of the urban working class during the 1850-1880 period. Wages for unskilled and semiskilled labor were never very high in the best of times, and unemployment was endemic to the economic system. These decades were punctuated by national financial panic in 1857, a postwar slump, and a prolonged depression in the 1870s."[19] The kind of historical and social analysis developed by Mandel regarding black poverty, and by George and Thernstrom in explaining poverty as a result of systemic forces in the nineteenth century, is missing from many contemporary public and scholarly discussions on this topic.

The Human Capital Explanation

One school of thought in the poverty literature focuses on limited "human capital" as an explanation of poverty. In other words, people are poor primarily due to a lack of education, training, or job skills, or due to language deficiencies; and this lack of "human capital" prevents economic mobility. While this explanation can be associated with "restricted opportunity" it focuses on the weaknesses of the individual. There is a presumption that the economic system is effective for anyone who is properly skilled and educated. Thus, poverty could be reduced significantly if only impoverished groups could obtain the skills necessary for the available jobs.

In Boston, Massachusetts, as in many other cities, for example, individuals who have not completed high school have been left out of many jobs in the changing labor market; presumably the absence of skills, or a "skills mismatch" has increased this group's chances of living in poverty or near-poverty. During the 1970s and 1980s, the central cities lost hundreds of thousands of "entry-level" jobs that could have been filled with people without a high school diploma. This loss occurred simultaneously with an increase in the number of "knowledge-intensive" jobs requiring fourteen or more years of schooling. This pattern has been especially evident in many of the larger cities in the Northeast, and in other regions as well.[20] Sociologist Vilma Ortiz reports the same pattern for New York City and Los Angeles: the number of jobs for the more-educated tended to increase much faster than jobs for the less-educated.[21]

Though these studies have formed many of the programmatic underpinnings for employment and training programs (i.e., "human capital" programs) around the country, several reports have pointed to an imprecise relationship between educational attainment and poverty, especially for blacks and Latinos.[22] While higher levels of education do reduce the chances of being poor among blacks and Latinos, education does not necessarily lessen a poverty or income gap between these groups and whites. This is illustrated in table 10.

TABLE 10
Percent of Household Heads Below Poverty Line
by Education and Race: 1985

Educational Attainment	Black	White	Difference
Less than 8 years*	34%	23%	11 points
8 years	37	13	24 points
High School 1-3 years	36	15	21 points
High School 4 years	27	7	20 points
College, 1 year or more	11	3	8 points

SOURCE: Derived from "Poverty Rates and Distribution of Black and White Populations by Various Demographic Characteristics, 1985" Gerald D. Jaynes and Robin M. Williams, Jr. *A Common Destiny: Blacks and American Society* (Washington, DC: National Academy Press, 1989), p. 288.
*Educational attainment of household heads, aged 25 and over.

As table 10 shows the gap in percentage points between blacks and whites below the poverty level actually *widens* as blacks obtain more education, up until one obtains at least one year of college. In 1990, while

22.6 percent of white families below the poverty level were headed by someone with less than eight years of schooling, the figure for comparable black families was 38.7 percent, and for Latino families it was 31.6 percent. While only 6.9 percent of all white heads of household who are high school graduates were living below the poverty level, for blacks and Latinos the comparable rates were 11.9 percent and 9.3 percent, respectively.[23] This qualification in the proposition that more education results in greater economic mobility was also noted by José E. Cruz regarding Puerto Ricans: "Low educational attainment 'explains' poverty to some degree; yet Puerto Rican educational levels are higher than Mexican American, while the poverty level of the latter is less."[24]

Norman Fainstein also takes issue with the human capital or skills mismatch explanation. He writes in an essay, "The Underclass/Mismatch Hypothesis as an Explanation for Black Economic Deprivation," that "the mismatch diagnosis is inadequate and misleading. Urban blacks are not particularly dependent on a declining manufacturing sector, rather they suffer from segmentation into low-wage employment in growth industries."[25] Fainstein implies that improving the skills of urban blacks may not necessarily produce more available jobs with above-poverty level wages. This discussion will be revisited in a subsequent section of this chapter.

Cultural, Moral, and Genetic Explanations

Another set of researchers and observers argue that improper social and work attitudes, including lack of moral standards, diminutive cultural attributes, or particular personal dispositions explain poverty and its persistence among some groups. Some have proposed, for instance, that "sexual recklessness" among young "lower-class" black males is one reason for the breakup of the family and resulting poverty. These arguments reflect Schiller's "flawed character" framework. There are two basic subsets in this school. One liberal variant is reflected in the mid-1960s work of sociologist Oscar Lewis, *La Vida*.[26] Lewis suggests here that many Puerto Ricans in New York City are poor because they do not have middle-class norms and values; such norms, he argues, can be imparted to poor people through education and proper socialization. Lewis's approach could also be called one of "restricted opportunity," because it suggests that the poor have not been allowed to develop the proper values and behavior for achieving middle-class status in America.

A conservative strand of thinking under the cultural school is reflected in a widely-read book by political scientist Edward C. Banfield, *The Unheavenly City*.[27] He argues that due to the innate "ethos" of some groups, the proper work habits, moral disposition, attitudes, and cultural norms necessary for social mobility cannot be transferred to these populations, regardless of government attempts to do so. Government should not waste resources in trying to change these innate cultural weaknesses, but rather should seek to constrain physical mobility and limit this group's potential to damage the chances of others in the black community.

George Gilder also emphasizes sexual immorality in his explanation of poverty in "The Collapse of the American Family": "Their problem is not poverty but a collapse of family discipline and sexual morality."[28] Gilder proposes in his 1989 essay "The Nature of Poverty," that poverty is inevitable for some in society and that the chances of impoverishment are determined by an individual's moral character.[29] Those who get stuck in poverty have rejected hard work, marriage and family, and religious faith. Manuel Carballo and demographer Mary Jo Bane remind us that this has been a major explanation of poverty used by political conservatives. Carballo and Bane state in *The State and the Poor in the 1980s* that "Conservatives from Hobbes to the present day have felt that the causes and cures of individual poverty are essentially not political or economic, but moral. Anyone willing to work hard can 'make it.' Therefore, those who have not made it must be unwilling to work and lazy. This theme has been behind every conservative solution to poverty from almshouses to 'workfare.'"[30]

Lawrence M. Mead focuses on the work ethic of certain sectors of the impoverished population as an explanation of their status. In his work, *The New Politics of Poverty*, Mead argues that a distinct sector of the impoverished population, the non-working poor, has lost a sense of work obligation. He states his belief that this sector, many of which are among the recipients of AFDC — blacks, the homeless, and drug abusers — suffer impoverishment due to their unwillingness to work. After neatly (too neatly, in my opinion) packaging other explanations — including racism and discrimination, low wages, loss of manufacturing jobs and unavailability of jobs, national economic recessions and downturns, lack of child care, disability, and lack of education and training — Mead concludes that it is the defeatist psychology of the black non-working poor that keeps them in this status: "The initial reason for most working-aged poverty is simply that fathers in ghetto areas tend not to provide for their children, while the mothers usually go on welfare rather than work themselves."[31]

Mead believes that "Resistance to low-wage jobs and a sense of defeatism appear to be the main deterents to work in the minds of the poor."[32] This resistance, he asserts, is imbedded in black culture:

> The culture of black America is the most significant for an understanding of today's nonwork and poverty. Although less than a third of blacks are poor in a given year, a majority of the long-term poor

come from this group. Evidently, the worldview of blacks makes them uniquely prone to the attitudes contrary to work, and thus vulnerable to poverty and dependency.[33]

Despite Mead's references to black culture, his claims touching upon black social experiences and misrepresentation of black leaders like Martin Luther King, Jr., reflect a woeful ignorance of black history. According to Mead, the only way to address this cultural/moral inadequacy, is to socialize blacks with a "work ethic," and instill personal responsibility with stringent workfare types of programs.

In another work by Gilder, *Wealth and Poverty*, the author does not delve deeply into whether the moral weaknesses of the poor are innate or reflect a group "ethos," as is argued by Banfield, but he does concur with Banfield's general theme that poverty reflects immorality and, like Mead, a lack of hard work.[34]

Many conservative writers focusing on poverty in the United States, and today many liberals as well, adopt a "moralistic" analysis, as is indicated in Mead's work. Gilder's moral tone is reflected in the following passage:

The only dependable route from poverty is always work, family, and faith. The first principle is that in order to move up, the poor must not only work, they must work harder than the classes above them. Every previous generation of the lower class has made such efforts. But the current poor, white even more than black, are refusing to work hard.[35]

Gilder continues:

The key to the intractable poverty of the hardcore American poor is the dominance of single and separated men in poor communities...The problem is neither race nor matriarchy in any meaningful sense. It is familial anarchy among the concentrated poor of the inner city, in which flamboyant and impulsive youths rather than responsible men provide the themes of aspiration. The result is that male sexual rhythms tend to prevail, and boys are brought up without authoritative fathers in the home to instill in them the values of responsible paternity: the provider role. "If she wants me, she'll pay," one young stud assured me in prison.[36]

Gilder suggests that the poor have a depraved morality that could be rectified by society. The correction can be made by draconian measures to punish and imprison the recalcitrant poor from a behavior considered negative by middle-class society.

While Banfield toys with the idea that poverty among blacks and Latinos may be related to innate native intelligence and genetic inferiority, in addition to moral inadequacy, Lowell E. Galloway wholeheartedly embraces this proposition in *Poverty in America*.[37] Galloway writes that

> If intelligence is treated as a physical aspect of man and economic rent is paid to those possessing unusual amounts of it, the very real possibility exists that poverty is transmitted from parent to child through the genetic mechanism. In the broadest sense, this implies that poverty is to some substantial extent hereditary in the physical sense...The thrust of our argument has been that a major source of the white-Negro income gap is probably differential endowments of genetic human capital.[38]

Galloway's claim of black genetic inferiority rests primarily on his sweeping contention that increasing educational expenditures have not been able to close the racial gap in educational achievement. As he argues, "What can explain the apparent lack of impact of per pupil expenditures on student performance? And, what are the implications of this in terms of the inheritance of poverty question? The answer to the first question may simply be that after some expenditure threshold is reached, the critical factor is the native ability (intelligence?) of the student population."[39]

Galloway concludes that given genetic ability as the major explanation of poverty status in America, the existence of poverty in society is quite "natural." He writes: "In assessing the nature of the poverty problem in the United States, we have placed great emphasis on the importance of differentials in the distribution of genetic human capital as a source of inequality in the distribution of income. This implies something 'natural' about the existence of relative poverty in this country."[40]

Challenging the "culture of poverty" ideas put forth by neo-conservatives such as Murray, Gilder, Banfield, and others, William J. Wilson argues that "the key theoretical concept...is not 'culture of poverty' but 'social isolation.'"[41] In essence, the poor may not behave under the norms of "middle-class" expectations, because they have become detached from this sector, and are therefore increasingly isolated from role models who reflect acceptable social behavior. One of the earliest, yet still most powerful critiques of the utilization of cultural or genetic explanations for poverty is sociologist Charles A. Valentine's *Culture and Poverty*.[42] Valentine examines the literature that has utilized culture as an explanation of poverty up to the time of his book's publication in 1968 and shows in the chapter, "The Pejorative Tradition Established by E. Franklin Frazier," how the work of this sociologist laid much of the foundation for the "culture of poverty" school. Valentine argues that those advocating culture as an explanation have not proven their case analytically.

The cultural approach in its various forms is easily advocated, however, because as Kenneth B. Clark suggests in his work, *Dark Ghetto*, "the cult of cultural deprivation...is seductive."[43] Valentine supports Clark's description of cultural explanations as a "subtle form of social class and racial snobbery and ignorance."[44] In his chapter "Postscript: A Proposal for Empowering the Poor to Reduce Inequality," Valentine proposes that the reason many social welfare programs aimed at eliminating or reducing poverty have not been effective is precisely due to the presumption of cultural deprivation; these programs have not empowered poor people "to act in behalf of their own interests, either individually or collectively."[45] Valentine's work is still relevant to issues of poverty in the current period. His recommendations do not merely call for more social welfare programs, but also for greater political mobilization on the part of poor people.

Two more recent critiques of the cultural explanation of black poverty include political economist Manning Marable's "The Contradictory Contours of Black Political Culture" and Cornel West's "Race and Social Theory: Towards a Genealogical Materialist Analysis."[46] Both Marable and West argue that the many discussions on the presumed pathology of black culture have not actually reflected community experiences. Both essays suggest that intellectuals focusing on fatalistic or culture-focused models for explaining black poverty represent the interests of a political, social, economic and cultural status quo that is antithetical to the well-being of poor people, or the elimination of poverty.

The Self-Serving Roles of Public Assistance Bureaucracies as an Explanation

Another strain of the poverty literature has focused on the roles of public assistance bureaucracies as an explanation for persistent poverty. This school also has two versions, each at a different end of the ideological spectrum. Some writers have proposed that the institutional inability to eliminate poverty can be explained in large part by the self-serving functions and roles of public assistance bureaucracies which have organizational interests in maintaining poverty.[47] This interpretation holds that poverty is functional for the political and organizational well-being of public assistance bureaucracies and necessary for the continued careers of bureaucrats administering services to the poor. It is argued, furthermore, that public assistance bureaucracies maintain poverty by inhibiting the natural entrepreneurial spirit of people who are poor.

Interestingly, both liberals and conservatives have identified the organizational nature and behavior of public assistance bureaucracies as a major obstacle in reducing poverty.[48] The policies called for by these various authors, however, are quite different. Some propose the elimination of public assistance bureaucracies and an unfettering of the free market; while other writers argue that only transferring power to the poor will guarantee opportunities for their social and economic mobility.

Macro-Economic and Demographic Explanations

The impact of broad economic and demographic changes at both the national and international level is another explanation for the problem of poverty. Joseph Persky, Elliot Sclar, and Wim Wiewel, writing for the Economic Policy Institute, point out that "Poverty is now more urban and more concentrated in poor neighborhoods within large cities than ever before...These changes have been caused primarily by factors related to the process of economic restructuring. Although the service sector in cities employs many unskilled and semi-skilled workers, the blue collar manufacturing jobs which black city residents, among others, used to hold in great numbers have disappeared."[49] Goldsmith and Blakely also posit that poverty is partially a result of radical change and transformation in global and domestic economies. But they add that these changes have exacerbated the problem of poverty in the United States due to inadequate political responses on the part of government: "We believe, in fact, that the recent upsurge in urban poverty has been generated not simply by transformations in the structure of the global and domestic economies, but by a particular set of American political responses, which have also helped guide these transformations."[50]

They write, further:

Three features dominate the current situation: America is less influential in world wide economic affairs; the international economy itself is less stable; and the landscape of domestic industry has been transformed. In these circumstances...it would be almost impossible to eradicate poverty by relying on the usual domestic economic policies, employment and training programs, or efforts that focus on jobs alone. Policies have not faced up to America's new place in the world.[51]

Sociologist Stanley Lieberson draws upon historical analysis of the structural changes in the U.S. economy as a major factor for the differing social and economic mobility patterns experienced by blacks and Latinos in comparison to white ethnics in American history. Lieberson states in his work, *A Piece of the Pie*, that the structural occupational context for blacks and Latinos is dramatically different today than it was for immigrant groups entering America at the turn of the century.[52] There were more jobs available during earlier periods that permitted some degree of security and social mobility. Lieberson's thesis is similar to that of political scientist Charles V. Hamilton, who proposes in an essay entitled "Political Access, Minority Participation, and the New Normalcy," that "Before we look at the black and Hispanic situation, it is useful to see the context in which earlier ethnic politics in this country developed. Those groups began arriving in America when industrial expansion was taking off. They could not have been more timely. Periodic depressions notwithstanding, there was a continually growing private-sector economy that could accommodate, indeed welcomed, growing masses of unskilled labor. That labor came...The need was mutual and the relationship mutually beneficial."[53]

Another way in which the broader economic context was historically more advantageous to whites than blacks is illustrated by Gerald D. Suttles, who reminds us that in earlier periods greater proportions of poor blacks lived in Chicago public housing than poor Italians, who tended to live in their own private homes.[54] This meant that the latter group had an opportunity to use their property as venture capital, to make their homes profitable by performing economic tasks like renting, or to use their homes as a basis for adding income to that received from outside salaried occupations. These kinds of opportunities were closed to many blacks due to discrimination and segregation in housing.

In the decades of the 1970s and 1980s the rapidly changing occupational structure of the national economy resulted in the increasing impoverization of the American city population. Mark Roseman, in his article "How the Poor Would Remedy Poverty," describes some of these changes:

The occupational structure of our nation is changing rapidly. Each year, two to three million workers lose jobs because of structural factors, in both urban and rural areas. Since 1981, two million manufacturing jobs have been lost...over 40% fewer jobs were created during the 1980s than in the last half of the prior decade...Approximately half of recently created jobs are 'contingent' positions from which workers are easily laid off. About 50% of new jobs created between 1979 and 1984 also paid less than $7,000 a year.[55]

Dennis Gilbert and Joseph A. Kahl also list occupational structure as one factor of central importance in explaining structural unemployment and diminishing job opportunities paying good living wages. In *The American Class Structure* Gilbert and Kahl write that,

The system of production was changing as factories became more automated. Manufacturing jobs for persons of low skill were shrinking as a proportion of the labor force, and many antiquated factories in the older cities were closing and shifting their production either to small towns or to foreign countries. Therefore, an excess of job seekers was competing for a diminishing supply of positions. A disproportionate number of those without jobs were from minority groups, American citizens living in the slums originally built for foreign immigrants.[56]

This systemic development continues today. According to professor of politics Peter Dreier this is a "root cause" of urban poverty; furthermore, "The electronics revolution has hastened the development of a global economy and footloose multinational corporations. Since the early 1970s, there has been a tremendous flight of previously high-wage (primarily manufacturing) industries from U.S. cities to locations with more 'favorable' business conditions — low wages, weak or nonexistent unions, and lax environmental laws."[57]

These kinds of figures and discussions are related to Wilson's focus on broad economic changes impacting cities and neighborhoods as an explanation for the growth of persistent poverty among some groups.[58]

Turning to economic downtowns and the decline in manufacturing jobs to explain poverty is also suggested in David Osborne's *Laboratories of Democracy*. Osborne argues that poverty and economic displacement not only reflect the general ill health of the economy, but an increasing disconnection from the economy's mainstream for large numbers of people:

Three groups are caught in the mismatch between available jobs and available workers: dislocated industrial workers; the urban poor; and the rural poor. Increasingly, these three groups live in isolated communities that have lost their connections to the economic mainstream. These communities are caught in a downward spiral of disinvestment, increasing poverty, and further disinvestment. A few of their members successfully make the jump into the economic mainstream, but as communities, they grow ever more isolated.[59]

Sociologist Vijai P. Singh summarizes this view as one of

> two competing explanations for the persistence of poverty and the emergence of the underclass in the United States. The first position is that recent changes in the American economy have substantially contributed to the growth of the underclass population...The pervasive elimination of blue collar, entry-level jobs and the emergence of knowledge-based jobs have not favored many blacks who did not possess sufficient levels of education, skill, or work experiences. Unemployment and growing isolation from the mainstream economy have led to unwed parenting, dependency, lawlessness, joblessness, and school failure among some blacks.[60]

This approach has been challenged in part by several studies showing that the relationship between economic growth and persistent poverty may not be as strong for various demographic groups as has been suggested by some observers.

Researchers Rebecca M. Blank and Alan S. Blinder report in "Macroeconomics, Income Distribution and Poverty" for instance, that:

> Poverty declined particularly rapidly during the boom years of 1965, 1966, and 1968 (which, of course, were also the years in which the Great Society programs were getting started) and then rose slightly during the mild recession of 1969-1970. When expansion resumed in 1971-1973, the poverty rate ratcheted down another notch — to 11.1 percent, its historic low; the deep recession of 1973-1975 pushed poverty back to 12.3 percent; the 1976-78 expansion trimmed the poverty rate once again; and back-to-back recessions in 1980 and 1981-82 raised poverty from 11.7 percent in 1979 to 15 percent in 1982. In 1982 and 1983 real GNP fell and then rose, the average unemployment rate was constant, and poverty crept upward to 15.2 percent.[61]

This supports, in part, Osborne's argument. But these authors also note that "only among white male-headed households" is this relationship between economic fluctuation and poverty rates so clear.[62] Along this line, researchers James Thornton, Richard Agnello, and Charles Link conclude that the lack of national economic growth as an explanation for pockets of poverty "has been overstated."[63] As was pointed out earlier, Theodore Cross, in his book *The Black Power Imperative*, shows that the relationship between economic growth and declining poverty during the decade of the 1970s may have been clear-cut for whites, but not necessarily for blacks.[64]

Does this also hold true for the 1980s? In 1980 the gross national product was $3,187 billion (in constant 1982 dollars); by 1988 this figure had increased by 29.2 percent to $4,118 billion. Professor Cross asks: did this kind of economic growth lift blacks and Latinos out of poverty? As was the case for the 1970s, the response to this question is again negative. As a matter of fact, according to the U.S. Bureau of the Census, an additional 214,000 white families became impoverished during the 1980s. For blacks and Latinos, the situation was even worse: an additional 257,000 black families became impoverished while another 382,000 Latino families became impoverished[65] — all during a period when the gross national product grew significantly. Table 11 illustrates this development.

TABLE 11
Number of Families Below Poverty Level by Race and Hispanic Origin: 1980-1988

	1980	1988	% Change
Gross National Product	3,187[a]	4,118[a]	+29.2%
Families Below the Poverty Level	*(in thousands)*		
Whites	4,195	4,409	+5.1%
Blacks	1,820	2,077	+13.7%
Hispanics	751	1,133	+50.2%

SOURCE: Derived from U.S. Bureau of Economic Analysis, *Survey of Current Business*, April 1991 (Washington, DC, 1991); and U.S. Bureau of the Census, *Statistical Abstract of the United States, 1992* (Washington, DC, 1992), table 724.
[a] billions of dollars, and in constant 1992 dollars.

Wilson and other writers, as does Osborne, remind us that the poor are becoming more socially isolated as a result of the broad economic and demographic changes described above. In an essay, "The Ghetto Underclass and the Changing Structure of Urban Poverty," Wilson and his co-authors offer statistics illustrating the growing isolation of the poor by showing the shift in racial composition of the poor in cities from 1970 to 1980.[66] This study makes reference to Chicago as an example to describe the out-migration of the non-poor from the city. The authors explain the social transformation that has occurred in the inner city characterized by increasing isolation: the poor are divorced from job networks, individual and positive role models, as well as community institutions. This suggestion has been challenged by several writers who show that the alleged flight of the black middle class is not the major culprit for increasing levels of poverty in predominantly black and poor neighborhoods. Furthermore, the claim of a halycon period of black ghetto life has been critiqued by Brett Williams in her essay, "Poverty Among African Americans in the United States," as "mythic history." She notes that "convincing evidence for this notion has yet to be offered."[67] Mark J. Stern also shares in this criticism noting that "the notion of the 'golden age' of the ghetto is flawed."[68] Stern uses census data from the 1940s and 1950s to illustrate this claim.

Employment Opportunities and Low Wages as Explanations

Low wages and the lack of jobs at "decent" wages may be one of the most important causes for poverty for all groups. This was cited earlier as a significant factor for the impoverization of individuals and groups in Henry George's study in the mid-nineteenth century: "The cause which produces poverty in the midst of advancing wealth is evidently the cause which exhibits itself in the tendency, everywhere recognized, of wages [being kept] to a minimum."[69] One article examining how some were able to overcome poverty in the 1930s cited a study by the Research Department of the AFL-CIO stating that low wages were a major cause of poverty during the Great Depression. This study, "The Low Paid Worker," concludes that poverty during the Great Depression was reduced primarily as a result of stabilizing and improving the wages and purchasing power of workers.[70] The report suggests that minimum wage policies could be effective in preventing impoverization of workers.

One of the most comprehensive earlier studies of the relationship between income and poverty is economist Gabriel Kolko's *Wealth and Power in America*.[71] Kolko identifies unemployment and low income, or "poverty wages," as the major causes of poverty. A study published in the early 1970s with a similar theme regarding the relationship between poverty and low wages is political economist Barry Bluestone's "Lower Income Workers and Marginal Industries."[72] Bluestone illustrates a strong connection between poverty and low wages by highlighting and discussing the characteristics of America's working poor. This idea is developed fully by Sar A. Levitan and Isaac Shapiro in *Working but Poor*.[73] A more recent and comprehensive study of the relationship of wages and poverty was, *No Escape: The Minimum Wage and Poverty*, sponsored by the Center on Budget and Policy Priorities and authored by Shapiro.[74]

A 1990 study by Linda R. Martin and Demetrios Giannaros, "Would a Higher Minimum Wage Help Poor Families Headed by Women?" concludes that a major explanation for poverty rates among women is low wages: "The most important empirical conclusion of this study is that, in relative terms, the real minimum wage plays a major role in explaining the feminization of poverty."[75] These researchers compare the effects of government transfer payments, unemployment rates, and fluctuations in economic activity, and find that it was the minimum wage levels set by the federal government that had the major impact on the extent of poverty among families headed by women. A similar conclusion about poor families is reached by Ronald B. Mincy in his article, "Raising the Minimum Wage." He concludes that the results of his study "appear to favor a higher minimum wage, but caution is necessary. Despite its inefficiency in reaching the poor, a higher minimum wage would significantly reduce poverty among working families."[76]

Racism, Discrimination, and Segregation as Explanations

Racism and discrimination cannot be discounted or dismissed as explanations for persisting poverty in communities of color. In a report published in the 1960s, political scientist Anthony Downs identified several ways — still current today — in which institutions discriminate against poor people and blacks in particular: through providing assistance in ways that emphasize dependency; through higher costs for goods and services; by omitting impoverished people from social insurance schemes; through denial of services (mortgage loans, credit, municipal services), and through maintenance of public schools at a lower level of quality.[77]

Carballo states in a work cited earlier that overlooking the problem of racism and discrimination is a major weakness in how conservatives approach the problem of poverty. He writes:

> The central missing element, by omission or commission, in the conservative view of poverty, drawn as it is from the intellectual roots of a then racially homogenous Great Britain, is its failure to grasp the basic relationship in multi-racial America between racism and poverty. While most of the poor are white, disproportionate numbers of the poor are black, Hispanic (that is, primarily mulatto or mestizo), and native American.[78]

He continues:

> Racism is by no means the sole or indeed perhaps even the primary cause of poverty among minorities...But racism does have a lot to do with the concentration of minorities in municipalities whose tax base cannot carry quality public education; in neighborhoods that make minorities the disproportionate victims of crime; in jobs that are part-time, low-wage, and without the benefits of health insurance, pensions, or even Social Security.[79]

Discrimination means that the skills necessary for economic mobility are inaccessible to people of color; it means that job promotions are unequally distributed on the basis of race and ethnicity; and that information about economic opportunities is not distributed uniformly or consistently.

The connections between discrimination and poverty are suggested in one case study of Massachusetts by sociologist James E. Blackwell. This author reviews the profile of and reasons for black youth unemployment in his study "Youth Unemployment in Massachusetts." According to Blackwell, people of color are subject to discriminatory practices, both formal and informal, which have detrimental consequences in the following areas: union apprenticeship programs; availability of mortgages; economic dislocation; job promotions; lesser wages for same the jobs; and availability of information and informational networks about employment opportunities.[80]

Racial segregation, as is suggested by sociologists Douglas Massey and Nancy A. Denton — and even earlier by Kenneth B. Clark in *Dark Ghettos: Dilemmas of Social Power* — goes hand in hand with racism and discrimination. Massey and Denton report that their research "indicates that racial residential segregation is the principal structural feature of American society responsible for the perpetuation of urban poverty and represents a primary cause of social inequality in the United States."[81] Massey writes that continuing racial segregation "acts to undermine the socioeconomic environment faced by poor blacks and leaves their communities extremely vulnerable to any downturn in the economy. Under conditions of high racial segregation, a rise in the black poverty rate produces a dramatic loss in potential demand in poor black neighborhoods, leading to the withdrawal, deterioration, and outright elimination of goods and services distributed through the market.[82] Racial segregation, in other words, exacerbates the ill effects of downturns in the economy among black families to a far greater extent than among whites. Understanding the relationship between racial segregation and poverty, according to Massey, provides insight into why the composition of the "underclass" is primarily black, and why this sector is concentrated in the Northeast and Midwest. Massey posits that "Segregation heightens and reinforces negative racial stereotypes by concentrating people who fit those stereotypes in a small number of highly visible minority neighborhoods — a structural version of 'blaming the victim' — thereby hardening prejudice, making discrimination more likely, and maintaining the motivation for segregation. The persistence of segregation, in turn, worsens the concentration of poverty."[83]

Family Structure as an Explanation

As suggested in many popular and academic forums, family structure is a popular explanation for poverty. Sometimes the so-called "breakdown" of the family is offered as a major reason individuals and families fall into poverty; this persists despite overwhelming and growing evidence that this link is much more complex than is suggested by the claim. In her 1986 article "Household Composition and Poverty," demographer Mary Jo Bane writes: "It has become common knowledge — whether true or not — that family structure is important in explaining contemporary poverty." But, "In fact, previous research...indicates that a rather small percentage of the changes in the poverty level over the past few decades can be attributed to demographic change."[84] As a result of her analysis Bane concludes that a focus on family structure is misspent: "the problem of poverty should be addressed by devoting attention to employment, wages, and the development of skills necessary for productive participation in the labor force rather than handwringing about the decline of the family."[85]

Despite increasing evidence to support this view, however, the family structure explanation suggested by sociologist Daniel Patrick Moynihan, and much earlier by sociologist E. Franklin Frazier, not only remains conventionally popular, but reflects much of current social welfare policy in the United States. Under the umbrella of family structure and poverty, the "feminization of poverty" has been turned to as a special feature of this relationship. This term is used to indicate that female-headed families are more susceptible to poverty than male-headed or two-parent families. This phrase was supposedly coined by Diana Pearce in a 1978 article, "The Feminization of Poverty: Women, Work, and Welfare."[86] While the term may be a recent one, Mimi Abramovitz shows in *Regulating the Lives of Women* that "women's impoverishment dates back to colonial America when from one-third to one-half of a town's poor were likely to be female."[87] Thus, the "feminization of poverty" may be a misnomer if it suggests that this is a new development in the national profile and history of poverty.

In an essay entitled "Politics and Policies of Feminization of Poverty," Bane provides a statistical overview of poverty characteristics and trends associated with female-headed households.[88] Barbara Ehrenreich, Holly Sklar and Karen Stollard in *Poverty and the American Dream* discuss how women are particularly exploited in the United States.[89] This qualitative study provides case studies of women experiencing poverty. One conclusion of the book is that "a job is not necessarily an antidote to poverty for women. On the contrary, the jobs available to women are part of the problem."[90] Women, according to these authors, are clustered in only 20 out of 420 occupations listed by the Bureau of Labor Statistics. These occupations tend to offer the lowest pay.

In her previously cited article Pearce suggests that race is not as significant a factor as gender in explaining the depressed economic condition of poor women.[91] But as shown by the extensive work of political economist Julianne Malveaux and others, it is not accurate to dismiss important racial distinctions in the poverty experiences of women. Malveaux describes how the labor experiences of black and white women differ significantly in her essay "The Political Economy of Black Women."[92] Goldberg and Kremin respond to Pearce by writing that "in the United States, black and Hispanic single mothers suffer poverty rates 50 percent greater than their white counterparts, and black women are three times as likely as white women to be in the economically vulnerable position of single motherhood. Three-fifths of poor, single-mother families in the United States, moreover, are women of color and their children."[93]

A strong precedent for utilizing family structure as an explanation for poverty is the 1965 "Moynihan Report," which proposed a link between the family structure of blacks and poverty:

> The circumstances of the Negro American community in recent years have probably been getting worse, not better...The fundamental problem, in which this is most clearly the case, is that of family structure...So long as this situation persists, the cycle of poverty and disadvantage will continue to repeat itself.[94]

Other observers, such as Banfield, have gone so far as to suggest a cultural predisposition on the part of "lower-class" groups not to maintain stable families, thus producing greater levels of poverty among these groups.[95]

In a book based on an analysis of U.S. Bureau of the Census data for 1980, *The Color Line and the Quality of Life in America*, researchers Reynolds Farley and Walter Allen conclude that:

the best single category of explanations for race differences in the organization of family life in contemporary U.S. society would seem to be those that attribute importance to race differences in functional relationship with the larger society and its institutions. Black-white differences in economic well-being, political power, and social standing — more so than differences in values and predispositions — explain the observed race differences in family organization and process.[96]

This finding has been confirmed by other studies. The Joint Center for Political and Economic Studies, for example, reports in *The Declining Economic Status of Black Children*, that:

While family structure is an important factor in determining whether a black child will be poor, the decline in marriage and the increased proportion of births occurring out of wedlock do not account fully for the decline in children's economic well-being. Indeed, the study revealed that the economic slippage experienced by all types of black families — whether headed by married couples, never-married women, or formerly-married women — played at least as great a role as family structure change in the worsening status of black children.[97]

It is clear that single, female heads of households have a higher poverty rate than single male-headed or two-parent households. But the implications of this relationship are not as conclusive as some would contend. And, as was discussed in chapter three, a poverty gap remains between black, white and Latino families of similar composition. White families contrasted to comparably structured black and Latino families tend to be better off in economic terms. This fact tends to dampen the unqualified claim that "family breakup" causes poverty.

There are other national social welfare systems that do not reflect a strong correlation between single, female heads of household and poverty status. Sweden is one such example. As Gertrude Goldberg and Eleanor Kremin write in *The Feminization of Poverty*: "In the United States it has long been assumed that there is a direct link between poverty and family composition or single motherhood. However, Sweden has gone far toward breaking this link — a notable achievement. Single motherhood is about as prevalent in Sweden as it is in the U.S. By using a combination of labor market and social policies...Sweden has achieved a relatively low rate of poverty for single parent families."[98]

The relationship between single, female heads of households and poverty status should not be approached fatalistically, as the case of Sweden shows. Even in the United States there have been some periods when an increasing labor force participation rate for women, coupled with decent wages, has reduced poverty status for single female-headed families. For example, in reviewing the immediate post-World War II period, Richard X. Chase reports in "Trends in Poverty Incidence and Its Rate of Reduction for Various Demographic Groups: 1947-1963," that increasing labor force participation rates for women during that period resulted in some reduction in the poverty rate of female-heads of households. His study shows that the incidence of poverty for all female-headed families was reduced from 51.5 percent in 1947, to 49.2 percent in 1956, to 47.6 percent in 1963. These slight reductions were due to the increasing labor force participation rate for women earning wages that enabled them to live above poverty status. During these same years, however, the incidence of poverty for male-headed families fell even faster, from 29.9 percent in 1947, to 19.8 percent in 1956, to 15.6 percent in 1963.[99]

Dependency and Poverty

Charles Murray argues in *Losing Ground* that the poor remain so because they have become psychologically and programmatically dependent on government largess.[100] If the public dole did not exist, Murray reasons, then presumably the poor would be forced to look for work, and to maintain stable two-parent families enabling them to eventually move out of poverty. This belief is held widely by both blacks and whites according to a survey reported by Sigelman and Welch. They report that 71 percent of blacks and 86 percent of whites believe that "welfare encourages people to work less."[101] "Permissiveness" or other generosity is the culprit explaining welfare dependency according to Lawrence M. Mead. He believes that poverty is perpetuated by the U.S. social welfare system because it permits people to receive benefits without demanding anything in return. Poor people, Mead argues, should be encouraged to become independent and competent by reflecting "good citizenship." This, he states, would reduce the number of unwed mothers and jobless men.[102]

Arguments that the welfare system is a major cause of increases in the number of single-female heads of household is not supported by hard data, as pointed out by Isabel V. Sawhill in "Poverty and the Underclass":

"the literature on the relationship between the welfare system and the growth of female-headed families suggests that welfare can account for no more than 15 to 25 percent of the growth in the incidence of women heading families over this period, or — at most — for a 0.4 percentage-point increase in the poverty rate."[103] The relatively high proportion and growth of single, female-headed households among blacks and Latinos should be of concern. But it cannot be shown definitively, or analytically according to political scientist Adolph Reed, Jr., that this growth reflects male irresponsibility or a pathological dependency on public assistance.[104] Dependency caused by government dole, although a popular and seductive explanation of persistent poverty, has little basis in hard evidence. As a matter of fact, between 1975 and 1983 there was a major decline in the proportion of families with female heads receiving public assistance and welfare income; growing dependency would instead show increasing rates of receipt of public assistance. In 1975, 47.1 percent of all black families with female heads, and 21.2 percent of all white families with female heads, received income from public assistance; by 1983, only 37.4 percent of all black families with female heads, and only 13.7 percent of similar white families, received income from public assistance.[105]

William J. Wilson and Kathryn M. Neckerman have shown that many studies focusing on the relationship between welfare benefits and out-of-wedlock births report that there is no association between these two factors. Furthermore, there is no relationship between varying state AFDC benefit levels and out-of-wedlock birth rates.[106] According to these two authors, one reason there is a higher level of single female heads of household in black communities is that the pool of "marriageable" black men has declined rapidly in the last two to three decades.[107] This means that the availability of black men with jobs that could support a family has declined considerably since World War II. As a result of continuing unemployment, there are fewer black men who can support families, thus the increase in black female-headed families since World War II. The Joint Center for Political and Economic Studies reported that "Nationally, less than 40 percent of black males aged 16 to 64 years are working full time, compared with almost 55 percent of white males."[108] The following table illustrates further the disparate labor force participation rates of black and white males.

TABLE 12
Labor Force Participation Rates of Males,
16 to 34 Years, by Race: 1950-1980

	1950	1960	1970	1980
Black (16-19)	55.8%	42.4%	35.8%	36.5%
White (16-19)	51.5	51.1	48.9	55.5
Black (20-24)	80.4	82.0	76.4	73.5
White (20-24)	82.1	86.8	81.6	84.3
Black (25-34)	86.2	88.5	87.6	83.5
White (25-34)	92.8	95.7	94.7	94.3

SOURCE: Derived from William J. Wilson and Kathryn M. Neckerman. "Labor Force Participation Rates by Age, Race, and Sex, 1940-1980." In *Fighting Poverty: What Works and What Doesn't*, eds. Sheldon H. Danziger and Daniel H. Weinberg (Cambridge, MA: Harvard University Press, 1986), table 10.4.

Wilson and Neckerman argue that black women with children are not marrying at a higher rate due to the relative lack of employed or employable, i.e. marriageable, black men. The differences in the labor force participation rates between black and white males help to explain the greater proportion of single female families among blacks. Although this proposition was made in earlier studies, the continuing decline of black male participation in the labor market has revived it as an explanation for the changing structure of black families.

Similar to Wilson and Neckerman, the report of the Center for the Study of Social Policy, "The Flip-Side of Black Female-Headed Families: Black Men," states:

Census and labor force data show that nearly half of the black male population age 16-64 is either unemployed, out of the labor force, in prisons, or their labor force status cannot be determined by available data. In contrast, only 23 percent of white men age 16-64 are in a similar situation...Corresponding increases in the number of black female-headed families may be rooted in the fact that many black men are jobless and thus unable to support families.[109]

Along this line of thought, Wilson and Neckerman point out that,

> In the 1960s scholars readily attributed black family deterioration to the problems of male joblessness. However, in the past ten to fifteen years, in the face of the overwhelming focus on welfare as the major source of black family break-up, concerns about the importance of male joblessness have receded into the background. We argue in this paper that the available evidence justifies renewed scholarly and public policy attention to the connection between the disintegration of poor families and black male prospects for stable employment.[110]

Economist William A. Darity, Jr. et al. focus on the lack of marriageable black men in an essay, "How Useful Is the Black Underclass?" In addition to considering declining labor force participation as a cause, Darity and his colleagues consider imprisonment, murder, suicide, drugs, and racial discrimination to be major explanations for the relatively small pool of marriageable black men.[111]

Another researcher who identifies the gender ratio in the black community as a factor related to family structure and economic well-being is political economist Manning Marable. In his internationally recognized work, *How Capitalism Underdeveloped Black America*, he proposes that black men are imprisoned at much higher rates than whites and that this is reflected in the deteriorating social and economic development of the black community.[112] According to political scientist Andrew Hacker this situation is not improving; the availability of black men is declining, which means that the relatively large presence of single black female households may be the norm for a long period. As Hacker writes: "The pool of 'marriageable' black men gets smaller every year...Over half a million black men are in jails and prisons, and as many more could be sent or returned there if they violate their parole or probation...Another large group is debilitated by drugs or alcohol or mental illness. In addition, the death rates for younger men have reached terrifying levels."[113]

Lack of Political Power as an Explanation

Lack of political power has been suggested as another explanation for the continuing status of poverty among some groups, especially those questionably labelled as the "black underclass." Social scientists Paul A. Baran and Paul M. Sweezy discussed the role of potential and real economic power in maintaining poverty during the mid-1960s. As they state in their article "Monopoly Capital":

The system has two poles: wealth, privilege, power at one; poverty, deprivation, powerlessness at the other...Today, Negroes are at the bottom, and there is neither room above nor anyone ready to take their place...For there may be nothing short of a complete change in the system — the abolition of both poles and the substitution of a society in which wealth and power are shared by all — that can transform their condition.[114]

This theme is repeated by professor of black studies Herman George, Jr., in his article "Black Americans, the 'Underclass' and the Subordination Process." He writes: "The subordination process is essentially a set of political-economic relationships which, dictated by U.S. capitalism, have determined the specific forms of inclusive exclusion which have characterized the histories of groups incorporated into the social order, in particular, people of African, Latin American, and Asian descent."[115] Political scientist Bette Woody also sees the political decisions of a conservative government as a major factor in the maintenance of poverty. This, she argues, is manifested by the government's refusal to respond to the negative impact of a changing economy on black income earners: "Two political factors have hampered fuller recognition of the impact of a changing economy on black earners. One is the absence of government response to the massive shift in the economy from production to services and a corresponding changeover in the gender composition of the American workforce. The second is the rise of an aggressive political conservatism in the United States, which uses selective indicators that emphasize social behavior as a cause of poverty."[116]

A political explanation for poverty and depressed economic opportunities for African-American women is offered by F. I. Ajanaku, M. L. Jackson, and T. S. Mosley in their article, "Underdevelopment in the U.S. Labor Market: The Case of African American Female Workers." They argue that the underdevelopment of black women and their economic potential has taken place at the same time that capital accumulation has benefited European Americans. This imbalance has not been rectified by black women due to the lack of political power to advocate effectively on their own behalf.[117]

Martin Luther King, Jr., in *Where Do We Go from Here: Chaos or Community?* defined the nature of persisting poverty fundamentally as one of political power and moral will on the part of those with wealth in society. He argued that only political power on the part of poor people can solve the problem of poverty in the United States; only power can transform the ghetto. Resolving the problem of poverty also requires confronting the growing militarization and imperialism of the United States government.

King also believed that capitalism — or at least the excesses of American capitalism rather than individual or group deficiencies — produces and is responsible for poverty.[118]

The National Conference of Catholic Bishops issued a "Pastoral Letter on the U.S. Economy" in November 1986 which implicitly endorsed King's earlier message regarding effective strategies for the elimination of poverty in American society. This pastoral letter calls for greater prioritization of the problem of poverty. As the pastoral letter states:

> If the U.S. were a country in which poverty existed amidst relatively equitable income distribution, one might argue that we do not have the resources to provide everyone with an adequate living. But, in fact, this is a country marked by glaring inequitable distribution of wealth and necessities...Gross inequalities are morally unjustifiable, particularly when millions lack even the bare necessities of life. In our judgement, the distribution of income and wealth in the U.S. is so inequitable that it violates this minimum standard of distributive justice.[119]

This statement defines poverty and growing social inequality as King did earlier — as both a national economic and moral crisis, and as one which requires a political response on the part of poor people and their advocates. Simply stated, poor people must organize and mobilize to demand more equitable redistribution of wealth in the United States. Mark J. Stern suggests that this was a critical element in maintaining economic progress in the 1970s, especially for the black poor. As Stern writes, "the urban jobless 'fell behind' during the 1970s not because overly generous welfare payments sapped their will to work or uphold family responsibilities, but because other groups grabbed a larger and larger share of the welfare pie."[120] The lack of political power on the part of the black poor prevented them from enjoying the fruits of racial welfare expansion during this period. This theme is repeated by Robin D. G. Kelley in her examination of poor people and their status in Birmingham between 1929 and 1970; she writes that "the Birmingham example offers important lessons for developing an approach to the problems of the black urban poor...In short, the poor need to play a more direct role in creating policies that affect them, particularly since they clearly understand the inner workings and contradictions of their world better than do middle-class politicians and academics."[121]

The implication of these kinds of reviews is that poor people must begin to advocate and "grab" for their economic interests in the political arena, as do other sectors such as corporations, banks, insurance and finance conglomerates, giant real-estate interests, and large hospitals. Only such political grabbing will allow poor people to utilize adequate resources for the reduction, and perhaps elimination, of poverty.

CHAPTER V
What Are the Major Characteristics and Themes Reflected in the United States Welfare System and Anti-Poverty Policies?

A family, living upon the scale allowed for in this estimate, must never spend a penny on railway fare or omnibus. They must never go into the country unless they walk. They must never purchase a half-penny newspaper or spend a penny to buy a ticket for a popular concert. They must write no letters to absent children, for they cannot afford to pay the postage. They must never contribute anything to their church or chapel, or give any help to a neighbor which costs them money. They cannot save, nor can they join sick or Trade Union, because they cannot pay the necessary subscription. The children must have no pocket money for dolls, marbles, or sweets. The father must smoke no tobacco and must drink no beer. The mother must never buy any pretty clothes for herself or for her children, the character of the family wardrobe as for the family diet being governed by the regulation, nothing must be bought but that which is absolutely necessary for the maintenance of physical health, and what is bought must be of the plainest and most economical description.

B. Seebohm Rowntree
Poverty, A Study of Town Life (1901)

The United States welfare system has traditionally reflected a dual view of the poor. As Paul Jacobs writes in his 1965 essay, "America's Schizophrenic View of the Poor,"

An ideological schizophrenia with a complex history characterizes the American view of poverty. On the one hand, we believe achievement is related primarily to self-reliance and self-help; on the other, we have been forced to concede that failure cannot always be laid on the door of the individual.[1]

A belief reflecting one side of this schizophrenic view of the poor is the presumption that the poor cannot be trusted; that they are continually attempting to "con" the system. As was discussed in the last chapter, it is also assumed implicitly, if not stated explicitly, that providing assistance on more than a temporary basis actually may be detrimental to the work ethic. The U.S. welfare system seems to reflect a belief that this work ethic is the best guarantee against poverty. As researcher David T. Ellwood explains in *Poor Support*,

When you give people money, food, or housing, you reduce the pressure on them to work and care for themselves. No one seriously disputes this proposition. Indeed, a very large part of the social science research on poverty in the past twenty years has been designed to answer the question of how much less people will work if they are given income support.[2]

This kind of thinking is evident in the Welfare Dependency Act of 1992 (S1256) introduced by U.S. Senator Daniel Patrick Moynihan. This bill mandates that the federal Department of Health and Human Services develop indicators of welfare dependency in order to track the extent of "dependency" over periods of time. The purpose of this is to determine the impact of welfare programs on welfare dependency. Much of the "welfare reform" movement in the 1980s focused on making recipients less dependent on public assistance. This is a strong and common link in a broad range of welfare reform initiatives at the state level. The message in these state initiatives is that the poor have generally become dependent on government dole and are not willing to work.[3]

Much of the general public's negative perception of the poor has been shaped by a long intellectual tradition in the United States. In 1914, for instance, Jacob Hollander wrote in *The Abolition of Poverty* that the poor are characterized by "shiftlessness," "malingering," and "the vagrancy of the work-shy."[4] This assessment was similar to that in Amos G. Warner's *American Charities*, published a few years earlier in 1894.[5]

The U.S. social welfare system and its anti-poverty efforts are, for the most part, based on Schiller's "flawed character" paradigm described in an earlier chapter. U.S. anti-poverty policies also reflect Rowntree's description of how the poor must be controlled by society. In terms of its organization, the U.S. social welfare system is fragmented and limited conceptually. As sociologist Fred Block writes, "The American welfare state is in many ways a flawed and fragmented creation, especially when compared to the more generous welfare states of the European capitalist societies."[6] One reason for this is that there is an implicit assumption reflected in the U.S. welfare system that the nation's economic system is viable for all.

This assumption of equal opportunity may partially explain the following description of policy characteristics of social welfare policy aimed at poverty found in Harrell R. Rodgers, Jr.'s *Poor Women, Poor Families*: "The emphasis is on dealing with families or individuals after they become poor or seriously ill...Assistance is designed to be temporary, varies significantly by state, and is limited mostly to families headed by single women who must remain single to receive help...Poor families can receive critical assistance (e.g. medical care) only if they stay on welfare...Most employed women cannot have a child without suffering serious wage loss, or even loss of their job."[7]

Conceptually, these kinds of social welfare policies are not significantly different from the English Poor Law of 1598, according to political scientists Ira Katznelson and Mark Kesselman. These two authors point out that major features of the U.S. system parallel "social welfare" for the poor in seventeenth-century England. These similarities include the "dual welfare" state; the element of forced labor in some form; the stigmatization of the poor, and the differentiation between the "deserving" and "undeserving" poor.[8]

As suggested by many writers and researchers, policies and programs within the U.S. welfare system do not reflect structural factors and developments as the major causes of poverty. Efforts aimed at eliminating poverty, in fact, focus on the presumed damaging effects of individual characteristics, including cultural or linguistic deficiencies, inadequate education or skills, dependency on government largesse, or changes in family structure. Within this shallow conceptual framework lies the dual, contradictory, and schizophrenic stance on how to approach poverty in America.

In his essay, "Historical Attitudes Toward Poverty," Herbert London describes a historical tug-of-war in America between "Darwinism" and "Progressivism," the latter emphasizing social responsibility regarding assistance to the poor, and the former contending that one social class has no right to demand anything of other groups of citizens.[9] This continuing tug can be witnessed in the goals and orientation of public policy related to alleviating poverty in this country in the current period.

The literature generally suggests that there are at least three broad societal goals of the U.S. welfare system directed at poverty: the relief of misery; the preservation of the social order; and regulation of the labor market by molding the work attitudes of the poor and near poor; Joe Feagin adds a fourth goal: "rehabilitation" of the poor.[10] While there have been many debates throughout American history regarding how to organize assistance to the poor and determining which of these three major goals should be the target of such assistance, there has been a consistent set of values underpinning the philosophical and programmatic characteristics of the U.S. welfare system. The literature has generally identified these values as: work ethic; the viability of entrepreneurship in the American economy, and the primacy of the nuclear family.

Social scientist Dorothy B. James in *Poverty, Politics, and Change* points to two major values that "have consistently dominated American thought and public policy from the seventeenth century to the present: ethnocentrism and liberalism."[11] She adds that the latter value is reflected in individualism and materialism. "These values are reflected in all aspects of public policy, including policy affecting the poor. Their strength has severely limited the degree to which Americans have been willing even to consider poverty a legitimate target of public policy, and has narrowly restricted the alternative policies that have been acceptable to the electorate."[12]

Some sectors of the poor population are perceived as not deserving assistance, as is indicated by the title of Michael B. Katz's book, *The Undeserving Poor*.[13] This is generally true, according to professor of social welfare Jane Axinn and her colleague Mark J. Stern, whether the poor are being viewed through the eyes of a liberal or conservative national administration. They write in *Dependency and Poverty*:

> Despite the enormous energy that has been expended on the issue, however, the analytical framework of welfare reformers has remained surprisingly unsophisticated. Welfare recipients have been seen — by both liberals and conservatives — as an "underclass" of poor women and men, who are either unwilling or unable to take advantage of the promise of American life.[14]

In addition to the schizophrenic view of the poor described here, the U.S. welfare system and its anti-poverty policies reflect selective treatment of poor people; some groups of the poor are treated more favorably than others. Note the following example: during the decade of the 1970s, benefits for Aid to Families with Dependent Children (AFDC) were cut by 13 percent. The majority of children in AFDC were black and Latino. In this same decade, however, benefits for Survivor's Insurance (SI) were increased by 53 percent; the majority of children in this program were white. Children in the latter program generally received three times the benefits received by children on AFDC.[15] Michael Sherraden adds that in neither case have the children themselves "earned these benefits...It happens that a large proportion of AFDC recipients are black or Hispanic, whereas the vast majority of SI recipients are white. SI benefits are tied to inflation, and real benefits are now almost three times more than the amount provided to AFDC children."[16]

Another example of this selective treatment is the recent 1994 directive of the current administration requiring that abortions performed on poor women impregnated due to rape or incest be paid by states through Medicaid.[17] While liberalizing this law is an important step in ensuring that poor women have the rights of others, the change only covers about one thousand women annually. Thus, these poor women are treated as "deserving," yet other thousands of poor women who may become pregnant unwantingly are forced to give birth because they are considered "undeserving."

Major United States Assistance Programs

There are two ways social welfare assistance is provided by the federal government: "means tested" and "non-means tested." In the former category recipients are targeted and scrutinized in terms of their income, personal assets, or family assets. Potential recipients cannot have income or assets in excess of an officially-determined level of eligibility. The other category of programs is administered on the basis of "universality." This includes anyone in a particular demographic or social group such as elderly, veterans, or the unemployed.

The following are non-means tested programs, providing cash assistance benefits:

Social Security Retirement (Old Age and Survivor's Insurance), established by the Social Security Act of 1935. The benefits of this program are now indexed to rise with inflation. In FY 1984 total expenditures were $162.4 billion doled out to 32.4 million recipients, for an average annual expenditure of $5,012 per individual.

Social Security Disability Insurance, established by the Amendment of 1956 to the Social Security Act. In FY 1984 expenditures were $18.5 billion doled out to 3.8 million recipients, for an average annual expenditure of $4,868 per individual.

Unemployment Insurance, established by the Social Security Act of 1935. In FY 1984 benefits distributed for the first 26 weeks of unemployment were $18.3 billion, for an average weekly expenditure per recipient of $119.

There are two major non-means tested programs, providing non-cash assistance benefits:

Medicare, established by the Amendment of 1965 to the Social Security Act. In FY 1984 total benefits expended were $62 billion, distributed to 29.6 million recipients, for an average annual expenditure per recipient of $2,095.

Subsidized School Lunch Program, established by the National School Lunch Act of 1946. In FY 1984 total expenditures were $800,000 doled out to 11.6 million students who receive a free or subsidized lunch on a daily basis.

There are two major means-tested programs that provide cash-assistance benefits:

Aid to Families with Dependent Children (AFDC), established by the Social Security Act of 1935. Benefits were expanded during the 1960s and then significantly reduced in the 1980s. Need for this kind of assistance is determined by states, but generally eligible families are those "with children under 18 years of age where one parent is absent owing to death, desertion, divorce, incapacitation, or incarceration." In FY 1984 total expenditures were $8.3 billion doled out to 10.9 million individuals, for an average annual expenditure of $761 per individual.

Supplemental Security Income, established by the Amendment of 1972 to the Social Security Act. Cash benefits are provided to the needy aged, blind, and disabled. In FY 1984 total expenditures were $8.5 billion distributed to 3.6 million recipients, resulting in an average annual expenditure of $2,361 per individual.

And finally, there are three major means-tested programs that provide non-cash-assistance benefits:

Medicaid, established by the Amendment of 1965 to Social Security Act. Covers medical costs for individuals in AFDC families and most individuals eligible for SSI. In FY 1984 total expenditures were $20.1 billion distributed to 21.9 million individuals, at an annual average cost of $918 per individual.

Food Stamps, established in 1961. Distributes food coupons to individuals and families with incomes below 130 percent of the poverty line; average value of coupons per recipient per month is $46; in the first year of this program 49,600 participants received food stamps, by 1986 this number had grown to 19,431,000.

Housing Assistance, established with the Housing Act of 1937. Assistance is provided in the form of public housing and rent subsidies to families with incomes below 80 percent (varies with some states) of median income for that area. In FY 1984, $9.9 billion was expended for 10 million families; the average annual expenditure was $990 per household.

Social Welfare Expenditures

It is important to note that, despite the size of social welfare programs in the United States, not all benefits are directed at the problems of poverty. Between 1961 and 1975, for example, three-quarters of all expenditures on social welfare went to the non-poor and elderly. There is a popular misconception that federal expenditures for social welfare are primarily expended on reducing poverty. This misconception is replete in both the popular and scholarly literature, as is reflected in the following statement made by John Silber in *Straight Shooting*: "Beginning with President Lyndon B. Johnson's War on Poverty and his vision of the Great Society, the amount we have spent on social welfare exceeds, in constant dollars, the amount we spent on World War II and, in fact, the total cost of any single project in any society throughout recorded history. Yet millions of Americans remain below the poverty line."[18] Adding the last phrase makes this statement a nonsequitur. It implies that the enormous social welfare budget of the United States is directed at reducing poverty.

Another scholar goes so far as to suggest that the enormous amount spent on the poor is evidence of a strong public spirit in American society: "Self interest cannot account, except through the grossest of contortions, for vast increases in spending for the poor that occurred in the 1960s and 1970s."[19] To the contrary, it can be argued that in at least one way the resources going to the poor have declined over the last ten years; while the absolute level of federal anti-poverty expenditures has increased slightly, the level of federal resources going to the poor on a *per capita* basis has declined by more than one-fifth between 1978 and 1987. The following table illustrates the decline in benefits to poor persons on a per capita basis between 1978 and 1987, although total social welfare expenditures for all persons have risen in absolute levels.

TABLE 13
Total Federal Government Anti-Poverty Expenditures
and Per Capita Expenditures: 1968-1987

	Federal Expenditures (Billions)	% Change 1978-1987	Federal Expenditures Per Capita Basis	% Change 1978-1987
1968	$38.6		$1,530	
1973	71.3		3,102	
1078	116.2		4,744	
1983	112.0		3,171	
1987	119.6	+2.9	3,675	-22.5

SOURCE: Derived from "Total Government Anti-poverty Expenditures Have Risen, but Outlay Per Poor Person Have Declined Since 1978 (1988 dollars)" in Sar A. Levitan, *Programs in Aid of the Poor* (Baltimore, MD: The Johns Hopkins University Press, 1990), table 6.

As table 13 illustrates, while total federal anti-poverty expenditures rose by slightly less than three percent (2.9) between 1978 and 1987, federal anti-poverty expenditures on a per capita basis declined by more than one fifth, or 22.5 percent! This reflects the fact that federal outlays have not kept pace with inflation, nor with increases in the number of poor persons.

Neither did poor people receiving AFDC fare well in 1991. As is pointed out by two scholars at the American Enterprise Institute for Public Policy Research,

Nineteen ninety-one was a bad year for welfare recipients. Nine states cut and 31 states froze benefits under the Aid to Families with Dependent Children program. At the same time, 14 states cut and another 13 froze general cash assistance payments — the program for poor people not eligible for AFDC.[20]

Douglas J. Besharou and Karen Baehler add that "By all accounts, when all the numbers are in, 1992 will turn out to have been worse."[21] According to one study, as a matter of fact, AFDC expenditures represent less than one percent of all federal expenditures in the current period.[22]

Even by the late 1960s and early 1970s, what some might describe as the relatively small amount committed directly to the poor was beginning to shrink rapidly. Political scientists David Robertson and Dennis Judd point out in their book *The Development of American Public Policy* that by 1971 several states staged "budget revolts" against welfare expenditures for the poor. These writers note that the power of the federal courts was not enough to expand participation in welfare. They write, "Despite the actions by federal courts to ease access to welfare, the American welfare system remained very limited and uneven. Of the thirty million citizens living in poverty, only ten million received some form of public assistance."[23] Research analysts Sar A. Levitan and Isaac Shapiro add to this point by stating that "AFDC payments leave most families in poverty. For a family of three living in a state with median AFDC support, the maximum AFDC grant combined with food stamp benefits yields less than three-quarters of the poverty-income threshold."[24] This is consistent with Levitan's finding that "When viewed in the context of the increase in the gross national product, the proportion of anti-poverty spending declined in the 1980s. Anti-poverty expenditures rose from 1.8 percent of GNP in 1968 to 3.9 percent in 1980 and then dropped slightly to 3.5 percent in 1987."[25]

This idea is related to one raised by researchers Sheldon H. Danziger and Daniel H. Weinberg who write in *Fighting Poverty* that "Social insurance transfers (primarily Social Security retirement, survivors, and disability payments, Medicare, and unemployment insurance) account for both the majority of spending in any year and for much of the spending growth: they rose from 3.3 percent of GNP in 1966 to 7.1 percent in 1984. None of these programs was specifically designed to reduce poverty."[26] David T. Ellwood and Lawrence H. Summers add, furthermore, that the "social insurance system is clearly geared to the middle-class."[27]

Reviewing and updating an important essay by Richard M. Titmus in 1965, "The Role of Redistribution in Social Policy," and the 1975 publication of Robert D. Plotnik and Felicity Skidmore, *Progress Against Poverty*, Mimi Abramovitz notes that, although social welfare spending nearly doubled between 1965 and 1972, the portion spent on the poor changed little, hovering around 40 percent of the total social welfare budget. Interestingly, however, today 40 percent seems "whopping" when compared with the proportions in later years. The Congressional Budget Office also reported that social welfare benefits often go to those least in need. In 1980, although 49 percent of federal expenditures were paid directly to individuals and families, only 13 percent of these dollars went for programs that used poverty or need as a criterion for receiving aid.[28]

Generally, federal budgets for non-means tested programs have increased much faster than social welfare expenditures based on a means test. Table 14 shows fiscal increases for means-tested and non-means tested programs between 1976 and 1984.

TABLE 14
**Federal Expenditures for Major Social
Welfare Programs: 1976 and 1984
(billions of 1984 dollars)**

	1976	*1984*	*% Change*
Social Security for elderly	152.2	205.6	+35.0
Medical protection for elderly	38.7	68.0	+75.7
Social Security for injured/disabled	24.5	26.1	+6.0
Employment-related benefits for injured/disabled	22.3	26.1	+17.0
Medical protection for injured/disabled	15.0	25.5	+70.0
Public assistance (primarily AFDC)	20.8	17.1	- 17.7
Food assistance (food stamps/ child nutrition)	14.4	16.2	+0.9
Housing and energy assistance for poor	5.5	7.4	+34.5
Employment, training, and social services for poor	12.5	9.3	-25.6
Medical protection for poor	12.4	15.7	+26.6

SOURCE: Derived from David T. Ellwood, *Poor Support* (New York: Basic Books, 1988), table 2.1; also see, William P. O'Hare, *Poverty in America: Trends and New Patterns* (Washington, DC: Population Reference Bureau, Inc., March 1987), pps. 26-30.

As shown in table 15 more updated data about federal social welfare and anti-poverty program expenditures is provided by Sherraden.

TABLE 15
Estimated Federal Direct and Tax Expenditures
for Social Welfare: Fiscal Year 1990
(billions of dollars)

	Direct Expenditures to Individuals[a]	Tax Expenditures[a]
Education	9.718	900 million
Employment	4.623	7.300
Social Services	8.466	4.200
Health Care	153.141	44.400
(Medicaid)[b]	37.398	
Income Security	366.800	89.800
(Suppl. Sec. Income)[b]	12.148	
(Family Support/ AFDC)[b]	11.180	
(Earn. Inc. Tax Cred.)[b]	3.841	
(Refugee Assist.)[b]	287 million	
(Low Inc. House Energy Assistance)[b]	1.125	
(Other)[b]	226 million	
Housing	17.626	47.200
(Subsidized Housing)[b]	13.645	
(Public Housing)[b]	1.652	
(Low Rent Public Housing)[b]	634 million	
(Emerg. Shelter)[b]	70 million	
Nutrition	21.458	
(Food Stamps)	13.606	

SOURCE: Derived from "Table 4-1, The Grand Welfare State: Estimated Welfare Expenditures to Individuals, Both Direct Expenditures and Tax Expenditures, Fiscal Year 1990" in Michael Sherraden, *Assets and the Poor* (Armonk, NY: M. E. Sharpe, 1991), p. 56.
[a]all figures in billions of dollars, unless otherwise indicated
[b]programs targeted to the poor

Sherraden reviews social welfare expenditures in the United States for fiscal year 1990 and finds a total social welfare budget of 775.6 billion dollars, including direct expenditures (581.832 billion) and tax expenditures (193.800 billion). Most of this amount is devoted to social insurance, or non-means tested programs, as is illustrated in table 15. Approximately 124.6 billion dollars or less than one-fifth of the grand total amount is devoted to programs assisting the poor. Medicaid, however, makes up almost one-third (30 percent) of this amount ($37.4 billion).

Furthermore, Sherraden points out that under education and nutrition, some assistance directly benefits the non-poor. In 1990, despite the attention it has received, family support payments (AFDC) and child support collection programs totaled $11.2 billion, or 1.4 percent of the nation's social welfare budget.[29] As Sherraden concludes, "In sum, the poor welfare state comprises only 16.0 percent of all welfare spending to individuals, while the nonpoor welfare state comprises 84.0 percent."[30] Programs aimed at the very poor either declined in dollars expended between 1976 and 1984, or at least did not increase as rapidly as was the case for the "universal" programs.

Table 15 also makes reference to tax expenditures. Although not receiving the attention that direct expenditures to poor people have, tax expenditures are much larger and represent a significant and integral part of American social welfare, comprising about $200 billion in 1990. Due to the size and impact of this kind of indirect spending, Christopher Howard argues that "The exclusion of indirect spending is impossible to justify."[31] A review of how tax expenditures are utilized shows that, in addition to being an integral part of social welfare and being distributed to millions of Americans, they tend to strongly benefit the non-poor and well-off sectors.

Conclusion

There is a consensus among the American public, reflected across a broad ideological spectrum, that U.S. social welfare directed towards anti-poverty efforts has been ineffective in terms of the large amounts of money devoted to reducing poverty. Evidence for this usually includes the documenting of increasing poverty, long-term unemployment, and lack of social mobility for millions of Americans, as well as an increasing rate of female-headed families. American social welfare in the area of anti-poverty efforts is considered and perceived by the public as expensive and ineffective. Researchers Cook and Barrett do report, however, that the criticism of anti-poverty programs reflects more a "vocal few" than it does American public opinion. Based on their national survey, they write: "One of the clearest conclusions we can draw from the data presented in this book is that there is no crisis of support. Judging from the beliefs expressed by respondents in this study, the crisis rhetoric of the 1980s seems to have been based on the eloquent speech of a vocal few and an overreliance on responses to a single yearly survey question about support for 'welfare'...There is a shared belief that the major programs of the welfare state should be at a minimum maintained."[32]

Unfortunately, this entrenched misperception of a "vocal few" regarding the amount of federal expenditures spent to fight poverty generates public debates that tend to focus on the perceived weaknesses of individuals and racial groups, rather than on the limitations and weaknesses of the structure, organization, and even philosophical underpinnings of the U.S. anti-poverty system. A failure to focus on the latter produces bizarre public policies that defeat the very purpose of helping Americans overcome poverty. There are several examples of policies and practices related to public assistance that illustrate how the characteristics and values described in this chapter take illogical and contradictory form in implementation. One example of this is current AFDC rules that penalize needy children because they happen to live in married-couple households. According to a press release by the Center on Budget and Policy Priorities,

> If a one parent family applies for AFDC and is poor enough, the family need only show that the other parent isn't home. But if a two parent family applies, they must show that one parent is either incapacitated or is unemployed and meets various "work history" rules. This screens out many families, especially young families that may not have much work history yet.[33]

Thus, here is one example of a programmatic approach that penalizes poor and married-couple families. Ironically, however, AFDC has come under increasing attack and public opprobrium because a large proportion of AFDC recipients are single females heading households. The Center on Budget and Policy Priorities points out further, that "Criticizing the AFDC program because so few of the parents are married is like criticizing Social Security for having so many recipients who are aged or disabled; the demography is a product of the program's design, not a commentary on the behavior of the recipients."[34] This is yet another illustration of the absence of strategies that focus on the well-being of the family — in whatever form — and the continuing attempt to separate the "deserving" poor from the "undeserving" poor.

Another illustration of the piecemeal, misdirected, and highly unrealistic approach evident in U.S. anti-poverty policies are the "learnfare" provisions for AFDC teens in some states, particularly Wisconsin and Ohio. These programs basically link a child or teenager's attendance in school with the distribution of an AFDC grant to the family. There are two assumptions inherent in the learnfare strategy. The first is that impoverishment is caused, or maintained, by the lack of schooling; the second is that AFDC recipients are so dependent on government dole that school attendance must be forced on them. These assumptions are erroneous. One major study showed that there is no significant difference in school attendance rates between welfare and non-welfare children. This study, "Do School Attendance Rates Vary Between AFDC and Non-AFDC Supported Children?" found that the mean attendance days for welfare children was 169 days, while for non-welfare children the figure was 172 days.[35] Other studies, cited by the Center for Law and Social Policy, also show that Learnfare approaches do not improve the graduation rates of teenagers receiving AFDC benefits.[36] In light of the findings of these kinds of studies, the Center for Law and Social Policy in Washington, D.C., concluded that,

> Education and social policy should help poor children have successful school outcomes. Learnfare may actually interfere with that goal. Instead of focusing on what a child needs, it shifts everyone's attention to disputes about how many days of school a child may or may not have missed two or more months ago. This happens because the correctness of the welfare grant turns on how many days the child missed, whether the absences were excused, whether there was a good cause. So, the schools, welfare department, and parents must put their attention on months-old attendance data rather than how to help the child. If there are resources available to help improve school outcomes for poor children, committing those resources to a complex attendance-tracking bureaucracy is a very bad use of them.[37]

These inconsistencies are supported by changing and increasingly weak public support for anti-poverty policies and programs in the United States. One term that has emerged, and that helps to maintain weak support for anti-poverty policies, is the dreaded "underclass." This is the subject of the next chapter.

CHAPTER VI

How Is the "Underclass" Defined and Explained?

The creation of a mass dependent underclass is by no means inevitable. It must be fought intellectually, socially, and morally.

Peter Townsend
Poverty in the United Kingdom (1979)

The term "underclass" has been used widely in the last several years. It is commonly used to describe people who are persistently impoverished, living in dilapidated housing, and permanently unemployed. To many, this term is associated with black (and Latino) youth who reflect social alienation in their behavior and are separated from economic productivity or employment. The term is conceptually imprecise, however, and it is used loosely by the media and by scholars and researchers. This is noted by Peter Weiss, vice president for the Center for Constitutional Rights, who writes that "'underclass' is one of those terms coined by a semanticist for the establishment who is charged with defanging militant words — probably the same person who substituted 'preventive defensive action' for 'nuclear strike,' or 'user-fee' for 'tax,' and 'underprivileged' for 'poor.'"[1]

In attempting to uncover the origin of this term, I discovered that David Matza used a term that is akin to underclass in the title of his essay "The Disreputable Poor" in 1966.[2] In another essay, "The 'Underclass' as Myth and Symbol," political scientist Adolph Reed, Jr. points out, however, that the term "underclass" is attributable to the Swedish economist Gunnar Myrdal.[3] Myrdal used the term "under-class" in his 1962 publication, *Challenge to Affluence*. He stated that "There is an under-class of people in the poverty pockets who live an even more precarious life and are increasingly excluded from any jobs worth having, or who do not find jobs at all."[4] In addition to Myrdal, other writers made reference to an "underclass" in earlier periods. Several policy analysts examining the distribution of municipal services in large cities started to make reference to the "underclass hypothesis" in the early 1970s.[5] But if this term is used to indicate those sectors in society that are socially and economically lower in status than the working class, or even lower in status than Marx's "lumpen proletariat," then perhaps there are yet earlier references to such a social sector or class.

Historian Mosei Ostrogorski is one writer who should be given credit for the antecedent of the term "underclass." In his 1901 work, *Democracy and the Organization of Political Parties*, he used the term "de-classed" in reference to the population that held a social and economic status even beneath that of the lowest sectors of the working-class.[6] Around this period, W. E. B. Du Bois also made reference to a class lower than the poor which included "the lowest class of criminals, prostitutes, and loafers; the 'submerged tenth.'" (Interestingly, Du Bois identified "political clubs and pool rooms" as a favorite hangout of this "submerged tenth.")[7] Another earlier writer who attempted to identify the persistently "lowest" social and economic sectors in society was Alfred Marshall, who made reference to a "Residuum" in 1895:

> [T]he conditions which surround extreme poverty, especially in densely crowded places, tend to deaden the higher faculties. Those who have been called the Residuum of our large towns have little opportunity for friendship; they know nothing of the decencies and the quiet, and very little even of the unity of family life; and religion often fails to reach them. No doubt their physical, mental, and moral ill-health is partly due to other causes than poverty...[8]

And even before Marshall, journalist Henry George's 1879 book on poverty, *Progress and Poverty*, makes reference to a sector wholly feared and despised even by the poor: "Upon streets lighted with gas and patrolled by uniformed policemen, beggars wait for the passer-by, and in the shadow of college, and library, and museum, are gathering the more hideous Huns and fiercer Vandals of whom Macaulay prophesied."[9] This is similar to historian John R. Alexander's reminder that even in colonial America "the disadvantaged were of two types. There were, first, the 'industrious' or 'deserving' poor...Below the industrious poor...were the 'indigent' or 'vicious' poor."[10] It is these kinds of historical events and information that have led one writer to query the presumed novelty of the term underclass. As historian Thomas Sugrue asks, "Are ominous reports of a new 'urban underclass' tangled in 'a web of pathology' indicative of a crisis of unprecedented depth and magnitude? Or have Americans simply rediscovered (as they seem to do every few decades) a persistent problem that is periodically marked by economic growth, by willful ignorance, or by political indifference?"[11]

Attempts to Define and Measure the "Underclass"

Returning to Reed's insightful essay, we find the theory that this term is basically a "powerful metaphor" whose "resonance has far outpaced its empirical content, and it has thrived as a concept in search of its object."[12] It has been contended that the "underclass" cannot be measured or characterized objectively and, according to researcher Mimi Abramovitz, is subject to political manipulation which "contributes to punitive policies" for the poor.[13] Michael B. Katz adds that attempts to define the underclass and its characteristics exclusively in terms of quantitative data — absent a broader context focusing on politics, the state, and social forces that have molded American institutions — represent incomplete and inaccurate analysis. He writes that "The method that compares past and present, documents the process of change, and explains the source of current institutional failure is, of course, historical. Nonetheless, it remains the method most neglected by researchers on the underclass and contemporary inner-city institutions."[14] Despite this, the Social Science Research Council's Committee on the Study of the Underclass has developed a massive "underclass data base" consisting of several indicators: low education level, single parenthood, poor work history, public assistance recipiency, and poverty. But focusing on these kinds of indicators without examination of social history may not be helpful in understanding the causes, nature, and resolution of poverty, according to writers like Reed and Katz.

These kinds of attempts to quantify the existence and characteristics of the underclass have, furthermore, been influenced heavily by journalistic accounts. In her essay "Poverty and the Underclass," Isabel V. Sawhill explains how journalism has molded the impressionistic definition or description of this term. She writes:

Recent journalistic accounts paint a picture that leaves little doubt that an underclass exists. This picture includes young men who father children with little or no expectation of supporting them. It includes unmarried women on welfare, raising children at taxpayers' expense and passing a life of poverty on to the next generation. It includes men who spurn regular work in favor of more lucrative but less legitimate or conventional means of earning a living, and alienated teenagers who drop out of school and remain semi-literate into their adult years. And whatever its contents, the picture is usually framed by a depressed urban landscape, and most of the faces are black.[15]

In a 1991 review for the Institute for Research on Poverty, William R. Prosser also advises caution about a term so conducive to subjective and confusing definitions. He writes: "Discussion of the underclass is further confused by differences between definitions used for theoretical, journalistic, and rhetorical purposes, and operational definitions used to study the underclass...Generally, the operational definitions have been arbitrary...[The term underclass] is no more precise than 'middle class,' as in 'middle class values,' or 'rich,' as in 'soak the rich.'"[16]

This warning is repeated by Martha Van Haitsma in her paper "The Underclass, Labor Force Attachment and Social Context":

All the most commonly used underclass indicators: chronic poverty, intergenerational poverty, spatial concentration, and non-normative patterns of income generation and family formation, are in some way problematic. Definitions based on chronic poverty do not tell us how we may distinguish in advance between the temporarily poor and the long term poor. Definitions based on intergenerational poverty similarly fail to offer structural distinctions between those poor whose parents or children are also poor and those whose poverty lasts only one generation. Not everyone who lives in an area of concentrated poverty is poor. Behavioral patterns such as unwed motherhood, criminal involvement and welfare dependency may arise from and lead to very different socioeconomic outcomes.[17]

Although "underclass" is a highly impressionistic and imprecise term, it has been used by some in the research community as if it is actually a well-defined concept. Frankly, this term seems more useful for ideological purposes than for analytical and theoretical study. Regarding this matter, Reed writes further: "Instead of clarifying or correcting the impressionistic generalities and simple-minded prejudices spewed by journalists...social scientists have legitimated them with an aura of scientific verity, surrounding them in an authenticating mist of quantification."[18]

Sociologist Christopher Jencks believes the term could be useful if we remember that there exist different categories of "the underclass." He describes these as the "impoverished underclass," "jobless female underclass," "educational underclass," "violent underclass," and the "reproductive underclass." Jencks argues that public policy based on a unitary concept of the underclass is doomed to failure because the various underclass populations may not necessarily be related to one another.[19]

There have been attempts to measure the size of the so-called underclass population. Sawhill writes that "Some researchers have equated the underclass with the able-bodied, persistently poor, a group estimated to number around 8 million people in the mid-1980s. Others have defined the underclass as people living in areas of concentrated poverty, a definition that yields considerably lower estimates. For example, in 1980, 2.4 million poor people lived in neighborhoods where the poverty rate was above 40 percent."[20] The definition of underclass, like the official definition of poverty, will in large part determine the size of the underclass. But in attempting to determine the definition of this term, the literature tends to reflect the biases of the researcher or the commentator, thereby predetermining both the existence and the size of this group.

Black Scholar, a premier journal of black social and political critique in the United States, devoted a special 1988 issue to the topic of "the underclass."[21] Most of the authors writing for this issue were skeptical about the analytical worth of this term. Troy Duster, the director of the Institute for the Study of Social Change at the University of California, writes in an essay, "Social Implications of the 'New' Black Urban Underclass," that "Any attempt at definition will simply provide a deflection to unproductive quibbling about the margins of the category."[22] And in the same journal in the article "Race, Class, and Black Poverty," economist Julianne Malveaux writes that "The concept of the 'underclass' has moved from nebulous to factual without a bent of data, from a whisper to a shout without a definition."[23] She suggests, furthermore, that attempts by some researchers to define this term are weak and open to manipulation. For example, defining an area where the poverty rate may be 40 percent or higher as an "underclass" neighborhood is arbitrary. This is but a sweeping generalization about individuals and families who live in an economically-depressed area.

Several essays included in Michael B. Katz's, *The Underclass Debate: Views from History* collectively suggest that mainstream researchers have unjustifiably overlooked historical, political, and institutional contexts in the development of an underclass sector. As Katz points out in his concluding essay, "Reframing the 'Underclass' Debate," utilizing history to understand "the source of current institutional failure...remains the method most neglected by researchers on the underclass and contemporary inner-city institutions."[24]

Another observation about the underclass debate is that there is a relatively small amount of literature on poverty in the Asian-American community. The underclass appears not to be associated with this community. There are some reports, however, suggesting that poverty among Asian-descent people is increasing, and that various Asian groups are experiencing poverty in different ways. Political scientists John Grove and Jiping Wu write, for instance, that "On closer examination of the Asian poor, it is equally apparent that Chinese poverty has increased at a greater rate than Japanese or Filipino poverty." But they add, "Other indicators such as unemployment rates and divorce rates do not suggest that Chinese poverty will result in a permanent underclass."[25]

Explanations for the Existence of the "Underclass" and Policy Implications

Some researchers and commentators have arbitrarily associated to "the underclass" a set of cultural patterns that are deviant from what is considered "normal" and presumably necessary behavior for social and economic mobility. For example, Nicholas Lemann argues in a 1986 essay, "The Origins of the Underclass," that "the underclass" has a distinctive culture, making it difficult for traditional public policy to assist this population.[26] In his words, the ghetto's "distinctive culture is now the greatest barrier to progress by the black underclass, rather than unemployment or welfare...The negative power of the ghetto all but guarantees that any attempt to solve the problems of the underclass *in the ghetto* won't work." He argues that what is needed in terms of public policy is "the imposition of a different, and more disciplined culture."[27]

This suggestion, though very popular among some scholars and government officials today, is not new. Attribution of dysfunctional cultural characteristics to "the underclass" is not novel when compared to the way pauperism was discussed at the turn of the century. Robert Hunter, in his 1904 book *Poverty*, states that he was perplexed by the deviant behavior of the "pauper and the vagrant." Hunter wrote:

> they clamored for alms, but they did not wish to alter their way of living. Even those who possessed the capacity for industrial usefulness and who might have become self-supporting did not wish to go back again into the factories, mills, or mines. In fact, so far as one could see, they were...unwilling...to alter their ways of living. However miserable their lot seemed to those of us on the Committees, to them it seemed to be, on the whole, acceptable enough to bring a certain sort of content. However malarious and poisonous and undrained, they loved their valley of idleness and quiet.[28]

He wrote further that in this state "they become merely breeders of children, who persist in the degeneration into which their fathers have fallen; and, like the tribe of Ishmael or the family of the Jukes, they have neither the willingness nor the capacity to respond to the efforts of those who would help, or force, them back again into the struggle."[29]

Both conclusions reached by Hunter are quite similar to arguments made by political scientist Edward C. Banfield almost 70 years later in his book *The Unheavenly City*. Banfield discusses how the "lower class" (i.e., underclass) lives with differing cultural reference points from what he considers "normal." For him, it is the innate, culturally-determined "ethos" associated with certain sectors of the poverty population that explains their social and economic status and their continuously depressed living conditions.[30] Thus, the lower class has been born into the economic abyss, according to Banfield, and, therefore, public policy will be ineffective in convincing these individuals to leave their world of poverty to partake of opportunities. Banfield's and Lemann's works enjoy popularity among the general public, as well as in government circles; it must be emphasized, however, that both authors have merely presented a polemic, rather than an analysis or conclusive information.

The view presented by writers like Banfield and Lemann is slightly different from that of John Silber, president of Boston University, in his book, *Straight Shooting*. For Silber, where the presence of an underclass is not culturally determined and inevitable, it is rather a result of society's promotion of negative behavior: "When young fathers are encouraged to evade elementary responsibility for their children, to brag that they have no intension of marrying the mother or of supporting the family, they are thereby encouraged to be irresponsible in everything else."[31] Again, like Banfield, Silber finds that a major reason for the status of "the underclass" is their sexual promiscuity.

According to writers like Banfield, Lemann, and others, the public's interest would be better served if public policy were aimed at restricting the mobility, freedom, and growth of the underclass — or, that sector which reflects a lower-class ethos. Silber offers a different approach by arguing that society must resolve the problem of the underclass by bringing them into the economic mainstream. He writes, "As Lincoln reminded us, a house divided against itself cannot stand. With an underclass perpetually denied the opportunities available to other Americans, we are divided against ourselves, and we shall not stand."[32] This warning brings one slightly closer to William J. Wilson's call for "National labor-market growth, and discouraging the use of unemployment as a way to slow inflation. These approaches would not be targeted to the poor, but tied to "opportunities in the private sector."[33] Obviously, Wilson does not believe as do Banfield and Lemann that underclass status is a permanent reflection of a particular cultural orientation. He has disavowed the term underclass, as a matter of fact, because it has become too closely tied to cultural determinism. Indeed, Wilson has accused several social scientists of misrepresenting the term.[34]

There are different approaches than that proposed by writers like Banfield, Lemann, and others that explain the existence of an "underclass," or what might be more appropriately called a continually impoverished sector in the black community. Two recent essays by political scientists Mack H. Jones and Charles P. Henry challenge some of the current research and conceptualization regarding the so-called underclass as reflected in the writings of Lemann and others. Both Jones and Henry suggest that what is ailing in the American city is not wayward and problem-filled black youth, but rather the economy. It is functional for dominant political and economic interests, however, that the public and government continue to focus on the presumed pathology of young blacks considered "underclass." Jones writes in his article "The Black Underclass as Systemic Phenomenon," that the current conditions ascribed to the black "underclass" are not novel. He notes that these social and economic conditions have "dogged the Black nation throughout American history...Rather than conceptualizing the current Black underclass as a new development, it may be more historically accurate and theoretically insightful to view it as a contemporary manifestation of a long existing phenomenon."[35] This social and historical fact, which tends to dampen the explanatory power of such factors as social attitudes and the parental or family structure, has been ignored by many poverty researchers, according to Jones.

Henry, too, criticizes the mainstream poverty research community for not only ignoring historical analysis regarding the nature of poverty in society but also for simplifying a complex social and economic development. Henry reminds poverty researchers that their approach to the problems of poverty are not conceptually different from those in much earlier periods. He adds that "class" as an analytical term is continually misused. Many poverty researchers, Henry argues, use the term class to describe their own views of behavior among unemployed black youth, rather than as an analytical tool to understand better the economic and social position of young blacks within society.[36] Similarly, economist Andrés Torres and sociologist Clara E. Rodriguez explain that some Puerto Rican researchers also criticize the use of the term underclass because it overlooks how individuals exhibit a range of behaviors in response to economic conditions; this term, they argue, tends to present the poor as a monolithic social construct.[37]

Another set of explanations for what is referred to as the underclass focuses on how structural and institutional factors generate an impoverished sector in the black community. One of the most insightful essays on the relationship between the development of a continually impoverished sector in the black community and technological change is found in Sidney M. Wilhelm's *Black in a White America*. In a chapter titled "The Economics of Uselessness," he argues that the poorest blacks have been made functionally unnecessary for U.S. economic development and that, therefore, the growth and existence of this sector is a matter of politics, i.e., how the government will exert control over the black underclass.[38] This is an explanation similar to that of historian Thomas F. Jackson, who writes in "The State, the Movement, and the Urban Poor: The War on Poverty and Political Mobilization in the 1960s," that "Powerlessness, both in relation to the electoral system and to the basic institutions touching the lives of the urban poor, has consistently remained a central feature of urban poverty," and that, "the central elements of a varied and developing African-American economic agenda were basically ignored in the 1960s and have been [ever] since."[39] This analysis differs from Wilson's, who implied a few years later in *The Truly Disadvantaged* that education and training in response to macro-level changes in the national economy could make the underclass economically functional in the American city.

The structural and institutional explanation was suggested earlier by social psychologist Kenneth Clark's pathbreaking work in the mid-1960s, *Dark Ghetto*. He showed the institutional origins of a sector in the black community that was associated with a "ghetto pathology."[40] This may remind people of today's concept of the underclass but, unlike some who attribute culture, ethos, or incorrigible deviancy to today's underclass, Clark showed that the individuals he worked with exhibited a "ghetto pathology" as a survival response to conditions imposed on the ghetto by external political and economic forces. Presumably, therefore, an appropriate response to eliminating ghetto pathology would be the elimination of these external forces. Clark could be included in a genre of writers who posit that so-called deviant behavior among poor people represents an adaptation among an oppressed population to structural isolation and marginalization.

One of the most important books written in the tradition of Clark's *Dark Ghetto* is professor of social welfare Douglas Glasgow's *The Black Underclass*.[41] Glasgow debunks three major explanations for the existence of what is referred to as an underclass in the black population: a lack of positive values; the feminization of poverty; and the theory that social programs have produced dependency among this population and thereby led to a refusal to work or to otherwise improve their own living conditions. Glasgow points out that these explanations confuse causes and symptoms and are ahistorical. He argues further that they ignore the ways in which the nature and cultural traditions of the black family are different from the image of the "normal" white family in America.

Other researchers utilizing or critiquing the underclass paradigm to examine Latino poverty include demographer Marta Tienda in "Puerto Ricans and the Underclass Debate" and economist Andrés Torres and sociologist Clara Rodriguez in "Latino Research and Policy."[42] As is pointed out by Torres and Rodriguez, an interesting difference in the public debate regarding the existence of a black and Puerto Rican underclass is the notion espoused by some researchers that, while such a designation of underclass characteristics may apply to a specific sector within the black community, it may be applicable to a much broader sector in the Puerto Rican community.[43] Melendez, however, argues against this contention, asserting that this term should not be used at all because it is "at best, a very ambiguous concept that has received a lot of criticism from both the left and the right." Melendez suggests that "to base one's argument on that model, one would have to really get into the conceptual usefulness of the concept of 'underclass.'"[44]

In conclusion, it can be stated that the literature on the underclass reflects controversy about the very use of this term. This controversy is based on the fact that the term is considered pejorative by many, and open to a broad range of definitions. This term also suggests that the underclass sector is different than the traditional poor. The underclass are characterized not only by poverty status but, as argued by some researchers, by a certain kind of behavior pattern associated with this sector. This behavior is considered negative and a barrier to socio-economic mobility. According to other researchers, however, this presumption about the nature of the underclass is simplistic and ahistorical. Therefore the focus on the underclass and attempts to define it are misspent; such attempts diverge energies from more concrete and useful anti-poverty strategies and proposals.

How Have the Poor Utilized Political Mobilization to Fight Poverty in the United States?

Poverty has been created for us by an irresponsible government; a government that puts far more money into death than into life; a government that speaks of a kinder gentler time then kills off its infants, women, children and elders...Poverty itself has become so acceptably institutionalized that we don't bat an eye anymore as we step over the bodies. Some of us get angry. All of us must become more angry, more visible and more vocal in our demands for fairness. To do less is a liberal copout. Maybe even a sin. So we must all speak out and be prepared for the hostility that follows.

> *Kip Tiernan and Fran Froehlich*
> Poor People's United Fund (1990)
> *Boston, Massachusetts*

In the last two decades many in the academic community, as well as in the mainstream media in the United States, have overlooked or de-emphasized how the poor and their own organizations have attempted to mobilize themselves politically in order to advocate policies and strategies for the elimination of poverty. As Robin D. G. Kelley argues, much of social science has tended "to focus on policy issues rather than on the lives and struggles of the poor themselves. The end result has been a failure to take into account opposition and human agency on the part of the poor. In particular, most social scientists overlook the role(s) of ideology and consciousness, the formation of oppositional movements among the inner-city poor, and various forms of individual and collective resistance."[1] Concomitantly, many researchers study poverty as if it had nothing to do with the particular distribution of political power in society. A recent series on poverty by *The New York Times* illustrates these kinds of oversights. Although the reporters for this series did point out that the "problem is not just one of policy but also one of politics," various attempts by poor people to utilize political power to reduce poverty were not raised in any of the three articles.[2] Perhaps the closest this series came to the relationship between political power and poverty was an allusion to the "empowerment" efforts of the Bush administration to enhance the choices available to the poor. But calls for the empowerment of the poor, as defined by current national efforts, are very different from the generating of political strategies and the mobilization and development of programmatic initiatives directly by the poor.

Yet, as stressed by U.S. Congressman Esteban Torres, the role of political power and whether poor people are politically organized are crucial factors in how a government responds to poverty: "There is persistent poverty by design, to keep a certain class of people in a syndrome of poverty, to serve a purpose in an economic society that exploits in order to make a profit. As long as there's no major turmoil — the fields aren't being burned, the factories aren't being seized, or businesses aren't under the gun from some federal agency — things will continue in that vein."[3]

The executive director of the Southern Regional Council, Steve Suitts, argues that: "Because poor Blacks remain without power in many places, the concepts of empowerment of the poor in racial America have a strategic future role in the work to reduce poverty...Strategies that encourage empowerment embrace democratic principles and thus are essential if the notion is to seriously address poverty."[4] This is a conclusion also reached by Marcia Bok, who asserts that only "grass-roots protest and mass movements in the United States" will elicit policies favorable to the well-being of the poor.[5] Professor of social work Ann Withorn proposes that the politicization of the poor in the 1960s resulted not only in new national social welfare polices, but also forced a redefinition of the federal government's role in human services.[6] Another earlier study, by Curt Lamb, found that political mobilization on the part of the poor resulted in important neighborhood benefits. In *Political Power in Poor Neighborhoods*, Lamb asserts that militancy does pay off in the effectiveness of poor neighborhoods and their leaders to engineer institutional changes that are responsive to their needs.[7]

Professor of social work Gloria Bonilla-Santiago suggests a theme similar to Bok's in her study of Puerto Rican migrant workers in New Jersey.[8] Her investigation is based on a case study of how Puerto Rican migrants experimented with various kinds of organizations to mobilize politically. Puerto Rican migrants realized that only by organizing themselves politically could they meet their basic living and social needs. William Goldsmith and Edward Blakely also suggest this idea when they write, "we believe better policy to minimize poverty will result only from new political forces, which are most likely to be rooted in the poverty of the central city. We believe, that is, that an urban political strategy is the most practical approach for attacking America's poverty problem."[9]

The development of an effective urban strategy requires strategies that are supported by political power. This approach is quite different from those focusing on the particular family structure of poor people or their cultural orientation as the causes for impoverishment. As Thomas F. Jackson writes, the concern of this approach "is with how to frame policies benefiting the poor in the context of the current political structure...[Policymakers] are less concerned with the possibilities for policy innovation and political mobilization of the poor to move in tandem."[10]

One source that has documented the politicization of the poor is an anthology on community organizing by Joan Ecklein, *Community Organizers*. Frances Fox Piven and Richard A. Cloward's *Poor People's Movements* also documents the political struggles of poor people in the United States. A few other works include Ann Withorn's *Serving the People: Social Services and Social Change*, Guida West and Rhoda Lois Blumberg's *Women and Social Protest*, Betty K.Mandell's *Welfare in America*, and Walda K. Fishman, et al., "African American Politics in the Era of Capitalist Economic Contraction" in Ralph C. Gomes and Linda F. Williams's *From Exclusion to Inclusion*.[11] The recent reader edited by Michael B. Katz, *The Underclass Debate: Views from History*, contains several essays that make various references to the political history of poor people, especially in the black community. I would also recommend Gary Delgado's *Organizing the Movement: The Roots and Growth of ACORN*. This book is a case study of the Arkansas Community Organizations for Reform Now, founded in part by the National Welfare Rights Organization; Delgado discusses ACORN's emergence and impact across the United States.[12]

A major reason for the lack of attention to the effect on the poor of the distribution of political power and its impact on social welfare policies is the focus of the research presumptions and paradigms that tend to dominate discussion in the U.S. academic community. Many researchers have overlooked the relationship of political power and poverty. Interestingly, this critique may be more applicable to researchers in the United States than to those in other countries.

One of the best comparisons of how research on poverty is approached by both European and American scholars is provided by Walter Korpi in his article "Approaches to the Study of Poverty in the United States."[13] Korpi believes that American scholarship on poverty is very limited when compared to European research. He writes:

[M]ajor weaknesses and imbalances are evident in American poverty research. A basic weakness is the reliance on the absolute definition of poverty, which cannot be scientifically justified in studies of changes in the extent of poverty over time. It also appears that the sectorially oriented poverty research in the United States could benefit from a greater pluralism, which should partly be of a disciplinary nature, and the present dominance of the economists should yield to a better balance among different disciplines. The social sciences have important differences in the ways in which they approach and define research problems.[14]

This critique is related to one made by Michael B. Katz who observed regarding his participation with the Social Science Research Council's

Committee for Research on the Urban Underclass:

> Since its preliminary writing in 1987, I have served as archivist to the Social Science Research Council's Committee for Research on the Urban Underclass. Listening to the discussions and reading the material, I was struck by the role of history in the way scholars, journalists, and politicians formulated the issues in the 'underclass' debate. Almost every major claim they made included either implicit or explicit assumptions about the past. Yet very few of them knew of the recent historical work related to their arguments, and what they said or implied about history often was incomplete, uninformed, or wrong.[15]

Susan H. Hertz made similar criticisms regarding the apolitical and ahistorical biases of much poverty research in the United States in *The Welfare Mother's Movement*:

> Until the last several years, there was a tendency in the social science literature to analyze the behavior of the poor as if they were isolated from the impact of urban and national institutions and events. The presumed autonomy and distinctiveness of people living in the ghettos, barrios, and reservations of the United States was particularly characteristic of the culture of poverty approach originally formulated by Lewis...While focusing exclusively on a poor, racial, or ethnic community provides a neat and manageable unit for research purposes, such a strategy does not do justice to the economic and political interdependencies which link all segments of our society together.[16]

As Peter Marris points in a recent report to the Rockefeller Foundation, "Research on poverty has always been directed far more on understanding the characteristics of people in poverty than on understanding the way the rest of us create the conditions of poverty by our collective behavior; and is this not the intellectual equivalent of blaming the victim?"[17]

Again Korpi writes,

> Insufficient attention has been paid to the explanation of poverty and inequality and to the development of alternatives to the prevailing policy strategies. The criteria used in program evaluation have focused too narrowly on target efficiency and have neglected other significant aspects of anti-poverty programs, such as their political consequences in inhibiting or encouraging political coalitions in support of continued efforts to reduce poverty and inequality.[18]

Despite weaknesses in American poverty research, social welfare analyst Fiona Williams acknowledges weaknesses in British social welfare research, also due to an arbitrary dismissal of political factors in determining the nature of poverty. She accuses mainstream British intellectuals and the government of doing this by generally:

a) neglecting issues of gender and race,
b) discrediting any ideological challenges to the social welfare system, and
c) ignoring the linkage between social welfare and patriarchy, racial domination in British society, as well as British imperialism.[19]

These kinds of biases in some poverty research literature, whether in the United States or in Britain, have not allowed a full appreciation of the call for political mobilization by poor people as a method for reducing poverty.

While some studies simply ignore political mobilization as a response to poverty, a few explicitly dismiss this strategy. For example, in "Strategies for the Powerless: The Welfare Rights Movement in New York City," Joyce Gelb and Alice Sardell argue that protest and community action has been ineffective in meeting the needs of the poor.[20] Another author, economist Thomas Sowell, suggests (inaccurately) that, because European immigrant groups settling in America did not rely on politics to achieve social and economic mobility, political power is useless for the poor in achieving social and economic mobility.[21]

Katherine O'Sullivan states, however, that overlooking or dismissing the role of power and politics in the persistence of poverty is unjustified; she writes, "Welfare usage and its precipitants and correlates have been among the most researched areas in poverty work. Yet, this is also one of the arenas in which the voices of the recipients have been least evident."[22] Frances Fox Piven and Richard A. Cloward, in one of their many studies documenting and analyzing poverty and the distribution of power, similarly state that "movements from below help to make history. But these movements have usually not been paid much heed by students of politics...Protest from the bottom, if acknowledged at all, is defined as a temporary interruption of political life...Nowhere are these distortions more marked than in the academic dismissal of contemporary social movements in the U.S."[23]

There are a few exceptions to this indictment, as noted earlier in this chapter, but generally the many attempts at mobilization by the poor as a response to their impoverished status have been ignored as legitimate policy or a political response. At least one recent exception to this oversight is an essay by Suitts, "Empowerment and Rural Poverty." In this essay, the author reminds us that "Strategies to empower the rural poor as a group have their origins in the American South more than a century ago and have reappeared in more recent times."[24] Suitts explains how the civil rights movement sparked a broad range of co-ops among poor blacks in the South that were used as both economic and political tools by the poor to exert control on the public policy process. In fact, Suitts points to a strong empowerment tradition among the black poor of the rural South that has forced government responsiveness to their needs:

> Political changes over the last three decades have ushered in a new era of Southern politics, one that has deepened the region's political support for Civil Rights and concern for the poor through government action. The changes represented a growing concern for policies and resources for the poor among government officials at a time when, in general, the government was diminishing its commitment and initiative to address poverty. In this respect these changes in political power among the rural Black poor created one of the few instances where government officials in the 1980s become more willing to address poverty than they were in the 1960s.[25]

The political mobilization of the poor, however, does not come easy — largely because it is threatening to the social and economic status-quo. Social psychologist Kenneth B. Clark and Jeanette Hopkins wrote in the late 1960s that the political mobilization of the poor has, indeed, been resisted by a broad array of forces. This was demonstrated in the era of the "Great Society" during President Johnson's tenure:

> As long as programs for the poor were philanthropic, ameliorative, welfare-oriented, based either on the hearty ward-boss political model, or the more chaste, less corrupt, but also less compassionate social agency model, political, social, or economic leadership felt no stirring of dread that the equation of power would shift. But when some of the poor, particularly the Negro poor and their advocates, took the War on Poverty seriously in a few cities like Syracuse and New York, organizing voters, demanding community control of schools...demanding that welfare recipients be treated as human beings, demanding an effective role in urban planning generally, the political forces in the cities deployed for counter attack.[26]

Even when there are governmental calls for the participation of the poor in decision-making, political mobilization of the poor is not treated seriously in the academic and policy communities. The call for "maximum feasible participation" during the Johnson administration, for example, did not mean political power or participation for the poor on behalf of themselves. As noted by Lillian B. Rubin in her article "Maximum Feasible Participation,"

> From the President's "Message on Poverty" on March 16, 1964, wherein he commended the bill to the Congress, to its passage five months later, there was no public discussion of the participation clause. Although a great deal of debate centered on the general provisions of Title II, congressional committee hearings reveal that, with the exception of the statement by then Attorney General Robert F. Kennedy, there is no mention of the clause by any other government official in several thousand pages of testimony...The congressional debates are equally devoid of discussion about "maximum feasible participation."[27]

During the Bush administration, calls for the "empowerment" of the poor on the part of government officials like Jack Kemp, the secretary of Housing and Urban Development, did not necessarily mean increased political power for the poor, but rather that the poor should become less "dependent" on government assistance.

To de-emphasize how the poor have utilized the political arena to fight poverty is unjustified, particularly given the role that political struggles have played in the development of welfare systems in the international arena. According to Eric S. Einhorn and John Logue in their recent book, *Modern Welfare States*:

> The origins of the modern welfare state in Scandinavia, as elsewhere, lie in the political struggles of the late nineteenth century occasioned by the rise of the labor movement. It was not coincidence that German Chancellor Otto von Bismarck inaugurated the world's first general pension, health, and disability insurance systems at the same time that he banned the German Social Democratic party in the 1880s. Nor is it an accident that the Scandinavian countries have both the strongest labor movements and the best-developed welfare states in the West. The success of the labor movement — and the fear of its success — and the development of the welfare state have been intimately related.[28]

Instances in American history when the poor have been able to convince national leaders and the public to consider their social and economic needs and interests have been due to the result of political struggle. As mentioned in chapter 1, it was "Coxey's Army" marching on Washington,

D.C., in 1894 and many other such "armies" that forced national consideration of the needs of the poor at that time.[29] In addition, the policies of the Great Depression were, in part, a response to the social and political unrest of millions of poor people. One example of this is the political struggles and demonstrations by blacks for jobs in the 1930s.[30]

Just as one cannot disregard the impact of Michael Harrington's book, *The Other America*, in changing some Americans' thinking about the problem of poverty in the 1960s, one must also not overlook the impact of the civil rights movement in forcing the Kennedy and Johnson administrations to pay more attention to the needs of the poor. As Harrington writes in *The New American Poverty*, "The anti-poverty program was not a civil rights program, but it was, in good measure, a result of the civil rights movement. Martin Luther King, Jr., focused upon the outrage of statutory segregation, not upon economics, but he knew full well that he led a people who were economic, as well as racial, pariahs."[31] A few years later Harrington wrote regarding this matter: the "civil rights struggle forced the country to see the shacks and tenements and rotting houses in which Negroes lived."[32] In the last two to three years of his life, King moved increasingly towards activism that would enhance the political power of poor people. In fact King's attempts to mobilize the poor were an extension of many earlier attempts and movements to mobilize in support of a political agenda as a response to the needs of poor people. This action on King's part was based on his belief that "powerlessness" is a fundamental explanation for the existence of poverty: "The plantation and the ghetto were created by those who had power both to confine those who had no power and to perpetuate their powerlessness. The problem of transforming the ghetto is, therefore, a problem of power."[33] Political scientist James W. Button also argues that at the local level blacks engaged in civil rights activities as a direct response to poverty; political equality was perceived as critical and a "fundamental precondition to advances in other aspects of life," as King also intimated.[34]

In the late 1960s and early 1970s, a major movement for education reform was organized in New York City by a coalition of poor and working-class parents. The "Community Control Movement" in this city, while sparked in the predominantly black community of Brownsville in Brooklyn, actually flowered in the lower East Side neighborhood of Manhattan, where poor Puerto Rican parents sought to influence school policies at the local level. This movement represented a merging of education and anti-poverty agendas for Puerto Rican, Asian and black parents.[35]

Some observers also point to the political participation of the elderly in the United States and abroad as an explanation for significant reduction in their rates of poverty. For example, Michael B. Fabricant and Steve

Burghardt write that,

> In 1960, 25 percent of the elderly were classified as poor, compared to 12.6 percent of the entire population. By the early 1980s, 14 percent of the elderly lived in poverty. By the mid-1980s, the percentages were reversed. For the first time, older Americans were marginally less poor than other Americans...The reasons for this economic shift relate to the increased size and political power of older Americans as a group. Recently, the elderly have pushed to straighten certain sections of the welfare state, especially Social Security and Medicare. Attacks leveled against Social Security by the Reagan administration and others have consistently failed because of the rapid and effective response of organization of the elderly.[36]

These few historical citations suggest that there are instances in American history when political power and mobilization had a major effect on resolving poverty for some groups.

In contrast to the claims of several authors mentioned above, poor people who have organized themselves as a group believe that political power is a necessary component of fighting poverty. A major focus of people living in poverty is acquiring political power within a context of economic justice and equity. One of the most prominent examples of this was the founding of the National Welfare Rights Organization (NWRO) in 1966. While NWRO was defunct by 1975, it did have significant impact on increasing and liberalizing welfare benefits for women and children. NWRO sought to organize poor women, in particular, on the basis of four principles: adequate income, dignity, justice, and democracy for all poor people.[37] Hertz concludes her study of NWRO by stating,

> The Welfare Mothers Movement did bring about a measure of political and personal change among many poor women who were effectively excluded from traditional women's or working class organizations, and who were not directly touched by the appeal of the feminist movement itself. The disappearance of the Welfare Mothers Movement in the mid-1970s, however, does not mean that the movement failed completely. For both individual participants as well as institutions in the established order...were different than they would have been had the Welfare Mothers Movement never existed.[38]

Additionally, in the late 1960s, poor people organized themselves nationally in response to the emergence of programs on behalf of the poor. Several conventions were held across the country during this period. On

April 13 and 14, 1966, about one thousand people from poor neighborhoods and rural areas across the country held a "Poor People's Convention" where the delegates severely criticized the anti-poverty efforts of Sargeant Shriver, the director for the Office of Economic Opportunity, as ineffective and paternalistic.[39] Delgado describes various instances of the political mobilization and impact of poor people in the 1970s and 1980s in his earlier cited work, *Organizing the Movement*.

Though sporadic at times, the efforts of poor people and their organizations to represent their own interests have continued to the current period. In a report based on a survey sponsored in 1988 by the Ford Foundation and the Coalition on Human Needs, "How the Poor Would Remedy Poverty," in-depth interviews were conducted with 202 low-income people around the country. The poor were asked what they thought were solutions to poverty and how they would change existing anti-poverty programs.[40] An overwhelming majority (82 percent) responded that they felt government had the responsibility to help poor people get out of poverty. The acquisition of better jobs and decent wages were the two most popular responses regarding the elimination of poverty in America. These findings have surfaced in other studies, as well.[41]

In reviewing the above study one journalist observed, "Most of those interviewed felt that they also had a responsibility to work. Nearly all who physically could work wanted to work, though most had reservations about traditional 'workfare' jobs. They didn't think workfare would help them get a 'regular job.' Their strongly expressed desire to get retraining that will lead to a good job undermines the argument that the welfare system produces dependence. The study found no support for the criticism of the welfare system as a morass of programs that provides so many benefits that people have no incentive to get a job."[42]

In an article titled, "The Colonizing Impact of Public Service Bureaucracies in Black Communities," Jacqueline Pope, a former activist with the NWRO, argues that poor people — and especially blacks — should revitalize efforts seeking to take control of public bureaucracies administering assistance. In "Women and Welfare Reform," Pope also calls for an "Economic Security Plan" that would include increasing the minimum wage; offering full-time employment; creating social salary for parenting, universal child care, and affordable housing; and lowering taxes for the working poor.[43] Pope's call is reminiscent of that found in *Poor People's Movements* by Frances Fox Piven and Richard A. Cloward. While Piven and Cloward's work is primarily a study of how the poor have sought to organize themselves and why their organizations have not generally been effective, an important theme of the work is that the political mobilization of the poor is necessary in order to resolve the problem of poverty.[44] This theme was echoed more recently in David Wagner's and Marcia Cohen's case study of the political struggles — and accomplishments — of the homeless and poor in Maine.[45]

In some states the poor have organized themselves in order to advocate for a more responsive government budget. These organizations, composed of poor people, have continuously rallied against welfare reform efforts perceived as punitive and shortsighted. In Massachusetts, for instance, the Massachusetts Human Services Coalition and the Coalition for Basic Human Needs have published a "Poor People's Budget FY92" that proposes major savings and greater balancing of the economic interests of the wealthy and the poor and working-class through progressive taxation policies. Dorothy Stevens, former welfare recipient and anti-poverty advocate in Massachusetts, ran for governor of Massachusetts in 1988 and, although she garnered slightly less than one thousand statewide votes, she was able to use the campaign as an important platform for showing the connection between impoverishment, politics, and power.[46] And in Detroit, an organization of welfare recipients and the homeless have electorally mobilized the poor community under a campaign, "Up and Out of Poverty Now," which targets elected officials for protest demonstrations.[47]

Another organization controlled by poor people and dedicated to eradicating poverty through a variety of means, including political mobilization and action, is based in Milwaukee and is known as Congress for a Working America (CFWA). As described by a reporter: "the group is also strongly committed to involving welfare recipients and the working poor in changing public policy...Within days of arriving at CFWA's office, job seekers may find themselves giving testimony at City Hall or at the State Capital in Madison."[48]

CFWA's political mobilization campaign to eliminate poverty has realized some important successes. In 1989 CFWA won a major legislative battle when the Wisconsin legislature adopted a statewide earned-income tax credit, which supplements the federal earned-income credit; thus "families with three children can get up to $1,038 extra per year from the state EIC on top of approximately $2,000 from the federal EIC. Only a handful of states have EICs, and, due to CFWA's urging, Wisconsin is the only one that ties the tax credit to family size."[49]

Similarly, the "Welfare Rights Committee of Up and Out of Poverty," based in Minneapolis-St. Paul, Minnesota, has organized welfare recipients, working poor people, and homeless people around legislative, electoral, and protest strategies. This organization has sought to maintain a presence in the Minnesota state legislature to discourage "welfare reform" considered anti-poor people. As a result of this kind of political work, attempts to make workfare mandatory in Minnesota were defeated.

Recently, this same group has started to organize against welfare reform ideas being floated by the Clinton administration.[50]

In 1992 the Boston Foundation sponsored several forums and seminars to determine what the poor in various racial and ethnic communities thought about the nature of poverty, and to solicit their ideas regarding adequate public policies for reducing poverty. A number of common themes about anti-poverty strategies and efforts emerged in these forums. These included:

Rejection of "deficit" or "pathological" explanation for poverty; rejection of terms like "underclass";

Emphasis on strengths and assets of people, communities; appreciation of cultural and linguistic backgrounds;

Appreciation of diversity within black, Asian, Latino, and white communities;

Policies for alleviating poverty should focus on children, youth and families;

Economic development and growth within a "community framework";

Importance of public policy that reflects a caring, civic/moral vision;

Individual self-responsibility within a context of strengthening and empowering the community is a critical element in effective anti-poverty efforts;

Self-determination for communities is important; community-based initiatives should decide how resources can be most effectively utilized in reducing or alleviating poverty;

Universal programs of social assistance and anti-poverty efforts are important, but they should be coupled with targeted efforts;

The question of why people are poor should be replaced with what are the characteristics of society that contribute to poverty;

Poor communities have utilized resources in ways that have allowed for economic and family survival; these resources should be identified and strengthened.[51]

It was generally agreed at these community forums that in order to have public policy reflect these principles and themes, however, the development of political leverage on the part of poor people is a critical element for success.

The message of these activists parallels the experiences of earlier poverty-stricken groups who ultimately were able to escape poverty. Political scientist Martin Kilson, author of "Black Social Classes and Intergenerational Poverty," points out that "Historically, the Anglo-Protestants in the agrarian South or in the grimy mining counties of West Virginia, the Irish, Slavic, Italian, Scandinavian, German, and other ethnic American lower classes in the industrial cities of the Northeast, and Midwest, approached the problem of poverty by searching out political power and institutional leverage — through populist movements, trade unions, pressure groups, and political parties."[52] Andrés Torres conducted research comparing the economic mobility of African-Americans and Puerto Ricans in New York City. He discovered that the degree of political power held by the former was indeed an important factor in explaining their greater economic well-being compared to the latter between 1960 and 1980.[53]

Barbara Ehrenreich, Holly Sklar, and Karen Stollard in *Poverty in American Dream*, also call for political mobilization on the part of the poor as a way to fight poverty. Their proposals for eliminating poverty include: guaranteed annual income, full employment, an end to employment discrimination, universal child care, reproductive rights, and taxation policies that would serve to redistribute wealth. These writers acknowledge that only through a politically mobilized poor population will there be an extraction of these kinds of public and social welfare policies from government.[54]

In a 1972 article by political scientist Charles V. Hamilton, "Urban Economics, Conduit Colonialism, and Public Policy," it is proposed that public funds normally used for public assistance in housing should instead be controlled and utilized by poor people as venture capital for economic entrepreneurial efforts. These efforts then could be managed and controlled by the poor and working-class.[55] According to Hamilton, the amount available for providing housing services to the poor is enormous, but misdirected:

By fiscal 1974, it is estimated that the public assistance program will have spent $1.8 or roughly $2 billion dollars in shelter allowance payments in New York City alone. There are roughly 7,000 buildings in the city in which more than half of the units are occupied by welfare households...The money comes into the Black communities, to the tune of millions of dollars per year, but it goes right out. It is paid to absentee landlords, to exploitative merchants, to credit gougers and loan sharks. The people we traditionally call "welfare recipients" are, in fact, really conduits. They conduct money from one segment of the economy (public treasury) to another (into the hands of private entrepreneurs). The real welfare recipients are those people who prey on the conduits every welfare-check day.[56]

By utilizing public funds as venture capital for the poor, poor people would finally be allowed realistic opportunities to develop the social and economic fabric of the community. As Hamilton suggests, such an approach could produce economically self-sufficient cooperative housing that would be less expensive to maintain and more efficient than welfare hotels which primarily benefit absentee landlords and real estate speculators.

Steven Wiseman calls for a more radical approach in his work, *The Politics of Human Services*.[57] He believes that poverty will not be eliminated until the poor, through political mobilization, force a significant redistribution of the nation's wealth. He writes "A new radical movement should strategically engage in electoral politics and efforts to legislate redistributions of wealth and power, but electoral politics should be only one of many interrelated vehicles for radical change. Such a mobilization can begin in the electoral arena if traditional divisions used to keep the poor on the defensive politically can be overcome."[58]

The notion of power and the political mobilization of the poor to reduce poverty may not be considered valid by some observers who believe that poverty status is inevitable for some people, or a reflection of individual or innate weaknesses. But apparently poor people have not given up on the idea that poverty reflects the lack of political and economic power. It is generally true that, when the poor have organized, their political demands — that is, their interests and well-being as defined by them, not others — have been put on the civic agenda. The civil rights movement may be the premier example of this kind of development. We can, of course, debate the merits of this political mobilization in responding effectively to poverty. But then again, given the historical record of the United States on this issue, we can also continue to debate the effectiveness of government proposals that have been put on the civic agenda on behalf of the poor — or in spite of them.

How Does Social Welfare Policy Directed at Poverty in the United States Compare to Social Welfare Systems in Other Countries?

The welfare state had begun under the conservative Junker, Bismarck, in the 1880s, in part as an act of feudal noblesse oblige, in part as an attempt to steal the thunder from a rising socialist movement. Sickness insurance came to Germany in 1883, to the UK in 1911; it has not yet come to the United States...Health insurance was introduced in Germany in 1880, in the UK in 1948, and in the United States in 1965 — but only for people over sixty-five years of age...Moreover, even when the United States did finally get around to legislating its most basic welfare-state programs, Social Security, it did so in an extremely limited way.

Michael Harrington
The New American Poverty (1984)

As suggested earlier the incidence of poverty is generally much greater and more widespread in the United States than in other Western industrial countries. In terms of the absolute poverty rate, or that rate based on the official definition of poverty as utilized by the United States, this nation — along with Australia and Britain — have reflected the highest levels of absolute poverty.[1] But in terms of relative poverty, which reflects disposable income below half the median of adjusted national income, between 1979 and 1982 the United States had a considerably higher rate (17.1 percent) than Australia (12.2 percent), Britain (9.7 percent), Canada (12.6 percent), Norway (5.2 percent), Sweden (5.3 percent), and West Germany (5.6 percent).[2] A few writers and researchers have examined differences and proposed some explanations.

Peter Townsend's work *Poverty in the United Kingdom* is considered a definitive study of British and European social welfare systems.[3] This study includes comparisons between social welfare policies in the United States and European nations. One of Townsend's most important conclusions in this seminal study is that poverty is caused by structural factors:

The chief conclusion of this report is that poverty is more extensive than is generally or officially believed and has to be understood not only as an inevitable feature of severe social inequality but also a particular consequence of actions by the rich to preserve and enhance their wealth and so deny it to others. Control of wealth and therefore of the terms under which it may be generated and passed on selectively or for the general good, is therefore central to any policies designed to abolish or alleviate the condition.[4]

Another of Townsend's conclusions, and one which reiterates the work of many other writers, is that American advances of the welfare state are newer and less universal compared to those of European countries. For example, Social Security in the United States was adopted in 1935; in Denmark in 1891; in Germany in 1889; France in 1905; and England and Sweden in 1908 and 1913 respectively.

Despite different methods being used to organize each country's political economy, European nations can still be grouped together in order to compare their social welfare systems to that of the United States. European systems, for example, tend to emphasize social welfare that is preventive rather than reactive; this means that services like health and income support are available in order to prevent people from falling into poverty, rather than serving them after impoverishment. The programs tend to reflect approaches associated with universality rather than targeted means-tested programs. Generally, there is a greater acceptance of a welfare state philosophy. In studying the Scandinavian countries' systems Eric S. Einhorn and John Logue write in *Modern Welfare States* that "Support for welfare programs in Western democracies rests on three basic motivations. The first is altruism, an unselfish desire to help others...The bulk of modern welfare state programs rest on a second principle, that of self-insurance..." And "While both altruism and social insurance have played roles in the historical development of the Scandinavian welfare states, in the last half century they have been superseded by a third principle: solidarity."[5] These kinds of values are very different than those reflected in the United States social welfare system, as explained in an earlier chapter.

The United States: An Incomplete Welfare State?

Jane Axinn and Mark J. Stern write in *Dependency and Poverty* that the United States "has always been viewed as an 'incomplete' welfare state."[6] Richard M. Titmus describes the United States' approach as the "residual welfare" model, where social welfare institutions occupy a secondary status to the market and family in meeting the needs of individuals and groups.[7] This theme reiterates what is described by Harold L. Wilensky and Charles N. Lebeaux in their 1965 work, *Industrial Society and Social Welfare*, as the United States' tendency to be "more reluctant than any rich democratic country to make a welfare effort appropriate to its affluence. Our support of national welfare programs is halting; our administration of services for the less privileged is mean...[W]e do it with ill grace, carping and complaining all the way."[8]

According to Harrell R. Rodgers, Jr. in *Poor Women, Poor Families*, the "United States is the only major Western industrial country that...does not have a uniform cash-benefit program for poor families; restricts cash-welfare benefits almost exclusively to single parent families headed by women; has designed its main cash-welfare program to discourage mothers from working; has no statutory maternity benefits; has no universal child-rearing benefits; and has no universal health-care benefits."[9] Professor of political economy Bette Woody refers to this as the absence of an entrenched, not-to-be-questioned "institutionalized welfare state" in the United States: "In stark contrast to other Western postindustrial states, the United States stands alone in the lack of an institutionalized welfare state. As an alternative, a set of fragmented programs has evolved that are isolated from macroeconomic planning and basic assumptions about the long-range employment picture."[10]

Another way of viewing the "incomplete" nature of the American welfare state in comparison with European systems is to note that in the latter a significantly higher proportion of the gross national product and gross domestic product is devoted to social welfare expenditures. In 1986, for example, the United States devoted only 13 percent of its GNP to social welfare expenditures, while England registered 17 percent, Belgium 25 percent, France 26 percent, West Germany 26 percent, and Sweden's share was 31 percent. In 1985, the United States registered 16.2 percent of its gross domestic product to social welfare; comparable figures for a few other nations include Canada at 22.6 percent, France at 34.2 percent, and Sweden at 32.0 percent.[11] Yet another study points out that the "United States stands in ignominious isolation: Among industrialized countries, the United States has the highest incidence of poverty among the non-elderly and the widest distribution of poverty across all age and family groups. It is also the country in which the poor experience the longest spells of poverty and the only western democracy that has failed to give a significant proportion of its poor a measure of income security."[12] One consequence of this is noted by Maria J. Honratty: "In Canada, social welfare programs bring one in two poor families out of poverty. In the U.S., the rate is one in five."[13] Higher levels of social welfare spending in other nations have meant less poverty.

According to some observers, it seems that the higher level of social welfare spending in European systems goes hand in hand with higher levels of economic growth and productivity. Between 1979 and 1988 the "productivity growth rates," or the average annual rate of gross domestic product per employed person, were higher for European nations and Japan than it was for the United States. Japan had a productivity growth rate of 3.0 percent per year during this period, France reached 2.0 percent, Italy reached 1.9 percent, and the United Kingdom, Germany, and Sweden marked rates of 1.8 percent, 1.6 percent, and 1.4 percent respectively. The United States had the lowest rate at 1.0 percent.[14]

Canada also offers important contrasts with U.S. policies:

Canadian social welfare programs differ from U.S. programs on three dimensions. First, Canada places much greater emphasis on universal, non-means tested benefits than does the United States. Canada runs a universal health insurance program, a universal old age security pension, and provides universal per-child payments (family allowances) to all households with children.[15]

Thus, as mentioned in an earlier chapter, in the United States children are in effect categorized into the deserving (SS recipients) and undeserving (AFDC) poor, while in Canada *all* children are assisted with a minimum flow of benefits.

Along with higher spending for the poor, there is also a greater level of governmental control and ownership of industries in other Western industrial nations in the areas of telecommunications, railroad, and electricity. This is discussed by Michael D. Reagan in *Regulation: The Politics of Policy*. He points out, for instance, that while the governments of England, France, Japan, Sweden and West Germany own one hundred percent of the telecommunications industry, in the United States this industry is totally privately owned.[16] And while the United States government owns about one-fourth of the railroad industry, the comparable portion of governmental ownership in Japan is three-quarters; in England, France, and West Germany the national governments have full ownership of railroads. This is noted because higher spending for the poor and social welfare may correspond with the greater public ownership of basic industries in some European nations; as there is less reliance on the private sector in these industries, there is also, concomitantly, less faith in the private sector's capacity to respond to the needs of the poor.

Higher social welfare expenditures in European systems in comparison to the United States may also be explained partially by the relatively greater political strength of labor in European nations. This is explained by Woody:

Along with the absence of national economic planning to meet a growing crisis in the economy, the United States has a major disadvantage in a weak tradition of organized labor...[T]he value of organized labor at the national level as a political balance against big economic interests is invaluable. Labor interest has been responsible for most social insurance and family assistance programs and has outweighed any disadvantage of deficit or inflation pressure.[17]

The role of a strong labor sector is also cited by Christopher Schenk and Elaine Bernard as a major explanation for more effective anti-poverty strategies in Canada.[18] Similarly, Einhorn and Logue point to labor power as a factor explaining why the Scandinavian countries have such an advanced form of social welfare. In these countries between 70 and 85 percent of all wage and salaried workers are unionized, while between 85 and 95 percent of all blue-collar workers are organized; even white-collar workers are organized at relatively high levels of between 50 and 80 percent. They write further, "By comparison, 20 to 60 percent of blue- and white-collar workers are organized elsewhere in Europe, and in the United States only about 18 percent are organized."[19]

Nathan Glazer has a different point of view regarding the extent of social welfarism in the United States and contends in *The Limits of Social Welfare Policy* that it is inaccurate to describe the American welfare state as incomplete. For him it is not the role of labor nor institutional confinements that explain less commitment to social welfare provided by government. Instead, according to Glazer the answer for the apparent passivity of the U.S. social welfare state has to do with the civic values held by Americans such as individualism, entrepreneurship, ethnicity, and materialism. These values, he argues, are reflected strongly in an American preference for a limited social welfare state. Glazer adds that the idea of increasing public dollars for anti-poverty programs is perceived as special treatment for blacks, thus motivating white Americans to oppose an aggressive social welfare state.[20]

There are other outstanding characteristics of social welfare in European nations that are different from what is found in the United States. Rodgers points to three major differences between U.S. and Western European social welfare policies in a previously mentioned work: "First, most of the Western industrial countries emphasize prevention of social problems, including poverty, by means of such policies as national health systems, extensive housing programs, and child or family allowances. Second, there is a belief that problems are best prevented if the most important programs are universal...Third, many of the countries try to ameliorate social problems by public intervention to keep the economy healthy."[21] And in a 1987 article titled "Long Waves in the Development of Welfare Systems," Massimo Paci adds that Western European nations, in comparison to the United States, do not support as strongly a "promarket and procompetition policy thrust."[22] In the same reader, in "Health Care and the Boundaries of Politics," Paul Starr and Ellen Immergut illustrate Paci's claim by reviewing national health policies in Western European nations.[23]

Margaret Weir, in "Ideas and Politics," compares the philosophical and policy framework of the British social welfare system with that of the United States by examining the acceptance and development of the ideas of John Maynard Keynes in both countries.[24] In the classic work cited earlier, *The General Theory of Employment, Interest and Money*, Keynes argues that national government could, and should, play a significant role in countering business downturns through fiscal and monetary policies.[25] According to Keynes, government should not shy away from an expanded and aggressive role as a major economic actor even if it means generating national deficits to spur economic activity. Weir believes that the greater acceptance of Keynesian ideas in Britain after World War II partially explains the greater role that national government performs in the areas of social welfare including health and housing.[26]

Weir suggests that a major difference between the social welfare systems of these two countries is their national institutional and administrative arrangements. She shows that between the Great Depression and World War II the relatively fluid and non-hierarchical national administrative and political system in the United States allowed for experimentation with Keynesian ideas, but that this same arrangement made it difficult after the Second World War to consolidate and fully implement these ideas. In Britain, a closed and hierarchical national bureaucracy worked towards discouraging new economic ideas with major social welfare implications but, again, this same arrangement made it easier after the war for Britain to embark to a greater degree than the United States on government expansionism.[27]

Race, Family, and the Feminization of Poverty

Three major differences between the U.S., Canadian, and European social welfare systems have to do with race, the role of family, and the feminization of poverty. In the United States the feminization of poverty is a much greater problem than in other social welfare systems. One excellent comparative study poverty among women across nations is *The Feminization of Poverty* edited by Gertrude S. Goldberg and Eleanor Kremin. This reader includes chapters on European and U.S. social welfare systems, as well as on the systems of Japan, Poland, and the Soviet Union.

Goldberg writes in this reader that "Family poverty has not been femi-
nized in Canada to the extent that it has in the United States, where [in
1986] 59 percent of poor families with children were single-mother
families...[while] the comparable Canadian figure is 42 percent."[28] Regarding Japan, Jane Axinn writes in "Japan: A Special Case" that "One of
the most striking differences between Japan and other developed countries is the apparent stability of Japanese marriages and the intergenerational
unity of Japanese families." She notes that in 1986 Japan's divorce rate was
the "lowest of any developed nation's."[29]

American social welfare policies generally do not focus on the family
unit to the extent that the policies of other nations do; American policies
tend to emphasize the individual or single parents rather than the well-
being of the family. Martin Rein and Hugh Heclo write in "What Welfare
Crisis?" regarding this emphasis: "American welfare ensures that any
emerging social need among these covered groups is likely to appear
critical and abnormal in relation to other more covert forms of social
dependency, including dependency among the relatively affluent."[30]

Similarities found in European social welfare systems when compared
to the United States should not obscure significant differences among
social welfare systems in Europe, as explained by John R. Freeman in
Democracy and Markets.[31] Freeman describes four basic political and
economic systems that are found among European nations, each with
implications for the nation's organization and extent of social welfare
policy: Pluralist/Private Economy, Pluralist/Mixed Economy, Corporat-
ist/Private Economy, and Corporatist/Mixed Economy. Each of these
systems produces different or slightly different kinds of social welfare.
Additionally, although the U.S. and European systems influence the
economic plight of women differently, researchers have observed that the
social position of women in all of these societies reflects inequality to the
status of men. As Hilda Scott writes in *Working Your Way to the Bottom*,
"Many years of study of the position of women in Eastern and Western
Europe have convinced me that the position of women throughout the
industrialized countries is more alike than it is different. This is true for the
countries that call themselves socialist, for the most committed of the
welfare states, and for militantly free enterprise countries like the
U.S....Overall, women's position in the industrialized countries is precarious."[32]

Despite major institutional and programmatic differences, there are
some similarities between the United States and Britain, in particular,
regarding the values that undergird social welfare and anti-poverty
policies. As in the United States, for example, a perceptual dichotomy
between a "deserving" and "undeserving" poor also exists in Britain. As

reported by political scientist Douglas E. Ashford, "The notion of 'deserving' and 'undeserving' poor dominated British thinking about social welfare for more than a century, and was incorporated into many of the twentieth-century welfare reforms.[33]

In *Social Policy: A Critical Introduction*, Fiona Williams discusses the major historical and philosophical underpinnings of social welfare public policy in Britain that are similar to those in the United States. According to Williams this welfare state has reflected three major values: reverence for the idea of the nuclear family with a breadwinner father, dependent wife and children; survival of the fittest; and a concern for maintaining the stock and culture of the British race.[34] These values, including the latter one — i.e., preservation of "white" American culture — have also resonated strongly in the social welfare history and policies of the United States.[35]

These values reflect three social functions that can be found in British and U.S. social welfare policies and practices: preservation of social harmony; maintaining favorable conditions for accumulation of wealth; and control of the non-working population.[36]

One common theme in all of the social welfare systems we have briefly described here is the huge impact of a growing aged population. The growth of this group has contributed to the rapid increase in social welfare expenses and has undergirded this population's rise as a politically influential national interest group in the United States and European nations. As Fred Pampel and John Williamson write, "the aged may be important for the sheer size of the programs that benefit them...[I]n the advanced democracies in 1980, over 60 percent of all social welfare expenditures went for two programs — pensions and medical care."[37]

As was stated earlier, race is also a significant variable in examining differences between the United States and European social welfare systems. It must be noted that the United States' social welfare system was founded, to a larger degree, on considerations of race in the domestic arena than is the case for European nations. Kenneth J. Newbeck and Jack L. Roach argue that "racism has long influenced welfare practice and policy in the U.S."[38] These authors chart the development and implementation of specific poverty policies that were directly and indirectly colored by racial considerations during the 1930s through the 1960s. While European nations were certainly not innocent of this kind of outlook, racial considerations were confined, to a certain extent, to colonial and foreign policy arenas. It will be interesting to note how social welfare and anti-poverty policies are adopted and pursued in European nations as racial differentiation increases in these places.

As is pointed out by Williams in her previously mentioned work *Social Policy*, there are similarities between the United States and Britain in particular, in how the social welfare systems treat racial minorities. The quarterly journal *Sage Race Relations Abstracts* also highlights a range of articles and reports illustrating important similarities between these two nations in terms of race and poverty. But until recently, many European nations have not had to openly and publicly respond to significant racial differentiation; the racial minorities in these European nations were either small in number, or were segregated as temporary workers. This is not to negate the central role that people of color in Europe and abroad have historically performed in that continent's economic development, as pointed out by Professor Louis Kushnick.[39] The demography of Europe as well as its economics are changing in such a way, however, that its social welfare systems may begin to reflect some of the racial and ethnic dynamics found in the United States.

The United States can learn how to reduce poverty more effectively by examining some of the features of anti-poverty strategies in the European, as well as Canadian, social welfare systems. As racial and ethnic differences and tensions increase in Europe, however, these nations should try to avoid the mingling of poverty and race as has happened in the United States. European nations, as well as Canada, must ensure that their citizens of color enjoy full social equality with whites, as demography changes their racial landscape.

The experience of some European nations shows that poverty can be reduced, if not eliminated totally. Such a goal calls for strategies and policies, this chapter would suggest, that guarantee a basic flow of income and services for all people in society that would allow them food, decent shelter, education, and health. It also means that the distinction between a deserving and undeserving poor must be challenged and eliminated in social welfare policies. Another lesson in this chapter is that poor people, as shown by the examples of the organized elderly and labor, must be mobilized politically to participate in all stages of the public policy process. The poor must be involved in conceptualizing adequate policy responses to problems associated with poverty, and they must be intricately involved in how such policies are implemented and evaluated.

CONCLUSION

This introduction to some of the major questions related to urban poverty in America illustrates that many of the issues and ideas raised about the nature of poverty and how it should be addressed are not new. Although a front page article in the summer of 1992 in the *New York Times* by Robin Toner was titled, "Rethinking Welfare,"in fact, there has been very little change in this nation's approach to poverty and welfare reform since the Nixon presidency.[1] Significant similarities can be found in literature separated by a quarter of a century or more. We have seen, for instance, that although "underclass" may technically be considered a new term, it is not novel when compared with terms like Ostrogorski's "de-classed" in his work published in 1901, or Marshall's "Residuum" appearing in 1914. Today's calls by political leaders for eliminating "dependency" on the part of the poor and for "training" programs to make them employable were spelled out more than three decades ago in the "Public Welfare Amendments Act of 1962."

Furthermore, the current view of poor people as lazy, uneducated and disinterested in improving their lot reflects a long tradition of thought and ideology. Interest in the well-being of the poor has changed from period to period before the backdrop of this tradition. Society's attention to poverty has fallen and risen on issues of economic affordability or social stability. Thus, as Joe R. Feagin pointed out twenty years ago,

> Concerns with poverty and welfare and for the very poor have been a roller coaster phenomenon over the last few centuries of Western history, rising and falling with such things as changes in economic conditions, in political protest, and the character of political leadership.[2]

One thing is certain, however: attempts to define and understand the nature of poverty for public policy purposes are still inadequate. While the literature has grown more technically sophisticated in terms of research methodologies, the nature of poverty and its causes are still being debated. The debate continues despite the fact that poverty has been written about throughout human history. When some observers today claim that the problem of poverty is one of individual weakness rather than a reflection of systemic causes, they are in fact repeating an idea that is very old in this society. It is interesting that George Gilder's claim that poverty is a reflection of moral weakness and disrespect for the institution of marriage is not really very different from the Humane Society's position in the colonial period that "Misery is ordained to be the companion and punishment of vice."[3] Similarly, Charles Murray's theme in *Losing Ground* that welfare assistance to the poor generates dependency on their part echoes precisely the report of the Poor Law Commission in 1834, which stated that by ignoring the "law of nature by which the effects of each man's improvidence or misconduct are borne by himself and his family," relief has produced a "train of evils: the loss of self-respect, responsibility, prudence, temperance, hard work..."[4]

The poor are still viewed through a double prism, as was suggested by Paul Jacobs three decades ago.[5] There is a continuing societal schizophrenia in the approach to the problem of poverty in America. In the 1860s several states attempted to reform efforts directed at the poor by separating the "worthy poor" from those dependents considered merely lazy.[6] As Michael B. Katz and others have shown, however, even today there exists the notion of a "deserving" and "undeserving" poor among the American public and the policy community. Current studies still reflect the debates regarding the cause of poverty or, more subtly, who or what is to be blamed for poverty. Thus, the writings of Henry George in the 1870s are relevant and enlightening for understanding how poverty is being discussed and analyzed today.[7]

The apparent failure or ineffectiveness of anti-poverty efforts in the black community is a theme that has been repeated in the poverty literature over the last 30 years. Note, for instance, Charles E. Silberman's sour assessment in the 1960s of public policy at that time: "Insofar as federal legislation can cope with the knotty problems of race, Congress has now done just about all that can be done. And yet we seem to be as far as ever from having solved the problem." Silberman adds that, "despite the efforts of the federal government, the median income of Negro families last year ($3,893) was only 56 percent that of white families—the same rate as ten years ago. No fewer than 45.8 percent of all Negro families earned less than $3,500 — i.e., less than the 'poverty income.' Unemployment among Negroes averaged 9.8 percent in 1964, versus 4.6 percent for whites. And more than one-quarter of all Negroes in the labor force were out of work at some time or other during the course of the year."[8]

The claim of ineffectiveness of anti-poverty funds and the claim that these efforts aggravate the problem of poverty have both been repeated in the 1980s and 1990s. The earlier cited works of Charles Murray, George Gilder, Thomas Sowell, and others are examples of this.

It is hoped, therefore, that this review of selected literature can serve to advance the general public's awareness and understanding of poverty in urban America. Minimally it should be clear that several concepts, indeed myths, about poverty must be questioned, and perhaps even discarded, from serious policy and civic discussions. These include the following:

That poverty is an "individual" problem

That poverty is a "local" problem

That poverty is an "apolitical" problem

That poverty reflects apathy among poor people

That poverty is an "isolated" problem, disconnected from other public policy issues

That poverty is a "black" or "Latino" problem

That poverty is experienced uniformly across all racial and ethnic groups

That poverty is an "unresolvable" problem

That the elderly are no longer impoverished

That poverty has been the target of relatively enormous amounts of public resources and dollars in an effort to eradicate it, and

That poverty results from a lack of "hard" work or from immorality on the part of poor people

Unfortunately, these myths about poverty in the United States are continually reflected in public discourse and in discourse among academics, government officials, and representatives of the media.

The problem of urban poverty in the United States is persistent and growing. American cities are beginning to reflect an "hour glass," to use a demographer's term, where the number of poverty-stricken families and children are growing at the bottom of the social and economic ladder at the same time that economically-mobile individuals are increasing in number at the top, while the middle sector is getting smaller.[9] The traditional center ground represented by working-class and lower middle-class families is rapidly declining in size as we increasingly become a society of the extremely rich and the extremely poor. Additionally, while poverty affects many groups, blacks and Latinos do continue to suffer disproportionately. This study has shown, furthermore, that by any number of measures, black poverty has been a permanent feature of U.S. society regardless of the period of time we may be investigating. All this does not bode well for the social and economic future of the United States.

The Changing Face of Urban Poverty

What is different today about the nature and current approaches to urban poverty is the particular social and economic context in which poverty is unfolding in America. A majority of the poor in the United States lived in rural areas and small towns in 1959, slightly more than a quarter lived in central cities, and 17 percent resided in American suburbs. Today, about 43 percent of all poor persons are found in the central cities. Another difference between current and earlier poverty has to do with the quantity and types of jobs available today and in previous times. Changes in employment, furthermore, have affected some groups more adversely than others. The once-abundant manufacturing positions offered better wages and greater job stability for groups who had access to them in earlier periods. The shift from a manufacturing to service economy began long before the 1980s, contrary to popular opinion. One aspect of this urban economic shift was reported in the late 1950s. Louis Ferman et al. noted that in 1956 white-collar jobs started to outnumber blue-collar jobs; furthermore, between 1962 and 1963 the growth of service sector jobs significantly outpaced the increase of manufacturing jobs. During the 1950s, 152,000 new manufacturing jobs were added to the nation's economy, compared to 283,000 service sector jobs.[10] As we now know, this was just the tip of the iceberg in terms of forthcoming economic changes in the decades of the 1970s and 1980s. William W. Goldsmith and Edward J. Blakely point out that "projections of future employment suggest that the trends toward increased inequality of pay and growing numbers of low-wage jobs will continue..."[11]

The role of government has also changed radically. The claim made by Michael Harrington in 1969 that "The new debate of the coming period will not be over whether the government should intervene in the economy, but how the intervention will take place" was, in retrospect, wrong.[12] Since 1980 a Keynesian-oriented political economy and policy framework has been rejected at the level of the national administration in the United States, as is pointed out by David McKay in *Domestic Policy and Ideology*.[13] The Reagan-Bush regime (1980-1992) has had a major impact on the kinds of public policies pursued in the area of poverty. Under the Reagan and Bush administrations the question was no longer what can government do about poverty, but rather, what can government do to reduce dependency? To some degree this seems to also reflect the Clinton administration's response to poverty, as is pointed out by Ann Withorn in her essay, "Playing by the Rules? Clinton and Poor People."[14] Such an approach, as suggested by political scientist M. E. Hawkesworth, is basically and ultimately based on an ideological conception of poor people as lazy, shiftless, and immoral.[15]

Besides the ideological and political changes that have been represented by Reagan's "New Federalism," during the decade of the 1980s there were social changes that represent a changing national context for the problem of poverty in American society. Jane Axinn and Mark J. Stern state, for instance, that the nation has experienced major demographic changes since the days before the Great Society.[16] These changes have important implications for social welfare policy. The population, for instance, has aged considerably; in 1950, 6 percent of all Americans were over 65 years of age; by 1980 this figure had increased to 8.1 percent and in 1985 it was 12 percent. The two-parent family is no longer as predominant as it was two or three decades ago. The latter decades of twentieth century America have also been characterized by the rapid growth of a two-tier service economy, concomitant with major losses in the number of manufacturing jobs, as mentioned earlier. And finally, the New Deal coalition, which made it possible to enact many politically popular social welfare programs, has been weakened considerably. I believe that it is this last political factor that is most critical in suggesting how the problem of poverty might be tackled effectively in the United States.

Politics, Power, and Poverty

There is a major resistance to viewing poor people within a political context. Is the reason for this because poverty is, in fact, for the greater good of society, as suggested by Aristophanes in his play *Plutos* (388 BC)? Others in modern times have made a similar suggestion. Sociologist Herbert Gans summarizes cogently how poverty is functional for modern American society in, "The Positive Functions of Poverty."[17] While Gans discusses fifteen functions that poverty performs for society, the following list covers some of the major "contributions" of poverty to the well-being of society that Gans sees:

1) the existence of poverty makes sure that "dirty work" is done;

2) the poor subsidize, directly and indirectly, many activities that benefit the affluent;

3) poverty creates jobs for a number of occupations and professions which serve the poor;

4) [the] poor buy goods that others do not want;

5) the poor can be identified and punished as alleged or real deviants in order to uphold the legitimacy of dominant norms;

6) poverty helps to guarantee the status of those who are not poor;

7) the poor perform several cultural functions. They have played an unsung role in the creation of "civilization" having supplied the construction labor for many of the monuments which are often identified as the noblest expressions and examples of civilization, for example, the Egyptian pyramids, Greek temples, and medieval churches.[18]

This idea was also reflected in "The Functions and Consequences of Anti-Poverty Views" by Joe R. Feagin in 1975.[19] More recently, sociologist Irene I. Blea adds to this point by stating in her work, *La Chicana and the Interaction of Race, Class, and Gender,* that "what some do not realize is that the rich need the poor in order to remain rich. If the poor do not adhere to prescribed roles, the rich do not maximize profit."[20] In another study she writes:

Poverty, in spite of its bad reputation, is functional. The treatment of the poor seems as a warning to American workers. The consequences of not being the norm are negative; but labor pools of the poor are always available to provide cheap labor and additional workers. When fewer workers are needed, the poor move into the reverse labor pool. Poverty also makes jobs. Many people have jobs helping the poor. Social workers, welfare workers, education and job counselors, food stamp personnel, and Medicaid and Medicare officers help poor people. Teachers, doctors, attorneys, nurses, politicians, business people, and many employers make money addressing the needs of the poor.[21]

Blea believes that "Anglo" positions of power and privilege are founded on the continuing existence of people of color having much less in terms of material goods. Thus, as Gans argues, poverty serves an important function in helping support power and privilege.

Although a few scholars cited in this literature have sought to analyze the problem of poverty as reflecting a particular distribution of wealth and power, this approach has not been part of many academic and research forums, as I have mentioned in earlier chapters. Michael B. Katz notes in *The Undeserving Poor* how curious it is that poverty and politics are divorced in American policy discussions: "When Americans talk about poverty, some things remain unsaid. Mainstream discourse about poverty, whether liberal or conservative, largely stays silent about politics, power, and equality. But poverty, after all, is about distribution; it results because some people receive a great deal less than others. Descriptions of the demography, behavior, or beliefs of subpopulations cannot explain the patterned inequalities evident in every era of American history. These result from styles of dominance, the way power is exercised, and the politics of distribution."[22]

This is exactly why economist Andrés Torres and sociologist Clara E. Rodriguez warn readers in *Hispanics in the Labor Force*, that it is unjustifiable to ignore the role of politics in transforming anti-poverty research into public policy. They write, "We would be remiss if we did not acknowledge the role that politics plays in transforming policy research into public policy. Policy agendas and recommendations may be driven as much, or more, by political conditions as by research findings...[T]he relationship between research agendas and policy prescriptions is often tenuous. Therefore, we should not mystify the role of researchers in the development of policy. Nor should we underestimate the power of political action in bringing about change."[23] I have also written that the growing human service and social crisis evident in black and Latino communities during the 1980s was primarily a result of political decisions made by government in defending the economic well-being of wealthier interests in the United States.[24]

Some scholars have called attention to how the interests of dominant groups influence and mold American social welfare and anti-poverty policies. For example, Thomas B. Edsall writes in *The New Politics of Inequality* that the two-tier nature of "social programs has functioned in practice to divide working-class Democrats from poor Democrats and has exacerbated racial splits within the party."[25] According to Edsall this has allowed the Republican Party to gain major electoral advantages at the national level. Governmental cutbacks of certain kinds of social welfare have been aimed primarily at maintaining a certain political balance rather than at responding to national economic concerns like reducing the deficit. Again, Edsall: "The cuts in food stamps and welfare were just a part of a much larger pattern of spending reductions, reductions that functioned more to alter the political balance of power than to reduce the size of the deficit...These cuts represent an ideological victory that runs even deeper than the numbers themselves."[26]

This is a major theme in a reader edited by sociologists David G. Gil and Eva A. Gil, *Toward Social and Economic Justice*. As they state in their introduction, "Injustice in social, economic, and political relations among individuals, classes, sexes, races, and nations is not inevitable; for humans themselves, not superhuman forces, have evolved unjust relations and can also overcome such relations by changing the patterns of their interactions and consciousness."[27] Additional evidence for this is provided in statements made by congressional representatives regarding their reasons for supporting, or not supporting, various social welfare programs. Based on interviews conducted by Fay L. Cook and Edith J. Barrett, it was found that the congressional representatives perceive the elderly to be "a strong and powerful interest group with a higher percentage of people who turn out to vote."[28] This perception allows for much support for public dollars targeted towards the elderly. Despite the apparent connection between politics, power and government benefits, many scholars have approached urban poverty with a presumption that it can be discussed and analyzed within a political vacuum.

The political mobilization of poor people to control the institutions and political processes that impact their lives has never been a sustained priority of any national administration's effort to eliminate poverty. As suggested in earlier chapters, some scholars and activists suggest that this is the only way to eliminate poverty in American society. Harrell R. Rodgers, Jr., for instance, has written that poverty, inequality, and racial discrimination "are a natural consequence of past and current political realities in our society. This is true not only because our political leaders allowed blacks to be suppressed and exploited for hundreds of years; but...because our political system is heavily biased in favor of upper socioeconomic status groups. Those who are favored by the system tend to prosper, those who are not may suffer. As long as these biases continue, many of our current social problems will persist."[29]

The strategies advocated by Douglas G. Glasgow for improving living conditions in poor and black communities are basically political ones. In his work, *The Black Underclass*, he proposes that "the creation and development of institutions — political, economic, social, and human resources — that provide quality services to the local population...means using a local institutional base to more effectively influence mainstream policies, program perspectives, and practices. Such a base could potentially counter and neutralize large-scale institutional rejection and social policies of benign neglect."[30] This echoes the theme found in the forward of Leslie W. Dunbar's edited work, *Minority Report*: "Essentially, our thought is that what in the past had been for the United States a problem first of all moral, or first of all constitutional, is now primarily political and economic...We see no disadvantages of American minorities likely to be much relieved without economic advance; we see no strong likelihood of that without enlarged political participation."[31] Several chapters in Dunbar's publication emphasize the role of institutions and their policies in explaining the social conditions of people of color in the United States.

Other publications that reflect a broad range of political responses to the problem of poverty in America are Gus Hall's *Fighting Racism*, and Lloyd Hogan's *Afro-Centric Principles of Black Political Economy*.[32] While the former calls for a class-based strategy that would unite communities of color with the white working-class in order to challenge the economic status quo, the Hogan study reflects a black nationalist and Afro-centric perspective. Hogan asserts that "an insignificant, but very powerful, number of non-blacks have been responsible for the material poverty of blacks."[33] He believes that the black community in the United States must seek to build bridges with blacks in Africa, as well as to control the land in which they are residing in the United States. This will allow blacks to pursue policies that are people-oriented, rather than profit-motivated. Only the former direction will allow blacks to overcome their deprived living conditions, according to Hogan.

Gil also states that the reduction of social and economic dislocation and poverty requires, in part, a political response. He writes in *Unraveling Social Policy* that "developing alternative social policies and understanding their dynamics and consequences are only first steps toward comprehensive, internally consistent, and humanly satisfying systems of social policies, steps which must be followed by consistent political action so that significant changes suggested by systematic policy analysis can become social realities."[34] Only the mobilization of poor people can guarantee that their interests and needs will be acted upon satisfactorily by those who control resources and processes to make and implement public policy.

The call for political mobilization on the part of the poor was, of course, a major theme of the National Welfare Rights Organization as described by Jacqueline Pope in her book. *Biting the Hand That Feeds Them.*[35] Similarly, Jill Quadagno writes in "Race, Class and Gender in the U.S. Welfare State," that "An important influence in welfare explosion was a shortlived but highly visible women's liberation movement, the National Welfare Rights Organization (NWRO). The NWRO was an organization of AFDC mothers whose activities were directed at class and gender issues...Although the NWRO was virtually defunct by 1970, at its peak it staged hundreds of sit-ins and confrontations at welfare offices and the percentage of eligible families applying for aid increased from about 33 percent in 1960 to more than 90 percent in some regions by 1971."[36]

Ann Withorn not only calls for the political mobilization of the poor as a resource for overcoming poverty, but reminds us that when this has occurred, major new social welfare policies have been enacted for the benefit of many. She writes that "Three major developments occurred in the early 1960s as a result of the poverty programs and the growing influence of the poor during this period: One was the passage of the 1962 social service amendments. Another was the passage of Medicaid in 1965. The third was the enactment of the Community Mental Health Centers Act in 1963...[T]he result of all these changes was to involve the federal government more in social services delivery than it had been since the days of the WPA."[37] And, as I have stated:

> At least one lesson we can extract from the educational and economic struggles that Blacks have engaged in throughout American history is that serious economic change, beneficial to Blacks, will not occur without Blacks having the power to demand it and to politically and economically punish those who stand in the way of justice and social equality for Blacks. Political power is the key to survival for Blacks in America.[38]

The call for the poor to mobilize politically, it should be noted, is not really different from saying that the poor should have the same opportunities to organize around their social and economic needs as any other interest group in pluralist America.

The British scholar Peter Townsend, in his earlier cited work *Poverty in the United Kingdom*, calls for the elimination of poverty through changing the social structure and its public policies. To him this means the abolition of excessive wealth and income; breaking down the distinction between earners and dependents; abolition of unemployment; the implementation of industrial democracy efforts; and the organization of social services based on home and family, not institutions. This line of thought is logical, given that the problems of the poor have only been put on the nation's public agenda as a result of political mobilization and threats of social instability. As Manuel Carballo writes in *The State and the Poor in the 1980s*, "One lesson of the past two decades is clear: Although concerned leaders such as Presidents Kennedy and Johnson may place poverty high on the national agenda, over time other issues such as war, the environment, and energy will overshadow it. During the 1980s, unless current economic policies once again give us a nation that is one-third ill-housed, ill-fed, and ill-clothed, there is every reason to believe that poverty will be in the background."[39]

Daniel Patrick Moynihan, writing about the War on Poverty in a previously cited work, takes issue with the suggestion that this effort arose as a result of political pressures. He states, "Nor did the War on Poverty come about because of any great surge of popular demand. The civil rights movement, while much involved with problems of poverty, was nonetheless at that time primarily directed to problems of civil rights as such...The origins of this effort simply cannot be explained in deterministic terms. It was more a rational than a political event."[40] But concern about the living conditions of the poor has never been an overwhelming motivation for the nation to pay attention to the causes and consequences of poverty. This was suggested by Nathan Glazer in his essay, "A Sociologist's View of Poverty": "It is the civil rights revolution that makes poverty a great issue in America, not merely poverty. And in other developed countries, it is the absence of a great social division coinciding roughly with the line of poverty that keeps poverty from becoming a great issue."[41]

A recent essay by urban scholars Charles V. Hamilton and Dona C. Hamilton illustrates that Moynihan's characterization of the agenda of the civil rights movement is incomplete. In fact, a broader social agenda was very much a part of the civil rights agenda. By studying the archives of various civil rights organizations, including the National Association for the Advancement of Colored People and the National Urban League, these two scholars note that in many instances since the New Deal the strictly civil rights agenda was sacrificed to the potential advancement of the social agenda.[42] Furthermore, Hamilton and Hamilton write, "It was the victories of the civil rights agenda — Supreme Court decisions, Civil Rights Act of 1964, Voting Rights Act of 1965, executive decrees of the early 1960s, Housing Law of 1968 — that set the stage for more concentrated attention to the social problems still persisting."[43]

Most observers would agree that the civil rights movement did have a major impact on poverty, both in terms of raising the public's awareness and in providing strategies for its resolution. The latter was most evident in the thinking and activism of Martin Luther King, Jr. King believed that politics and the distribution of power were inseparable from the possibility of better living conditions for the poor. As he wrote in 1967, "When a people are mired in oppression, they realize deliverance only when they have accumulated the power to enforce change."[44] He added that it was political mobilization and organization that allowed other groups to escape poverty and explained that "Jews progressed because they possessed a tradition of education combined with social and political action...[U]niting social action with education competence, Jews became enormously effective in political life. Those Jews who became lawyers, businessmen, writers, entertainers, union leaders and medical men did not vanish into the pursuits of their trade exclusively. They lived an active life in political circles, learning the techniques and arts of politics."[45] Politicizing the poor, King felt, would mean that they would question, challenge, and change their lower social and economic status in society.

Consistent with the spirit of King's words, this selective review of the literature on urban poverty in the United States will end with a quotation from a book by David and Eva Gil, *Toward Social and Economic Justice:*

In order to develop effective strategies toward human survival and meaningful lives for all, we need to STOP, THINK, and QUESTION assumptions, values and practices which we have come to take for granted, and SEARCH for philosophical and institutional alternatives to prevailing ways of life.[46]

Similarly, I hope that this review of the literature will encourage all concerned to stop and become aware about the problem of poverty in the United States and to challenge how we have been socialized to think incorrectly about poverty, and to thereby reach for ways to make the United States a more just and equal society for all.

NOTES

Introduction

1. Adolph Reed, Jr., "The Underclass as Myth and Symbol: The Poverty of Discourse About Poverty," *Radical America* 24, no. 1 (Summer 1991).

2. Barry R. Schiller, *The Economics of Poverty and Discrimination* (Englewood Cliffs, NJ: Prentice-Hall, 1976), p. ix.

3. Ibid.

4. Daniel Patrick Moynihan, "Toward a National Urban Policy," *The Public Interest*, no. 9 (Fall 1969), p. 8.

5. Nathan Glazer, *The Limits of Social Policy* (Cambridge, MA: Harvard University Press, 1988).

6. Lee Sigelman and Susan Welch, *Black Americans' View of Racial Inequality: The Dream Deferred* (New York: Cambridge University Press, 1991), p. 159.

7. Reed, "Underclass as Myth and Symbol," p. 4.

8. Michael Wiseman, "How Workfare Really Works," *The Public Interest*, no. 89 (Fall 1987), p. 36.

9. Carlton Sagara and Peter Kiang, *Recognizing Poverty in Boston's Asian American Community* (Boston: The Boston Foundation Persistent Poverty Project, 1992).

10. See Charles Sullivan and Kathlyn Hatch, *The Chinese in Boston, 1970* (Boston: Action for Boston Community Development, 1973); Franklin Williams, "The Forgotten Minority: Asian Americans in New York City" (U.S. Commission on Civil Rights, Washington, DC, 1977); and John Grove and Jiping Wu, "Who Benefited from the Gains of Asian-Americans, 1940-1980?" in *Racism and the Underclass*, ed. George W. Shephard, Jr., and David Penna (Westport, CT: Greenwood Press, 1991).

11. Cynthia M. Duncan and Stephen Sweet, "Poverty in Rural America" in *Poverty In America*, ed. Cynthia M. Duncan (Westport, CT: Auburn House, 1992), p. xxii.

Chapter 1

1. Daniel H. Weinberg is cited in Jason DeParle, "In Rising Debate on Poverty, the Question: Who Is Poor?" *The New York Times*, September 3, 1990, p. 10.

2. Peter Townsend, *Poverty in the United Kingdom: A Survey of Household Resources and Standards of Living* (Berkeley: University of California Press, 1979).

3. B. Seebohm Rowntree, *Poverty: A Study of Town Life* (London: Longman, Green and Co., 1901).

4. Referenced in Rowntree, ibid.; also see Townsend, *Poverty in the United Kingdom*, p. 263; and E. J. Hobsbawn "Poverty," in *New International Encyclopedia of the Social Sciences*, ed. D. L. Sills, vol. 12 (London: Macmillan, 1968).

5. Quoted in Townsend, *Poverty in the United Kingdom*, p. 33.

6. Michael Sherraden, *Assets and the Poor* (Armonk, NY: M. E. Sharpe, 1991), p. 21.

7. Robert J. Lampman, *Ends and Means of Reducing Income Poverty* (Chicago: Markham Publishing Co., 1971); also see Robert Hunter, *Poverty* (New York: MacMillan, 1904).

8. U.S. Bureau of Labor Statistics, *Handbook of Labor Statistics*, Bulletin No. 694 (Washington, DC, 1941).

9. Gabriel Kolko, *Wealth and Power in America: An Analysis of Social Class and Income Distribution* (New York: Praeger Publishers, 1962), p. 97. Also see Works Progress Administration, "Intercity Differences in Costs of Living in March 1935: 59 Cities," Research Monograph 12, (Washington, DC: U.S. Government Printing Office, 1987).

10. Michael Harrington, *The Other America: Poverty in the United States* (New York: MacMillan, 1969).

11. DeParle, "In Rising Debate on Poverty."

12. Joyce E. Allen and Margaret C. Simms, "Is a New Yardstick Needed to Measure Poverty?" *Focus*. 18, no. 2 (February, 1990), p. 6

13. Mollie Orshansky, "How Poverty Is Measured," *Monthly Labor Review* 92, no. 2 (February 1969), pp. 37-41.

14. U.S. Bureau of the Census, *Statistical Abstract of the United States: 1992* (Washington, DC, 1992), p. 426; also see U.S. General Accounting Office, *Poverty Trends, 1980-1988: Changes in Family Composition and Income Sources Among the Poor* (Washington, DC, September 1992), p. 10.

15. This information is cited in Michael Harrington, *The New American Poverty* (New York: Penguin Books, 1985),

16. Harrington, *The New American Poverty*, p. 81.

17. Reynolds Farley, *Blacks and Whites: Narrowing the Gap* (Cambridge, MA: Harvard University Press, 1984), p. 157.

18. Diane Colasanto, "Bush Presidency Tarnished by Growing Public Concern about Poverty," *Gallup Report*, no. 287 (August 1989), p. 5.

19. John Kenneth Galbraith, *The Affluent Society* (New York: New American Literary, 1958), p. 251; also see Anthony Downs, "Who Are the Urban Poor?" (New York: Committee for Economic Development, 1970).

20. Lawrence E. Gary, "Poverty, Stress and Mental Health: Perspectives from the Black Community," in *Mental Health: A Challenge to the Black Community*, (Philadelphia: Dorrance, 1978), p. 60.

21. Barry R. Schiller, *The Economics of Poverty and Discrimination* (Englewood Cliffs, NJ: Prentice-Hall, 1976), p. 10.

22. Victor Fuchs, "Redefining Poverty and Redistributing Income," *Public Interest*, no. 8 (Summer 1967).

23. Townsend, *Poverty in the United Kingdom*, p. 31.

24. Louis A. Ferman, Joyce L. Kornbluh, Alan Haber, *Poverty in America* (Ann Arbor: University of Michigan Press, 1969), p. 5.

25. Adam Smith, *The Wealth of Nations* (1776; reprint, New York: Modern Library, 1937), p. 821.

26. Michael B. Katz, *The Undeserving Poor: From the War on Poverty to the War on Welfare* (New York: Pantheon Books, 1990).

27. Mimi Abramovitz, "Everyone Is on Welfare: The Role of Redistribution in Social Policy," in *Social Welfare Policy: Perspectives, Patterns and Insights*, ed. I. C. Colby (Chicago: Dorsey Press, 1989).

28. Bertram M. Beck, "How Do We Involve the Poor?" in *Poverty, Power, and Politics*, ed. Chaim Isaac Waxman (New York: Gosset & Dunlop, 1968); also see Charles V. Hamilton, "The Patron-Recipient Relationships and Minority Politics in New York City," *Political Science Quarterly* 94, no. 2 (Summer 1979).

29. Beck, "How Do We Involve the Poor?" p. 270.

30. S. M. Miller and Pamela A. Roby, *The Future of Inequality* (New York: Basic Books, 1970), p. 3.

31. See Frances Fox Piven and Richard A. Cloward, *Regulating the Poor* (New York: Pantheon, 1971); also see Milton Friedman, *Capitalism and Freedom* (Chicago: The University of Chicago Press, 1982).

32. Robert Rector, "How 'Poor' are America's Poor?" *Backgrounder*, no. 791 (September 21, 1990), pps. 1-22.

33. Robert Greenstein, press release issued October 1, 1993, by the Center on Budget and Policy Priorities, Washington, DC.; this information was disseminated via the Handsnet Electronic Bulletin Board.

34. Robert D. Plotnick and Felicity Skidmore, *Progress Against Poverty: A Review of the 1964-1974 Decade* (New York: Academic Press, 1975).

35. Farley, *Blacks and Whites*, p. 166.

36. Ibid.

37. U.S. Bureau of the Census, *Current Population Reports* "Measuring the Effect of Benefits and Taxes on Income and Poverty: 1990" Series P-60, no. 176-RD (Washington, DC, 1991), see pp. 3-8.

38. Lawrence Mischel and David M. Frankel, *The State of Working America* (Armonk, NY: M. E. Sharpe, 1991), p. 166.

39. Ibid.

40. "Smaller Slices of the Pie: The Growing Economic Vulnerability of Poor and Moderate Income Americans" (Washington, DC: Center on Budget and Policy Priorities, 1985), p. 38.

41. Ibid., p. 39.

42. Jane Axinn and Mark J. Stern, *Dependency and Poverty: Old Problems in a New World Order* (Lexington, MA: Lexington Books, 1988).

43. Mischel and Frankel, *The State of Working America*, p. 167.

44. Robert Greenstein, "Attempts to Dismiss the Census Poverty Data." (Center on Budget and Policy Priorities, Washington, DC, September 28, 1993) p. 3; unpublished paper.

Chapter 2

1. Charles V. Hamilton and Dona C. Hamilton, "The Dual Agenda: Social Policies of Civil Rights Organizations, New Deal to the Present" (Paper delivered at the 1991 Annual Meeting of the American Political Science Association, Washington, DC, August 29-September 1, 1991), p. 6.

2. David McKay, *Domestic Policy and Ideology: Presidents and the American State, 1964-1987* (London: Cambridge University Press, 1989).

3. Edward D. Berkowitz, *America's Welfare State: From Roosevelt to Reagan* (Baltimore: The Johns Hopkins University Press, 1991), p. 2.

4. Robert X. Browning, *Politics and Social Welfare Policy in the United States* (Knoxville: The University of Tennessee Press, 1991), p. 115.

5. See Donald S. Howard, *WPA and the Federal Relief Policy* (1943; reprint, New York: Da Capo Press, 1973).

6. Robert C. Weaver, "Poverty in America: The Role of Urban Renewal," in *Poverty in America*, ed. Margaret S. Gordon (San Francisco: Chandler Publishing Co., 1965).

7. Martin Anderson, *The Federal Bulldozer* (Cambridge: Massachusetts Institute of Technology Press, 1964), p. 495.

8. Berkowitz, *America's Welfare State*, p. 5.

9. Mimi Abramovitz, *Regulating the Lives of Women: Social Welfare Policy from Colonial Times to the Present* (Boston: South End Press, 1989).

10. Dorothy B. James, *Poverty, Politics and Change* (New York: Prentice-Hall, 1972), p. 51.

11. Michael B. Katz, *In the Shadow of the Poorhouse: A Social History of Welfare in America* (New York: Basic Books, 1986).

12. Michael B. Katz, *The Undeserving Poor: From the War on Poverty to the War on Welfare* (New York: Pantheon, 1989).

13. Neil Gilbert, *Capitalism and the Welfare State* (New Haven, CT: Yale University Press, 1983).

14. John Maynard Keynes, *General Theory of Employment, Interest and Money* (1936; reprint, New York: Harcourt, Brace and Jovanovich, 1965).

15. William J. Wilson, *The Truly Disadvantaged: The Inner City, Poverty, and Public Policy* (Chicago: The University of Chicago Press, 1987), p. 119.

16. Hamilton and Hamilton, "The Dual Agenda," p. 6; also see John Hope Franklin, *From Slavery to Freedom: A History of Negro Americans* (New York: Knopf, 1968), p. 396.

17. Nancy L. Grant, *TVA and Black Americans: Planning for the Status Quo* (Philadelphia: Temple University Press, 1990).

18. Theda Skocpol, "Universal Appeal: Politically Viable Policies to Combat Poverty," *The Brookings Review*, 9, no. 3 (Summer 1991), p. 31.

19. Gilbert, *Capitalism and the Welfare State*, p. 70.

20. Alberto Rivera-Fournier, "Social Security Administration Underserves Hispanic Population," *NPRC Reports* (Washington, DC: National Puerto Rican Coalition, October 1992), p. 6.

21. Fay L. Cook and Edith J. Barrett, *Support for the American Welfare State* (New York: Columbia University Press, 1992), p. 226.

22. Robert Greenstein, "Relieving Poverty," *The Brookings Review* 9, no. 3 (Summer 1991), p. 34.

23. Mark J. Stern, "Poverty and Family Composition Since 1940," in *The Underclass Debate: Views from History*, ed. Michael B. Katz (Princeton, NJ: Princeton University Press, 1993), p. 237.

24. E. W. Kelley, *Policy and Politics in the United States* (Philadelphia: Temple University Press, 1987), p. 223.

25. Richard E. Dawson and James A. Robinson, "The Politics of Welfare," in *Politics in the American States*, eds. Herbert Jacob and Kenneth Vines (Boston: Little, Brown, and Co., 1965).

26. Michael Harrington, *The Other America: Poverty in the United States* (New York: MacMillan, 1969); and Dwight McDonald, "Our Invisible Poor," *The New Yorker*, January 16, 1963.

27. Kelley, *Policy and Politics in the United States*, p. 240.

28. Lillian B. Rubin, "Maximum Feasible Participation: The Origins, Implications, and Present Status," *The Annals*, 385 (September 1969), p. 20.

29. Ibid.

30. Henry Allen, "A Radical Critique of Federal Work and Manpower Programs, 1933-1974," in *Welfare in America*, ed. Betty Reid Mandell (Englewood Cliffs, NJ: Prentice-Hall, 1975), p. 32.

31. Robert J. Lampman, *Ends and Means of Reducing Income Poverty* (Chicago: Markham, 1971), p. 7; also see Sar A. Levitan, *The Great Society's Poor Law : A New Approach to Poverty* (Baltimore: The Johns Hopkins University Press, 1969).

32. Gilbert, *Capitalism and the Welfare State*, p. 142.

33. Ibid., pp. 39-63.

34. Sheldon H. Danziger and Daniel Weinberg, *Fighting Poverty: What Works and What Doesn't* (Cambridge, MA: Harvard University Press, 1986), p. 4.

35. Sar A. Levitan, *The Great Society's Poor Law: A New Approach to Poverty* (Baltimore: The Johns Hopkins University Press, 1969).

36. Louis A. Ferman, Foreword, *The Annals*, 385 (September 1969), p. ix.

37. See Sanford Knavitz and Ferne R. Rolodner, "Community Action: Where Has It Been? Where Will It Go?" in ibid., pp. 3-40.

38. Daniel Patrick Moynihan, *Maximum Feasible Misunderstanding: Community Action in the War on Poverty* (New York: The Free Press, 1970).

39. Leslie W. Dunbar, *Minority Report: What Has Happened to Blacks, Hispanics, American Indians, and Other Minorities in the 1980s?* (New York: Pantheon Books, 1984), p. 201.

40. Peter Marris and Martin Rein, *Dilemmas of Social Reform* (1967; reprint, Chicago: The University of Chicago Press, 1982).

41. Ibid., p. 92.

42. Ibid., p. 90.

43. Roger Wilkins, "Don't Blame the Great Society," *The Progressive* 56, no. 7 (July 1992), p. 17.

44. Susan H. Hertz, *The Welfare Mothers' Movement: A Decade of Change for Poor Women?* (Washington, DC: The University Press of America, 1981), p. 22.

45. United States Kerner Commission, *Report to the National Advisory Commission on Civil Disorders* (New York: Bantam Books, 1968).

46. John Charles Boger, "Race and the American City: The Kerner Commission in Retrospect," *North Carolina Law Review* 71, no. 5 (June 1993), p. 1340.

47. Thomas Gladwin, *Poverty USA* (Boston: Little Brown and Co., 1967).

48. James A. Morone, *The Democratic Wish: Popular Participation and Limits of American Government* (New York: Basic Books, 1990), p. 219; also see S. M. Miller and Martin Rein, "Participation, Poverty, and Administration," *Public Administration Review*, no. 29 (January-February 1969), pp. 15-24.

49. S. M. Miller and Pamela Roby, "The War on Poverty Reconsidered," in *Poverty: Views from the Left*, eds. Jeremy Larner and Irving Howe (New York: William Morrow and Co., 1968), p. 69.

50. Chaim Isaac Waxman, *Poverty, Politics and Power* (New York: Gosset and Dunlap, 1968).

51. Saul Alinsky, "The War on Poverty: Political Pornography," in ibid., p. 173.

52. Theodore J. Lowi, *The End of Liberalism: The Second Republic of the U.S.* (New York: W. W. Norton and Co., 1979), p. 200.

53. Hugh Heclo, "The Political Foundations of Anti-poverty Policy," in *Fighting Poverty*, eds. Danziger and Weinberg.

54. Ibid., pps. 321-324.

55. Lowi, *The End of Liberalism*, p. 190; also see Daniel Patrick Moynihan, *The Politics of Guaranteed Annual Income: The Nixon Administration and the Family Assistance Plan* (New York: Vintage Books, 1973); and Lucy Creighton and Sally Geis, "Income Maintenance and Then What?" *Social Policy* 6, no. 1, (May/June 1975).

56. Martha Derthwick, *Uncontrollable Spending for Social Service Grants* (Washington, DC: The Brookings Institute, 1975), p. 8.

57. Browning, *Politics and Social Welfare Policy*, p. 51.

58. Marc L. Miringoff, *1992 Index of Social Health: Monitoring the Social Well-Being of the Nation* (Tarrytown, NY: Fordham Institute for Innovation in Social Policy, 1992), p. 6.

59. See Kenneth Dolbeare and Murray J. Edelman, *American Politics: Policies, Power and Change* (Lexington, MA: DC Heath, 1974), p. 148.

60. Henry Allen, "A Radical Critique of Federal Work and Manpower Programs," p. 38.

61. David Greenstone and Paul Peterson, *Race and Authority in Urban America* (New York: Russell Sage, 1974).

62. See Daniel Patrick Moynihan, *The Negro Family: The Case for National Action* Washington, DC: U.S. Department of Labor, 1965. A critique of the Moynihan Report and examination of how it was used to focus on the symptoms, rather than the causes, of poverty is found in: Carl Ginsburg, *Race and Media: The Enduring Life of the Moynihan Report* (New York: Institute for Media Analysis, 1989).

63. Harrell R. Rodgers, Jr., *Poor Women, Poor Families: The Economic Plight of America's Female-Headed Households* (Armonk, NY: M.E. Sharpe, 1990), p. 124.

64. Ellen Teninty, "Tax Credits Divide and Conquer," *Equal Means* 1, no. 4 (Winter 1993). (New York: Ms. Foundation for Women).

65. K. Sue Jewell, *Survival of the Black Family: The Institutional Impact of U.S. Social Policy* (Westport, CT: Praeger, 1988), p. 57.

66. James R. Storey, Robert Harris and Frank Levy, *The Better Jobs and Income Plan: A Guide to President Carter's Welfare Reform Proposal* (Washington, DC: The Urban Institute, 1978).

67. David McKay, *Domestic Policy and Ideology*, pp. 109-137.

68. Robert H. Haveman, "The Changed Face of Poverty: A Call for New Policies," *Focus* 11, no. 2 (Summer 1988). Institute on Research and Poverty, University of Wisconsin, Madison.

69. Theresa Funiciello, "The Poverty Industry: Do Government and Charities Create the Poor?" *MS*, November/December, 1990.

70. Anthony Downs, "Who Are the Urban Poor?" in *The Urban Economy*, ed. Harold M. Hochman (New York: W. W. Norton and Co., 1976), p. 19.

71. John F. Kain and Joseph J. Persky, "Alternatives to the Gilded Ghetto," in ibid., p. 214.

72. Roger Starr, "Which of the Poor Shall Live in Public Housing?" *The Public Interest*, no. 23 (Spring 1971).

73. Edward C. Banfield, *The Unheavenly City* (Boston: Little, Brown and Co., 1973).

74. Lowi, *The End of Liberalism*, p. 210.

75. David Stoesz, "Poor Policy: The Legacy of the Kerner Commission for Social Welfare," *North Carolina Law Review* 71, no. 5 (June 1993), p. 1680.

76. Anthony S. Campagna, *U.S. National Economic Policy, 1917-1985* (New York: Praeger, 1987), p. 505.

77. William P. O'Hare, *Poverty in America: Trends and New Patterns* (Washington, DC: Population Reference Bureau, 1987), p. 35.

78. Ibid., pp. 35 and 36; also see "Smaller Slices of the Pie: The Growing Economic Vulnerability of Poor and Moderate Income Americans" (Washington, DC: Center on Budget and Policy Priorities, 1985).

79. Information about details of the latter can be found in: Douglas Hibbs, *The Political Economy of Industrial Democracies* (Cambridge, MA: Harvard University Press, 1987); also see Sheldon Danziger, "Poverty and Inequality Under Reaganomics," *Journal of Contemporary Studies* 1 (Summer 1982).

80. Rodgers, *Poor Women, Poor Families*, p. 120.

81. Jewell, *Survival of the Black Family*, p. 14.

82. Browning, *Politics and Social Welfare Policy*, p. 164.

83. John Donahue, *The Privatization Decision* (New York: Basic Books, 1989), pps. 179-211.

84. Charles S. Bullock, "Expanding Black Economic Rights," in *Racism and Inequality: The Policy Alternatives*, ed. Harrell R. Rodgers, Jr. (San Francisco: W. H. Freeman and Co., 1975), p. 122.

85. Donahue, *The Privatization Decision*, p. 209.

86. Ibid., p. 210.

87. Andrew W. Mellon, *Taxation, the People's Business* (New York: MacMillan, 1924).

88. Frank Ackerman, *Hazardous to Our Wealth: Economic Policies in the 1980s* (Boston: South End Press, 1984), p. 28.

89. Campagna, *U.S. National Economic Policy*, p. 487.

90. Lawrence B. Lindsay, *The Growth Experiment: How the New Tax Policy Is Transforming the U.S. Economy* (New York: Basic Books, 1990), p. 82.

91. Charles A. Murray, *Losing Ground: American Social Policy, 1950-1980* (New York: Basic Books, 1984).

92. David B. Robertson and Dennis R. Judd, *The Development of American Public Policy* (Glenview, IL: Scott, Foresman and Co., 1989), p. 220.

93. Lawrence M. Mead, "Social Programs and Social Obligations," *The Public Interest* 69, no. 3 (Fall 1982), pp. 17-32.

94. M. E. Hawkesworth, *Theoretical Issues in Policy Analysis* (Albany: State University of New York Press, 1988), p. 174.

95. Richard A. Cloward and Frances Fox Piven, "The Fraud of Workfare," *The Nation*, May 23, 1993, p. 693.

96. See George Sternlieb and David Listokin, *New Tools for Economic Development: The Enterprise Zone, Development Bank and RFC* (New Brunswick, NJ: Rutgers University Press, 1980).

97. Danziger, "Poverty and Inequality under Reaganomics," p. 28.

98. Also see Michael A. Stegman, "National Urban Policy Revisited," *North Carolina Law Review* 71, no. 5 (June 1993), pp. 1759-60.

99. This statement is by Jack Kemp, secretary for the Department of Housing and Urban Development, and is cited in Stegman, ibid.

100. George Berlin and Andrew Sum, *Toward a More Perfect Union: Basic Skills, Poor Families and Our Economic Future* (New York: Ford Foundation and Project on Social Welfare and the American Future, 1988).

101. Ibid., p. 29.

102. Michael Morris and John B. Williamson, "Workfare: The Poverty/Dependence Trade Off," *Social Policy* 17, no. 4 (Summer 1987), p. 16.

103. Bette Woody, "U.S. Employment Policy: Success and Failure in Reaching Black Women Workers: Recent Theory and Evidence," research report (Boston: The University of Massachusetts, The Trotter Institute, forthcoming), p. 37.

104. Bette Woody, "Welfare Reform: A Summary and Analysis of Current U.S. Congressional Debate Over the Family Support Act of 1988," *Trotter Review* 3, no. 2 (Spring 1989).

105. Linda McCart, "A Governor's Guide to the Family Support Act: Challenges and Opportunities," National Governor's Association Report (Washington, DC: National Governors' Association, 1990); also see Rodgers, *Poor Women, Pooor Families*, p. 116.

106. José E. Cruz, *Implementing the Family Support Act: Perspectives of Puerto Rican Clients* (Washington, DC: National Puerto Rican Coalition, 1991), p. 25.

107. Thomas Corbett, "Child Poverty and Welfare Reform: Progress or Paralyses?" *Focus* 15, no. 1 (Spring 1993), p. 4; Institute on Research and Poverty, University of Wisconsin, Madison.

108. Rodgers, *Poor Women, Poor Families*, p. 150.

109. Kathleen Sylvester, "Welfare: The Hope and the Frustration," *Governing*, (November, 1991).

110. Laurie Udesky, "Welfare Reform and Its Victims," *The Nation*, September 24, 1990.

111. Morris and Williamson, "Workfare."

112. Ibid., p. 50.

113. Cynthia Rexroat, *The Declining Economic Status of Black Children: Examining the Change* (Washington, DC: Joint Center for Political and Economic Studies, 1990), p. 13.

114. Marcia Bok, *Civil Rights and the Social Programs of the 1960s* (Westport, CT: Praeger, 1992), p. 46.

115. Ibid., p. 47.

116. Katherine McFate, "Welfare Reform Short-Changed," *Focus* 18, no. 8 (August 1990), p. 7.

117. "Economic Empowerment Task Force," White House memorandum, Office of the Press Secretary, February 27, 1991.

118. For a summary and critique of H.O.P.E., see Frank Smizik, "Public Housing: It's Not Politically Correct," *Equal Times*, June 1991.

119. See "Expanding Choice and Opportunity for Individuals, Families, and Communities," fact sheet, Office of the Press Secretary, White House, February 27, 1991.

120. See Dick Thornburgh, "Economic Empowerment Task Force," Domestic Policy Control, White House memorandum, September 4, 1990.

121. Robert J. Lampman, *Ends and Means of Reducing Income Poverty* (Chicago: Markham Publishing, 1971), p. 64.

122. The figures for the poverty gap are from Sheldon H. Danziger, Robert H. Haveman, and Robert D. Plotnick, "Anti-poverty Policy: Effects on the Poor and the Nonpoor," in Danziger and Weinberg, *Fighting Poverty*, p. 59.

123. See David Futrelle, "Surplus Values," *In These Times* 18, no. 1 (November 29, 1993), p. 14.

124. Randy Abelda, "The Misogyny Behind Welfare Reform," *The Boston Globe* (December 29, 1993), p. 15.

125. Michael Abramowitz, "Doledrums," *The New Republic* 206 (March 30, 1992) pp. 16-18.

126. Penelope Lemov, "Putting Welfare on the Clock," *Governing* (November 1993), p. 30.

127. See "Enterprise and Empowerment Zones," background briefing paper, White House, May 4, 1993.

Chapter 3

1. John Kenneth Galbraith, *The Affluent Society* (London: Houghton Mifflin, 1958), p. 323.

2. Mollie Orshansky, "Counting the Poor: Another Look at the Poverty Profile," *Social Security Bulletin* 28, no. 1 (January 1965).

3. Isaac Shapiro, *Poverty in America* (Washington, DC: Center on Budget and Policy Priorities, October 1992).

4. Elizabeth Evanson, "Social and Economic Changes Since the Great Depression: Studies of Census Data, 1940s-1980s," *Focus* 11, no. 3 (Fall 1988).

5. George L. Beckford, *Persistent Poverty: Underdevelopment in Plantation Economics of the Third World* (London: Oxford University, 1972).

6. Sar A. Levitan and Isaac Shapiro, *Working but Poor: America's Contradiction* (Baltimore: The Johns Hopkins University Press, 1987), p. 25; also see Sar A. Levitan, *Programs in Aid of Poor* (Baltimore: The Johns Hopkins University Press, 1990), p. 7.

7. Ibid., p. 9.

8. Ibid.

9. Ibid.

10. Ibid., p. 21.

11. U.S. Bureau of the Census, *Money, Income and Poverty Status of Families and Persons in the U.S., 1989* (Washington, DC, 1990).

12. Isabel V. Sawhill, "Poverty and the Underclass," in *Challenges to Leadership: Economic and Social Issues for the Next Decade* (Washington, DC: The Urban Institute Press, 1988), p. 215.

13. Luxembourg Income Study, 1986.

14. Sawhill, "Poverty and the Underclass," p. 226.

15. U.S. General Accounting Office, *Poverty Trends, 1980-1988: Changes in Family Composition and Income Sources Among the Poor* (Washington, DC, September 1992), p. 29.

16. Dorothy B. James, *Poverty, Politics and Change* (Englewood Cliffs, NJ: Prentice-Hall, 1972).

17. Emory Burton, *The Poverty Debate: Politics and the Poor in America* (Westport, CT: Praeger, 1992), p. 14.

18. William H. Frey, *Metropolitan America: Beyond the Transition* (Washington, DC: Population Reference Bureau, July 1990), p. 36.

19. William P. O'Hare and Brenda Curry-White, *The Rural Underclass: Examination of Multiple-Problem Populations in Urban and Rural Settings* (Washington, DC: Population Reference Bureau, March 1992).

20. William J. Wilson, *The Truly Disadvantaged: The Inner City, the Underclass and Public Policy* (Chicago: The University of Chicago Press, 1987).

21. This finding is different from an earlier conclusion reported in the mid-seventies by sociologist Donald Warren in *Black Neighborhoods: An Assessment of Community Power* (Ann Arbor: University of Michigan Press, 1975). He found that black urban communities tended to reflect greater social class mixture (i.e., "social compression") than white communities. At the time he wrote his book, the black middle, working, and poor sectors tended to live in the same community to a much greater extent than in the current period.

22. Peter Dreier, "America's Urban Crisis: Symptoms, Causes, Solutions," *North Carolina Law Review* 71, no. 5 (June 1993), p. 1364.

23. Cited in W. E. B. Du Bois, *The Philadelphia Negro: A Social Study* (1899; reprint, New York: Schocken Books, 1976), p. 269.

24. U.S. Bureau of the Census, *Statistical Abstract of the United States: 1992* (Washington, DC, 1992), table 724.

25. Katherine McFate, *The Metropolitan Area Fact Book: Statistical Portrait of Blacks and Whites* (Washington, DC: Joint Center for Political and Economic Studies, 1988), p. 2.

26. Ibid.

27. Julia Teresa Quiroz, *Twenty-Two Hispanic Leaders Discuss Poverty* (Washington, DC: National Council of La Raza, November 1990), p. i.

28. Harriet Romo, *New Directions for Latino Public Policy Research* (Austin: The University of Texas, Center for Mexican American Studies and Inter-University Program Office, 1990).

29. Marta Van Haitsma, "The Underclass, Labor Force Attachment and Social Context: Are People of Mexican Origin Joining the Urban Underclass?" (Paper

delivered at the Midwest Sociological Association Meeting, St. Louis, Missouri, April 5 - 10, 1989), p. 1.

30. Jennifer Juarez Robles, "Hispanic Poverty: Hispanics Emerging as Nation's Poorest Minority Group," *Chicago Reporter* 17, no. 6 (June 1988), p. 1.

31. Raymond F. Clapp, "Spanish Americans of the Southwest," in *Poverty in America*, eds. Louis A. Ferman, Joyce L. Kornbluh, Alan Haber (Ann Arbor: University of Michigan Press, 1969).

32. Jeremiah Cotton, "Toward a Theory and Strategy for Black Economic Development," in *Race, Politics, and Economic Development: Community Perspectives*, ed. James Jennings (London: Verso Press, 1992).

33. Gerald D. Jaynes and Robin M. Williams, Jr. *A Common Destiny: Blacks and American Society* (Washington, DC: National Academy Press, 1988), p. 278.

34. Reynolds S. Farley and Walter R. Allen, *The Color Line and the Quality of Life in America* (New York: Oxford University Press, 1989).

35. Theodore Cross, *The Black Power Imperative: Racial Inequality and the Politics of Non-Violence* (New York: Faulkner Press, 1987), p. 480.

36. Andrew Hacker, *Two Nations: Black and White, Separate, Hostile and Unequal* (New York: Charles Scribner's Sons, 1992), p. 92.

37. McFate, *The Metropolitan Area Fact Book*, p. 10.

38. William R. Prosser, "The Underclass: Assessing What We Have Learned," *Focus* 13, no. 2 (Summer 1991), p. 4. Institute on Research and Poverty, University of Wisconsin, Madison.

39. William P. O'Hare, Kelvin Pollard, Taynia L. Mann, and Mary M. Kent, *African Americans in the 1990s* (Washington, DC: Population Reference Bureau, July 1990), p. 32.

40. Alfred N. Garwood, *Black Americans: A Statistical Sourcebook* (Boulder, CO: Numbers and Concepts, 1992), p. 261.

41. Lucius J. Barker, "Jesse Jackson's Candidacy in Political-Social Perspective: A Contextual Analysis," in *Jesse Jackson's 1984 Political Campaign*, eds. Lucius J. Barker and Ronald W. Walters (Chicago: University of Illinois Press, 1989), p. 6.

42. Gertrude S. Goldberg and Eleanor Kremin, *The Feminization of Poverty: Only in America?* (New York: Praeger, 1990), p. 1.

43. Harrell R. Rodgers, Jr. *Poor Women, Poor Families: The Economic Plight of America's Female-Headed Households* (Armonk, NY: M. E. Sharpe, 1990).

44. Mary Jo Bane, "Politics and Policies of the Feminization of Poverty," in *The Politics of Social Policy in the United States*, ed. Margaret Weir, Ann S. Orloff and Theda Skocpol (Princeton, NJ: Princeton University Press, 1988), p. 384.

45. Mary Jo Bane, "Household Composition and Poverty," in Sheldon H. Danziger and Daniel H. Weinberg, *Fighting Poverty: What Works and What Doesn't* (Cambridge, MA: Harvard University Press, 1986), pps. 214-230.

46. Harrell R. Rodgers, Jr., *The Cost of Human Neglect* (Armonk, NY: M.E. Sharpe, 1982).

47. Sonia M. Perez, "Puerto Rican Young Men and Economic Instability: Implications for Puerto Rican Family Poverty," (Paper prepared for the National Council of La Raza, Washington, DC, April 1992), p. 7.

48. Lawrence Mischel and David Frankel, *The State of Working America* (Armonk, NY: M. E. Sharpe, 1991), p. 184.

49. William Darity, Jr., et al. "Race and Inequality in the Managerial Age," in *African-Americans: Essential Perspectives*, ed. Wornie L. Reed (Westport, CT: Auburn House, 1993), p. 50.

50. Joyce E. Allen and Margaret C. Simms, "Is a New Yardstick Needed to Measure Poverty?" *Focus* 18, no. 2 (February 1990).

51. Jaynes and Williams, *A Common Destiny*, p. 281.

52. Frank Hobbs and Laura Lippman, *Children's Well-Being: An International Comparison* (Washington, DC: Center for International Research, 1990); see also *Education Week*, "The Growth of Single Parent Families," January 16, 1991.

53. Barry R. Schiller, *The Economics of Poverty and Discrimination* (Englewood Cliffs, NJ: Prentice-Hall, 1976), p. 100.

54. Mischel and Frankel, *The State of Working America*, p. 186.

55. National Council of La Raza, "Child Poverty Up Nationally, in 33 States, and in 84 Major Cities," *Poverty Project Newsletter* 4, no. 2 (Summer 1992).

56. Judith Weitz, *Kids Count Data Book* (Washington, DC: Center for Study of Social Policy, March 1992).

57. U.S. Bureau of the Census, *Statistical Abstract of the United States: 1992* (Washington, DC, 1992), table 718.

58. Mischel and Frankel, *The State of Working America*, p. 177.

59. David J. Eggebeen and Daniel T. Lichter, "Race, Family Structure, and Changing Poverty Among American Children," *American Sociological Review* 56, no. 6 (December 1991), p. 802.

60. U.S. Bureau of the Census, *Statistical Abstract: 1992*, table 719.

61. Mischel and Frankel, *The State of Working America*, p. 177; also see Suzanne M. Bianchi, *America's Children: Mixed Prospects* (Washington, DC: Population Reference Bureau, 1990).

62. Pérez, "Puerto Rican Young Men," p. 7.

63. U.S. Bureau of the Census, *Statistical Abstract: 1992*, table 721.

64. Scott Bass, "Poverty Sting Can Be Sharpest for Elderly," *Boston Globe*, August 16, 1992.

65. Ibid.

66. Burton, *The Poverty Debate*, p. 17.

67. U.S. Bureau of the Census, *Statistical Abstract: 1992*, table 721.

68. "Smaller Slices of the Pie: The Growing Economic Vulnerability of Poor and Moderate Income Americans," (Washington DC: Center on Budget and Policy Priorities, 1985).

69. Ibid., p. 7.

70. John L. Palmer and Isabel V. Sawhill, eds. *The Reagan Record: An Assessment of America's Changing Domestic Priorities* (Cambridge, MA: Ballinger, 1984).

71. Mischel and Frankel, *The State of Working America*, p. 169.

72. David T. Ellwood, *Poor Support* (New York: Basic Books, 1988).

73. U.S. Bureau of the Census, *Money, Income and Poverty Status*.

74. Ellwood, *Poor Support*, table 2.1.

75. Mischel and Frankel, *The State of Working America*, p. 177.

76. U.S. Bureau of the Census, *Workers with Low Earnings: 1964 to 1990* (Washington, DC, 1992).

77. Levitan and Shapiro, *Working but Poor*, p. 16.

78. Michael Harrington, with Robert Greenstein and Eleanor Holmes Norton, *Who Are the Poor: A Profile of the Changing Faces of Poverty in the United States,* reprint prepared for Justice for All, Washington, DC, 1987, p. 148.

79. Mischel and Frankel, *The State of Working America*, p. 116.

80. Ibid., p. 119.

81. Levitan and Shapiro, *Working but Poor*, p. 49.

82. Lawrence M. Mead, *The New Politics of Poverty* (New York: Basic Books, 1992).

Chapter 4

1. Karl Polanyi, *The Great Transformation: The Political and Economic Origin of Our Time* (Boston: Beacon Press, 1944), p. 91.

2. Ibid., p. 93.

3. W. E. B. Du Bois, "The Revelation of Saint Orgne the Damned," *W. E. B. Du Bois Speaks: Speeches and Addresses* ed. Philip S. Foner (New York: Pathfinder Press, 1970), p. 107.

4. William W. Goldsmith and Edward J. Blakely, *Separate Societies: Poverty and Inequality in U.S. Cities* (Philadelphia: Temple University Press, 1992).

5. Barry R. Schiller, *The Economics of Poverty and Discrimination* (Englewood Cliffs, NJ: Prentice-Hall, 1976), p. 40.

6. Lee Sigelman and Susan Welch, *Black Americans' View of Racial Inequality: The Dream Deferred* (New York: Cambridge University Press, 1991), p. 86.

7. Schiller, *The Economics of Poverty and Discrimination*, p. 40.

8. Michael Sherraden, *Assets and the Poor* (Armonk, NY: M. E. Sharpe, 1991), p. 35.

9. Chaim Isaac Waxman, *The Stigma of Poverty* (New York: Pergamon Press, 1983), p. 1.

10. Jay R. Mandel, *The Roots of Black Poverty: The Southern Plantation Economy After the Civil War* (Durham, NC: Duke University Press, 1978).

11. W. E. B. Du Bois, *Black Reconstruction in America 1860-1880* (1935; New York: Atheneum, 1985), p. 696.

12. Mandel, *The Roots of Black Poverty*, p. 121.

13. James Jennings and Monte Rivera, eds. *Puerto Rican Politics in Urban America* (Westport, CT: Greenwood Press, 1984).

14. Elizabeth H. Pleck, *Black Migration and Poverty, Boston 1865-1900* (New York: Academic Press, 1979), p. 199.

15. See Harold X. Connally, *A Ghetto Grows in Brooklyn* (New York: New York University Press, 1977); and Gilbert Osofsky, *Harlem: The Making of a Ghetto, Negro New York, 1890-1930* (New York: Harper and Row, 1966); and Kenneth L. Kusmer, *Black Cleveland 1870-1930* (Chicago:University of Illinois Press, 1976).

16. Cesar A. Iglesias, *Memorias de Bernardo Vega* (Puerto Rico: Ediciones Huracan, 1980).

17. Henry George, *Progress and Poverty: An Inquiry into the Cause of Industrial Depressions and of Increase of Want with Increase of Wealth* (1879; reprint, New York: Robert Schalkenbach Foundation, 1971).

18. Ibid., p. 296.

19. Stephen Thernstrom, *Poverty and Progress: Social Mobility in a Nineteenth Century City* (New York: Atheneum, 1969), p. 131.

20. William J. Wilson, *The Truly Disadvantaged: The Inner City, the Underclass, and Public Policy* (Chicago: The University of Chicago Press, 1987), p. 40; also see John D. Kasarda, "Urban Change and Minority Opportunities," in *The New Urban Poverty*, ed. Paul E. Peterson (Washington, DC: The Brookings Institute, 1985), p. 50.

21. Vilma Ortiz, "Latinos and Industrial Change in New York and Los Angeles," in *Hispanics in the Labor Force*, eds. Edwin Melendez, et al. (New York: Plenum Press, 1991), p. 125; also see John D. Kasarda, in *The New Urban Poverty*.

22. Jeanne E. Griffith, Mary J. Frase, John H. Ralph, *American Education: The Challenge of Change* (Washington, DC: Population Reference Bureau, December 1989), pp. 9 and 10; also see Dawn M. Beskerville, "Poverty vs. Academic Achievement," *Black Enterprise*, (March 1991), p. 37.

23. U.S. Bureau of the Census, *Statistical Abstract of the United States: 1992* (Washington, DC, 1992), table 725.

24. José E. Cruz, *Developing a Puerto Rican Agenda for Research and Research Advocacy* (Washington, DC: National Puerto Rican Coalition, June 1992), p. 7.

25. Norman Fainstein, "The Underclass/Mismatch Hypothesis as an Explanation for Black Economic Deprivation," *Politics and Society* 15, no. 4 (1986-87), p. 403.

26. Oscar Lewis, *La Vida: A Puerto Rican Family in the Culture of Poverty* (New York: Random House, 1966).

27. Edward C. Banfield, *The Unheavenly City* (Boston: Little, Brown & Co., 1973).

28. George Gilder, "The Collapse of the American Family," *The Public Interest*, no. 89 (Fall 1987), p. 20.

29. George Gilder, "The Nature of Poverty," in *Social Welfare Policy: Perspectives, Patterns and Insights*, ed. I. C. Colby (Chicago: Dorsey Press, 1989).

30. Manuel Carballo and Mary Jo Bane, *The State and the Poor in the 1980s* (Westport, CT: Auburn Publishing, 1984), p. xxi.

31. Lawrence M. Mead, *The New Politics of Poverty* (New York: Basic Books, 1992), p. 14.

32. Ibid., p. 145.

33. Ibid., p. 148

34. George Gilder, *Wealth and Poverty* (New York: Basic Books, 1981).

35. Ibid., p. 69.

36. Ibid., p. 71.

37. Lowell E. Galloway, *Poverty in America* (Columbus OH: Grid, 1973).

38. Ibid., p. 91.

39. Ibid., p. 67.

40. Ibid., p. 159.

41. William J. Wilson, "The Ghetto Underclass and the Social Transformation of the Inner City," *Black Scholar* 19, no. 3 (May/June 1988), p. 16.

42. Charles A. Valentine, *Culture and Poverty: Critique and Counter Proposals* (Chicago: The University of Chicago Press, 1968).

43. Kenneth B. Clark, *Dark Ghetto: Dilemmas of Social Power* (New York: Harper and Row, 1965), p. 130.

44. Valentine, *Culture and Poverty*, p. 82.

45. Ibid., p. 155.

46. Manning Marable, "The Contradictory Contours of Black Political Culture"; and Cornel West, "Race and Social Theory: Towards a Genealogical Materialist Analysis," in *The Year Left 2*, eds. Mike Davis, Michael Sprinker, Manning Marable and Fred Pfeil (London: Verso Press, 1987).

47. Robert L. Woodson, *On the Road to Economic Freedom* (Washington, DC: Regnery Gateway, 1987); Nathan Glazer, *The Limits of Social Policy* (Cambridge, MA: Harvard University Press, 1989).

48. Frances Fox Piven and Richard A. Cloward, *Regulating the Poor* (New York: Pantheon, 1971); Charles V. Hamilton, "A Patron-Recipient Relationship and Minority Politics in New York City," *Political Science Quarterly* 94, no. 2 (Summer, 1979).

49. Joseph Persky, Elliot Sclar, and Wim Wiewel, *Does America Need Cities?* (Washington, DC: Economic Policy Institute, 1991), p. 30.

50. Goldsmith and Blakely, *Separate Societies*, p. 11.

51. Ibid, p. 59.

52. Stanley Lieberson, *A Piece of the Pie: Blacks and White Immigrants Since 1880* (Berkeley: University of California Press, 1980).

53. Charles V. Hamilton, "Political Access, Minority Participation, and the New Normalcy," in *Minority Report: What Has Happened to Blacks, Hispanics, American Indians, and Other Minorities in the Eighties*, ed. Leslie W. Dunbar (New York: Pantheon Books, 1984), p. 8.

54. Gerald D. Suttles, *The Social Order of the Slum* (Chicago: The University of Chicago Press, 1968).

55. Mark Roseman, "How the Poor Would Remedy Poverty: A Review Essay," *Social Policy* 18, no. 4, (Spring 1988), p. 62.

56. Dennis Gilbert and Joseph A. Kahl, *The American Class Structure: A New Synthesis* (Chicago: Dorsey Press, 1987), p. 294.

57. Peter Dreier, "America's Urban Crisis: Symptoms, Causes, Solutions," *North Carolina Law Review* 71, no. 5 (June 1993), p. 1372.

58. Wilson, *The Truly Disadvantaged.*

59. David Osborne, *Laboratories of Democracy: A New Breed of Governor Creates Models for National Growth* (Cambridge, MA: Harvard Business School Press, 1990), p. 289.

60. Vijai P. Singh, "The Underclass in the United States: Some Correlates of Economic Change," *Sociological Inquiry* 61, no. 4 (November 1991), p. 509.

61. Rebecca M. Blank and Alan S. Blinder, "Macroeconomics, Income Distribution, and Poverty," in *Fighting Poverty: What Works and What Doesn't*, eds. Sheldon H. Danziger and Daniel H. Weinberg (Cambridge, MA: Harvard University Press, 1986), p. 189.

62. Ibid., p. 184.

63. James Thornton, Richard Agnello and Charles Link, "Poverty and Economic Growth: Trickle Down Peters Out," *Economic Inquiry* 16, no. 3 (1978), pp. 385-393.

64. Theodore Cross, *The Black Power Imperative* (New York: Faulkner, 1984).

65. U.S. Bureau of the Census, *Statistical Abstracts of the United States, 1992* (Washington, DC, 1992), table 724.

66. William J. Wilson, Robert Aponte, Joleen Kirscheman, and Lois J. O. Wocquaint, "The Ghetto Underclass and the Changing Structure of Urban Poverty," in *Quiet Riots: Race and Poverty in the United States*, eds. Fred Harris and Roger Wilkins (New York: Pantheon Books, 1988).

67. Brett Williams, "Poverty Among African American in the United States," *Human Organization* 51, no. 2 (1992), p. 167.

68. Mark J. Stern, "Poverty and Family Composition Since 1940," in *The Underclass Debate: Views from History*, ed. Michael B. Katz (Princeton, NJ: Princeton University Press, 1993), p. 221.

69. George, *Progress and Poverty*, p. 17.

70. "The Low Paid Worker," in *Poverty in America*, eds. Louis A. Ferman, Joyce L. Kornbluh, and Alan Haber (Ann Arbor: University of Michigan Press, 1969), p. 190.

71. Gabriel Kolko, *Wealth and Power in America: An Analysis of Social Class and Income Distribution* (New York: Praeger Publishers, 1962).

72. Barry Bluestone, "Lower Income Workers and Marginal Industries," in *Poverty in America*, eds. Ferman, Kornbluh, Haber.

73. Sar A. Levitan and Isaac Shapiro, *Working but Poor: America's Contradiction* (Baltimore: The Johns Hopkins University Press, 1987).

74. Isaac Shapiro, *No Escape: The Minimum Wage and Poverty* (Washington, DC: Center on Budget and Policy Priorities, 1987).

75. Linda R. Martin and Demetrios Giannaros, "Would a Higher Minimum Wage Help Poor Families Headed by Women?" *Monthly Labor Review* 113, no. 8 (August 1990), p. 36.

76. Ronald B. Mincy, "Raising the Minimum Wage: Effects on Family Policy," *Monthly Labor Review* 113, no. 7 (July 1990), p. 24.

77. Anthony Downs, "Who Are the Urban Poor," in *The Urban Economy* ed. Harold H. Hochman (New York: W. W. Norton and Co., 1976)

78. Carballo, *The State and the Poor*, p. xxii.

79. Ibid.

80. James E. Blackwell, *Youth Employment and Unemployment: Outreach Initiatives in Massachusetts and the City of Boston*, monograph. (Boston: William M. Trotter Institute, University of Massachusetts, 1987).

81. Douglas S. Massey and Nancy A. Denton, *American Apartheid: Segregation and the Making of the Underclass* (Cambridge, MA: Harvard University Press, 1993), p. viii.

82. Douglas S. Massey, "American Apartheid: Segregation and the Making of the Underclass," *Poverty and Race* 1, no. 4 (September 1992), p. 2.

83. Ibid., p. 4.

84. Mary Jo Bane, "Household Composition and Poverty," in *Fighting Poverty*, eds. Danziger and Weinberg, p. 209.

85. Ibid., p. 231.

86. Diana Pearce, "The Feminization of Poverty: Women, Work and Welfare," *Urban and Social Change Review* 11 (February 1978).

87. Mimi Abramovitz, *Regulating the Lives of Women: Social Welfare Policy from Colonial Times to the Present* (Boston: South End Press, 1989), p. 76.

88. Mary Jo Bane, "Politics and Policies of Feminization of Poverty," in *The*

Politics of Social Policy in the U.S., eds. Margaret Weir, Ann S. Orloff and Theda Skocpol (Princeton, NJ: Princeton University Press, 1988).

89. Barbara Ehrenreich, Holly Sklar and Karen Stollard, *Poverty and the American Dream: Women and Children First* (Boston: South End Press, 1983).

90. Ibid., p. 18.

91. Pearce, "The Feminization of Poverty," p. 34.

92. Julianne Malveaux, "The Political Economy of Black Women," in *Race, Politics and Economic Development: Community Perspectives*, ed. James Jennings (London: Verso Press, 1992).

93. Gertrude S. Goldberg and Eleanor Kremin, *The Feminization of Poverty: Only in America?* (New York: Praeger, 1990) p. 5.

94. Daniel P. Moynihan, *The Negro Family: The Case for National Action* (Washington, DC: U.S. Department of Labor, 1965).

95. Banfield, *The Unheavenly City*.

96. Reynolds Farley and Walter Allen, *The Color Line and the Quality of Life in America* (New York: Oxford University Press, 1989), p. 187.

97. Cynthia Rexroat, *The Declining Economic Status of Black Children: Examining the Change* (Washington, DC: Joint Center for Political and Economic Studies, 1990), p. 4.

98. Goldberg and Kremin, *The Feminization of Poverty*, p. 202.

99. Richard X. Chase, "Trends in Poverty Incidence and Its Rate of Reduction for Various Demographic Groups: 1947-1963," Unpublished Ph.D. dissertation, University of Maryland, 1966; *Collected Papers on Poverty Issues* 1, ed. Doris Yokelson (New York: Hudson Institute, June 1975).

100. Charles A. Murray, *Losing Ground: American Social Policy, 1950-1980* (New York: Basic Books, 1984); also see by Murray, "The Two Wars Against Poverty: Economic Growth and The Great Society," *The Public Interest*, no. 69 (Fall 1982).

101. Sigelman and Welch, *Black Americans: View of Racial Inequality*, p. 141.

102. Lawrence M. Mead, *Beyond Entitlement: The Social Obligations of Citizenship* (New York: Free Press, 1986).

103. Isabel V. Sawhill, "Poverty and the Underclass," in *Challenges to Leadership: Economic and Social Issues for the Next Decade* (Washington, DC: The Urban Institute Press, 1988), p. 220.

104. Adolph Reed, Jr. "The Underclass as Myth and Symbol: The Poverty of Discourse About Poverty," *Radical America* 24, no. 1 (Summer 1991).

105. William Darity, Jr. "Race and Inequality in the Managerial Age," in *African-Americans: Essential Perspectives*, ed. Wornie L. Reed (Westport, CT: Auburn House, 1993), p. 65.

106. William J. Wilson and Kathryn M. Neckerman, "Poverty and Family Structure: The Widening Gap Between Evidence and Public Policy Issues," in Danziger and Weinberg, *Fighting Poverty*, p. 248.

107. Ibid., see pps. 252-259.

108. Katherine McFate, *The Metropolitan Area Fact Book: Statistical Portrait of Blacks and Whites* (Washington, DC: Joint Center for Political and Economic Studies, 1988), p. 8.

109. "The Flip Side of Female-Headed Families: Black Adult Men," (Center for the Study of Social Policy, Washington, DC 1985), p. i.

110. Wilson and Neckerman, "Poverty and Family Structure," p. 256.

111. William A. Darity, Jr., Samuel L. Myers, William J. Sobol, and Emmett Carson, "How Useful Is the Black Underclass?" *Focus* 13, no. 2 (Summer 1991), p. 12, Institute on Research and Poverty, University of Wisconsin, Madison; also see William P. O'Hare, Kelvin M. Pollard, Taynia L. Mann, and Mary M. Kent, *African Americans in the 1990s* (Washington, DC: Population Reference Bureau, July 1991), p. 17.

112. Manning Marable, *How Capitalism Underdeveloped Black America* (Boston: South End Press, 1983); see chapters "The Black Poor" and "Black Prisoners."

113. Andrew Hacker, *Two Nations: Black and White, Separate, Hostile, and Unequal* (New York: Charles Scribner's Sons, 1992), p. 75.

114. Paul A. Baran and Paul M. Sweezy, *Monopoly Capital: An Essay on the American Economic and Social Order* (New York: Monthly Review Press, 1966), p. 279.

115. Herman George, Jr. "Black Americans, the 'Underclass' and the Subordination Process," *Black Scholar* 19, no. 3 (May/June 1988), p. 48.

116. Bette Woody, *Black Women in the Workplace: Impacts of Structural Change in the Economy* (Westport, CT: Greenwood Press, 1992), p. 9.

117. F. I. Ajanaku, M. L. Jackson, and T. S. Mosley, "Underdevelopment in the U.S. Labor Market: The Case of African American Female Workers," *The Urban League Review* 14, no. 2 (1990), pps. 29-41.

118. See Martin Luther King, Jr. "Martin Luther King Jr. Defines Black Power," *New York Times Magazine*, (June 11, 1967); and, Martin Luther King, Jr., *Where Do We Go from Here: Chaos or Community?* (Boston, MA: Beacon Press, 1968).

119. National Conference of Catholic Bishops, *Economic Justice for All: Pastoral Letter on Catholic Social Teaching and the U.S. Economy* (Washington, DC: National Conference of Catholic Bishops, 1986).

120. Stern, "Poverty and Family Composition," p. 230.

121. Robin D.G. Kelley, "The Black Poor and the Politics of Opposition in an New South City, 1929-1970," in *The Underclass Debate*, ed. Katz, p. 332.

Chapter 5

1.   Paul Jacobs, "America's Schizophrenic View of the Poor," in *Poverty: Views from the Left*, eds. Jeremy Larner and Irving Howe (New York: William Morrow and Co., 1968), p. 40.

2.   David T. Ellwood, *Poor Support* (New York: Basic Books, 1988), p. 19.

3.   Dierdre Martinez, "States Offer New Strategies for Welfare Policy," *Poverty Project Newsletter* 4, no. 2 (Washington, DC: National Council of La Raza, Spring 1992).

4.   Jacob Hollander, *The Abolition of Poverty* (Boston: Houghton Mifflin, 1914).

5.   Amos G. Warner, *American Charities* (1894; reprint, New York: Russell and Russell, 1971).

6.   Fred Block, Richard A. Cloward, Barbara Ehrenreich, and Frances Fox Piven, *The Mean Season: The Attack on the Welfare State* (New York: Pantheon Books, 1987), p. xi.

7.   Harrell R. Rodgers, Jr. *Poor Women, Poor Families: The Economic Plight of America's Female-Headed Households* (Armonk, NY: M. E. Sharpe, 1986), p. 104.

8.   Ira Katznelson and Mark Kesselman, *The Politics of Power: A Critical Introduction to American Government* (New York: Harcourt, Brace, and Jovanovich, 1975), p. 434.

9.   Herbert London, "Historical Attitudes Toward Poverty," (New York: The Hudson Institute, 1975), p. 1-33.

10.   Joe R. Feagin, *Subordinating the Poor: Welfare and American Beliefs* (Englewood Cliffs, NJ: Prentice-Hall, 1975), p. 52.

11.   Dorothy B. James, *Poverty, Politics and Change* (Englewood Cliffs, NJ: Prentice-Hall, 1972), p. 21.

12.   Ibid.

13.   Michael B. Katz, *The Undeserving Poor: From the War on Poverty to the War on Welfare* (New York: Pantheon, 1989).

14.   Jane Axinn and Mark J. Stern, *Dependency and Poverty: Old Problems in a New World Order* (Lexington, MA: Lexington Books, 1988), p. 5.

15.   Daniel P. Moynihan, "Our Poorest Citizens — Children," *Focus* 11, no. 1 (Spring 1988), p. 5.

16.   Michael Sherraden, *Assets and the Poor* (Armonk, NY: M. E. Sharpe, 1991), p. 54.

17.   The use of Medicaid funds to pay for abortions was denied under the Hyde Amendment, which prohibited this unless a woman's life was in danger.

18.   John Silber, *Straight Shooting: What's Wrong with America and How to Fix It* (New York: Harper and Row, 1989), p. 204.

19.   Steven Kelman, *Making Public Policy: A Hopeful View of Government* (New York: Basic Books, 1987), p. 250.

20.   Douglas J. Besharou and Karen Baehler, "The Perverse Federal Incentives for Welfare Cuts," *Governing* (February, 1993), p. 11.

21.   Ibid.

22.   Eugene Smolensky, Eric Everhouse, and Siobhan Reilly, "Welfare Reform in California" (Berkeley: University of California, Institute of Governmental Studies Press, 1992).

23.   David B. Robertson and Dennis Judd, *The Development of American Public Policy* (Glenview, IL: Scott, Foresman and Co., 1989), p. 226.

24.   Sar A. Levitan and Isaac Shapiro, *Working but Poor: America's Contradiction* (Baltimore: The Johns Hopkins University Press, 1988), p. 100.

25.   Sar A. Levitan, *Programs in Aid of the Poor* (Baltimore: The Johns Hopkins University Press, 1990), p. 30.

26.   Sheldon H. Danziger and Daniel H. Weinberg, *Fighting Poverty: What Works and What Doesn't* (Cambridge, MA: Harvard University Press, 1986), p. 4.

27.   David T. Ellwood and Lawrence H. Summers, "Poverty in America: Is Welfare the Answer or the Problem?" in *Fighting Poverty*, eds. Danziger and Weinberg, p. 84.

28.   Mimi Abramovitz, "Everyone Is on Welfare: The Role of Redistribution in Social Policy Revisited," *Social Work* 28, no. 6 (November/December 1983), p. 441; also see Richard M. Titmus, "The Role of Redistribution in Social Policy," *Social Security Bulletin* 28, no. 1 (June 1965); and Robert D. Plotnick and Felicity Skidmore,

Progress Against Poverty: A Review of the 1964-1974 Decade. (New York: Academic Press, 1975).

29. Sherraden, *Assets and the Poor*, pps. 54-70.

30. Ibid., p. 69.

31. Christopher Howard, "The Hidden Side of the American Welfare State," *Political Science Quarterly* 108, no. 3 (Fall 1993), p. 404.

32. Fay L. Cook and Edith J. Barrett, *Support for the American Welfare State* (New York: Columbia University Press, 1992), p. 218.

33. Center on Budget and Policy Priorities, "Welfare Rules Should Stop Penalizing Married Families," press release disseminated via Handsnet Electronic Bulletin Board, November 8, 1993.

34. Ibid.

35. William F. McMahon, Marc Thomas, Sammie B. White, and John F. Zipp, "Do School Attendance Rates Vary Between AFDC and Non-AFDC Supported Children?" (The Urban Research Center, University of Wisconsin, Milwaukee, September 28, 1989).

36. See "The Rush to Reform: 1992 State AFDC Legislative and Waiver Activities" (Center for Law and Social Policy, Washington, DC, February 21, 1992).

37. Ibid., p. 3.

Chapter 6

1. Peter Weiss, "The Human Rights of the Underclass," in *Racism and the Underclass*, eds. George W. Shepherd, Jr., and David Penna (Westport, CT: Greenwood Press, 1991), p. 15.

2. David Matza, "The Disreputable Poor," in *Social Structure and Mobility in Economic Development*, eds. Neil Smelser and Seymour M. Lipset (Chicago: Aldine, 1966).

3. Adolph Reed, Jr. "The Underclass as Myth and Symbol: The Poverty of Discourse About Poverty," *Radical America* 24, no. 1 (Summer 1991).

4. Gunnar Myrdal, "The War on Poverty," *New Republic* 150 (February 8, 1964), p. 14.

5. See James Jennings, "Measuring the Quality of Municipal Services in Black Urban Communities: Unresolved Research Issues," *Urban Resources* 2, no. 3 (Spring 1985).

6. Mosei Ostrogorski, *Democracy and the Organization of Political Parties* (1901; reprint, Chicago: Quadrangle Books, 1964).

7. W. E. B. Du Bois, *The Philadelphia Negro: A Social Study* (1899; reprint, New York: Schocken Books, 1976), p. 311.

8. Alfred Marshall, *Principles of Economics* (London: MacMillan and Co., 1924), pp. 2-4.

9. Henry George, *Progress and Poverty: An Inquiry into the Cause of Industrial Depressions and of Increase of Want with Increase of Wealth, the Remedy* (1879; reprint, New York: Robert Schalkenback Foundation, 1971), p. 7.

10. John R. Alexander, "Poverty, Fear and Continuity: An Analysis of the Poor in Late Eighteenth-Century Philadelphia," in *The Peoples of Philadelphia*, ed. Allen F. Davis and Mark H. Haller (Philadelphia: Temple University Press, 1974), p. 16.

11. Thomas J. Sugrue, "The Structure of Urban Poverty: The Reorganization of Space and Work in Three Periods of American History," in *The Underclass Debate: Views from History*, ed. Michael B. Katz. (Princeton, NJ: Princeton University Press, 1993), p. 85.

12. Reed, "The Underclass as Myth and Symbol," p. 22.

13. Mimi Abramovitz, "Putting an End to Doublespeak About Race, Gender, and Poverty," *Social Work* 36, no. 5 (September 1991), p. 383.

14. Michael B. Katz, "Reframing the 'Underclass' Debate," in *The Underclass Debate: Views from History* (Princeton, NJ: Princeton University Press, 1993), p. 473.

15. Isabel V. Sawhill, "Poverty and the Underclass," in *Challenges to Leadership: Economic and Social Issues for the Next Decade* (Washington, DC: The Urban Institute Press, 1988), p. 227.

16. William R. Prosser, "The Underclass: Assessing What We Have Learned," *Focus* 13, no. 2 (Summer 1991), p. 3.

17. Martha Van Haitsma, "The Underclass, Labor Force Attachment and Social Context: Are People of Mexican Origin Joining the Urban Underclass?" (Paper delivered at the Midwest Sociological Association Meeting, St. Louis, Missouri, April 5 - 10, 1989), p. 3; also see by same author "A Contextual Definition of the Underclass" *Focus* 12, no. 1 (Spring/Summer 1989), p. 27, Institute on Research and Poverty, University of Wisconsin, Madison.

18. Reed, "The Underclass as Myth and Symbol," p. 24.

19. Christopher Jencks, *Rethinking Social Policy: Race, Poverty and the Underclass* (Cambridge, MA: Harvard University Press, 1992), see pps. 143-203.

20. Sawhill, *Poverty and the Underclass*, p. 229.

21. See *Black Scholar* 19, no. 3 (May/June, 1988).

22. Troy Duster, "Social Implication of the 'New' Black Urban Underclass," ibid., p. 3.

23. Julianne Malveaux, "Race, Class, and Black Poverty," ibid., p. 18.

24. Michael B. Katz, ed., *The Underclass Debate: Views from History* (Princeton, NJ: Princeton University Press, 1993), p. 473.

25. John Grove and Jiping Wu, "Who Benefited from the Gains of Asian-Americans, 1940-1980?" in *Racism and the Underclass*, eds. Shepherd and Penna, p. 107.

26. Nicholas Lemann, "The Origins of the Underclass," *The Atlantic Monthly*, July 1986.

27. Ibid., p. 67.

28. Robert Hunter, *Poverty* (New York: Macmillan, 1904), pp. 318-340.

29. Ibid.

30. Edward C. Banfield, *The Unheavenly City* (Boston: Little, Brown and Co., 1973).

31. John Silber, *Straight Shooting: What's Wrong with America and How to Fix It* (New York: Harper and Row, 1989), p. 203.

32. Ibid.

33. William J. Wilson, *The Truly Disadvantaged: The Inner City, the Underclass and Public Policy* (Chicago: The University of Chicago Press, 1987), p. 151.

34. See William J. Wilson, "Another Look at 'The Truly Disadvantaged'," *Political Science Quarterly* 106, no. 4 (Winter 1991-92), p. 654.

35. Mack H. Jones, "The Black Underclass as Systemic Phenomenon," in *Race, Politics, and Economic Development: Community Perspectives*, ed. James Jennings (London: Verso Press, 1992), p. 54.

36. Charles P. Henry, "Understanding the Role of the Underclass: The Role of Culture and Economic Progress," in ibid, p. 83.

37. Andrés Torres and Clara E. Rodriguez, "Latino Research and Policy: The Puerto Rican Case," in *Hispanics in the Labor Force*, eds. Edwin Melendez, Clara Rodriguez, and Janis Barry Figueroa (New York: Plenum Press, 1991).

38. Sidney M. Wilhelm, *Black in a White America* (Cambridge, MA: Schenkman, 1983); and see Wilson, *The Truly Disadvantaged*.

39. Thomas F. Jackson, "The State, the Movement, and the Urban Poor: The War on Poverty and Political Mobilization in the 1960s," in *The Underclass Debate*, ed. Katz, p. 407.

40. Kenneth B. Clark, *Dark Ghetto: Dilemmas of Social Power* (New York: Harper and Row, 1965).

41. Douglas G. Glasgow, *The Black Underclass: Poverty, Unemployment and Entrapment of Ghetto Youth* (San Francisco: Jossey-Bass Publishers, 1980).

42. Marta Tienda, "Puerto Ricans and the Underclass Debate," *Annals*, 501 (January 1989); also see Andrés Torres and Clara E. Rodriguez, "Latino Research and Policy."

43. Torres and Rodriguez, "Latino Research and Policy," p. 256.

44. Edwin Melendez, "Commentary," in *The Puerto Rican Exception: Persistent Poverty and the Conservative Social Policy of Linda Chavez*, eds. Angelo Falcon and John Santiago (New York: Institute for Puerto Rican Policy, 1992), p. 11.

Chapter 7

1. Robin D. G. Kelley, "The Black Poor and the Politics of Oppression in a New South City, 1929-1970," in *The Underclass Debate: Views from History*, ed. Michael B. Katz (Princeton, NJ: Princeton University Press, 1993), p. 294.

2. Jason DeParle, "Suffering in the Cities Persists as U.S. Fights Other Battles," *New York Times*, January 27, 1991; Peter Applebome, "Urban Blight Worsens but Many Never Feel It," *New York Times*, January 28, 1991; and Applebome and DeParle, "Ideas to Help Poor Abound, but a Consensus Is Wanting," *New York Times*, January 29, 1991.

3. Julia Teresa Ortiz, *Twenty-Two Hispanic Leaders Discuss Poverty* (Washington, DC: National Council of La Raza, November 1990), p. 9.

4. Cited in Cynthia Duncan, ed. *Rural Poverty in America* (Westport, CT: Auburn House, 1992), p. 248.

5. Marcia Bok, *Civil Rights and the Social Programs of the 1960s* (Westport, CT: Praeger, 1992), p. 150.

6. See Ann Withorn, *Serving the People: Social Services and Social Change* (New York: Columbia University, 1984).

7. Curt Lamb, *Political Power in Poor Neighborhoods* (Cambridge, MA: Schenkman, 1975), see his chapter, "Does Militancy Pay?"

8. Gloria Bonilla-Santiago, *Organizing Puerto Rican Migrant Farmworkers* (New York: Peter Lang Publishing, 1988).

9. William W. Goldsmith and Edward J. Blakely, *Separate Societies: Poverty and Inequality in U.S. Cities* (Philadelphia: Temple University Press, 1992), p. 139.

10. Thomas F. Jackson, "The State, the Movement, and the Urban Poor: The War on Poverty and Political Mobilization," in *The Underclass Debate*, ed. Katz, p. 404.

11. For a sampling of the available literature, see Joan Ecklein, *Community Organizing* (New York: John Wiley and Sons, 2nd. ed., 1984); Ann Withorn, *Serving the People: Social Services and Social Change* (New York: Columbia University Press, 1984); Guida West and Rhoda Lois Blumberg, *Women and Social Protest* (New York: Oxford University Press, 1990); Frances Fox Piven and Richard A. Cloward, *Poor People's Movements: Why They Succeed, How They Fail* (New York: Pantheon Books, 1977); Betty K. Mandell, *Welfare in America: Controlling the Dangerous Classes* (Englewood Cliffs, NJ: Prentice-Hall, 1975); Ralph C. Gomes and Linda F. Williams, *From Exclusion to Inclusion* (Westport, CT: Greenwood Press, 1992); and Fred Block, et al., *The Mean Season: The Attack on the Welfare State* (New York: Pantheon Books, 1987).

12. See Katz, *The Underclass Debate*; and Gary Delgado, *Organizing the Movement: The Roots and Growth of ACORN* (Philadelphia: Temple University Press, 1986).

13. Walter Korpi, "Approaches to the Study of Poverty in the United States: Critical Notes from a European Perspective," in *Poverty and Public Policy: An Evolution of Social Science Research*, ed. Vincent J. Covello (Cambridge, MA: Schenkman 1980).

14. Ibid., p. 308.

15. Katz, *The Underclass Debate*, p. vii.

16. Susan H. Hertz, *The Welfare Mothers' Movement: A Decade of Change for Poor Women?* (Washington, DC: University Press of America, 1981), p. 31.

17. Peter Marris, "Strategy and Context: Reflections on the Community Planning and Action Programs," report to Rockefeller Foundation, January 1991, p. 39.

18. Korpi, "Approaches to the Study of Poverty," p. 308.

19. Fiona Williams, *Social Policy: A Critical Introduction* (New York: Blackwell Publishers, 1989).

20. Joyce Gelb and Alice Sardell, "Strategies for the Powerless: The Welfare Rights Movement in New York City," *American Behavioral Scientist* 17, no. 4 (March/April 1974).

21. Thomas Sowell, *Civil Rights: Rhetoric and Reality* (New York: William Morrow, 1984), pps. 29-35.

22. Katherine O'Sullivan, "Approaching Poverty in the U.S.," *Social Problems* 38, no. 4 (November 1991), p. 429.

23. Frances Fox Piven and Richard A. Cloward, "Preface," in *The National Welfare Rights Movement: The Social Protest of Poor Women*, ed. Guida West (New York: Praeger, 1981), p. vii.

24. Steve Suitts, "Empowerment and Rural Poverty," in Duncan, *Rural Poverty in America*, p. 236.

25. Ibid., p. 241.

26. Kenneth B. Clark and Jeanette Hopkins, *A Relevant War Against Poverty* (New York: Harper and Row, 1970), p. vii.

27. Lillian B. Rubin, "Maximum Feasible Participation: The Origins, Implications, and Present Status," *The Annals* 385 (September 1969), p. 15.

28. Eric S. Einhorn and John Logue, *Modern Welfare States: Politics and Policies in Social Democratic Scandinavia* (New York: Praeger, 1989), p. 13.

29. See D. L. McMurry, *Coxey's Army: A Study of the Industrial Movement of 1894* (1929; reprint, Seattle: University of Washington Press, 1968); and Carlos Schwantes, *Coxey's Army: An American Odyssey* (Lincoln: University of Nebraska Press, 1985).

30. Robert Brisbane, *The Black Vanguard* (Valley Forge, PA: Judson Press, 1969); see especially pps. 133-158.

31. Michael Harrington, *The New American Poverty* (New York: Penguin Books, 1985) , p. 18.

32. Michael Harrington, *Fragments of the Century* (New York: Saturday Review Press, 1973), p. 94.

33. Martin Luther King, Jr. *Where Do We Go from Here? Chaos or Community* (New York: Harper and Row, 1967), p. 36.

34. James W. Button, *Blacks and Social Change: Impact of the Civil Rights Movement in Southern Communities* (Princeton, NJ: Princeton University Press, 1989), p. 3.

35. See James Jennings, "Community Control: A Grassroots Response," *Journal of Education* 161, no. 4 (Fall 1979).

36. Michael B. Fabricant and Steve Burghardt, *The Welfare State Crisis and the Transformation of Social Service Work* (Armonk, NY: M. E. Sharpe, 1992), p. 15.

37. West, *The National Welfare Rights Movement*, p. 39.

38. Hertz, *The Welfare Mothers Movement*, p. 186.

39. Clark and Hopkins, *A Relevant War Against the Poor*, p. 195.

40. Coalition on Human Needs, "How the Poor Would Remedy Poverty," (Washington, DC: Author, 1988).

41. See Kathryn Edin, "Summing the Welfare System: How AFDC Recipients Make Ends Meet in Chicago," *Social Problems* 38, no. 4 (November 1991).

42. Timothy Saasta, "Community Change," *Social Policy* 19, no. 2, (Fall 1989), p. 61.

43. See Jacqueline Pope, "The Colonizing Impact of Public Service Bureaucracies in Black Communities," in *Race, Politics and Economic Development: Community Perspectives*, ed. James Jennings (London: Verso Press, 1992); and Jacqueline Pope, "Women and Welfare Reform," *Black Scholar* 19, no. 3 (May/June 1988).

44. Frances Fox Piven and Richard A. Cloward, *Poor People's Movements: Why They Succeed How They Fail* (New York: Pantheon Books, 1979).

45. David Wagner and Marcia B. Cohen, "The Power of the People: Homeless Protesters in the Aftermath of Social Movement Participation," *Social Problems* 38, no. 4 (November 1991).

46. Interview with Massachusetts gubernatorial candidate Dorothy Stevens; see also "Candidate Raps Vote Counting," *The Boston Globe*, February 22, 1991.

47. Camille Colastosti, "Governor Shreds Michigan Safety Net," *The Guardian*, December 4, 1991.

48. Robin Epstein, "Workfair," *In These Times*, March 8, 1993, p. 18.

49. Ibid., p. 19.

50. Deb Konechne, "Hard Times: Fighting for Basic Needs," *Forward Motion* 12, no. 5 (December 1993), p. 14.

51. James Jennings, "Major Themes and Strategies Reflected in Boston Foundation's 'Persistent Poverty' Roundtable," report submitted to Boston Foundation Persistent Poverty Project, June 18, 1992.

52. Martin Kilson, "Black Social Classes and Intergenerational Poverty," *Public Interest*, no. 64, (Summer 1981), p. 69.

53. Andrés Torres, "Labor Market Segmentation: African-American and Puerto Rican Labor in New York City, 1960-1980," *The Review of Black Political Economy* 20, no. 1 (Summer 1991).

54. Barbara Ehrenreich, Holly Sklar, and Karen Stollard, *Poverty and the American Dream: Women and Children First* (Boston: South End Press, 1983).

55. Charles V. Hamilton, "Urban Economics, Conduit Colonialism, and Public Policy," *Black World* 21, no. 10 (October 1972).

56. Ibid., p. 41.

57. Steven Wiseman, *The Politics of Human Services: A Radical Alternative to the Welfare State* (Boston: South End Press, 1984).

58. Ibid., p. 16.

Chapter 8

1. See Isabel V. Sawhill, "Poverty and the Underclass," in *Challenges to Leadership: Economic and Social Issues for the Next Decade* (Washington, DC: The Urban Institute Press, 1988); also see Katherine McFate, "First World Poverty," (Washington, DC: Joint Center for Political and Economic Studies, November 1991).

2. Ibid., p. 217.

3. Peter Townsend, *Poverty in the United Kingdom: A Survey of Household Resources and Standards of Living* (Berkeley: University of California Press, 1979).

4. Ibid., p. 893.

5. Eric S. Einhorn and John Logue, *Modern Welfare States: Politics and Policies in Social Democratic Scandinavia* (New York: Praeger, 1989), p. 141.

6. Mark J. Stern and Jane Axinn, *Dependency and Poverty: Old Problems in a New World Order* (Lexington, MA: Lexington Books, 1988), p. 1.

7. Richard M. Titmus, *Social Policy: An Introduction* (New York: Pantheon Books, 1975).

8. Harold L. Wilensky and Charles N. Lebeaux, *Industrial Society and Social Welfare* (New York: Free Press, 1965), p. xviii.

9. Harrell R. Rodgers, Jr. *Poor Women, Poor Families: The Economic Plight of America's Female-Headed Households* (Armonk, NY: M. E. Sharpe, 1990), p. 104.

10. Bette Woody, *Black Women in the Workplace: Impact of Structural Changes* (Westport, CT: Greenwood Press, 1992), p. 164.

11. Gertrude S. Goldberg and Eleanor Kremin, *The Feminization of Poverty: Only in America?* (New York: Praeger, 1990), p. 8.

12. Katherine McFate, "Poverty, Inequality and the Crisis of Social Policy,"

(Washington, DC: Joint Center for Political and Economic Studies, 1991), p. 21.

13. Maria J. Honratty, "Why Canada Has Less Poverty," *Social Policy* 23, no. 1 (Summer 1992), p. 32.

14. Samuel Bowles, David M. Gordon and Thomas Weiskopf, *After the Wasteland: A Democratic Economics in the Year 2000* (Armonk, NY: M. E. Sharpe, 1991), p. 6.

15. Honratty, "Why Canada Has Less Poverty," p. 34.

16. Michael D. Reagan, *Regulation: The Politics of Policy* (New York: Little, Brown, and Co., 1987), p. 11; also see Charles F. Andrain, *Politics and Economic Policy in Western Democracies* (North Scituate, MA: Duxbury Press, 1980), p. 23.

17. Woody, *Black Women in the Workplace*, p. 16

18. Christopher Schenk and Elaine Bernard, "Social Unionism: Labor as a Political Force," *Social Policy* 23, no. 1 (Summer 1992), p. 38.

19. Einhorn and Logue, *Modern Welfare States*, p. 231.

20. Nathan Glazer, *The Limits of Social Policy* (Cambridge, MA: Harvard University Press, 1988).

21. Rodgers, *Poor Women, Poor Families*, p. 103.

22. Massimo Paci, "Long Waves in the Development of Welfare Systems," in *Changing Boundaries of the Political: The Evolving Balance Between State and Society, Public and Private in Europe*, ed. Charles S. Maier (Cambridge: Cambridge University Press, 1987), p. 180.

23. Paul Starr and Ellen Immergut, "Health Care and the Boundaries of Politics," in ibid.

24. Margaret Weir, "Ideas and Politics: The Acceptance of Keynesianism in Britain and the United States," in *The Political Power of Economic Ideas*, ed. Peter Hall (Princeton, NJ: Princeton University Press, 1989).

25. John Maynard Keynes, *The General Theory of Employment, Interest and Money* (1936; reprint, New York: Harcourt, Brace, & Jovanovich, 1965).

26. Weir, *Ideas and Politics*.

27. Ibid., p. 59.

28. Gertrude S. Goldberg, "Canada: Bordering on the Feminization of Poverty," *The Feminization of Poverty*, eds. Goldberg and Kremin, p. 81.

29. Jane Axinn, "Japan: A Special Case," in ibid., p. 101.

30. Martin Rein and Hugh Heclo, "What Welfare Crisis? A Comparison Among the United States, Britain and Sweden," *The Public Interest*, no. 33 (Fall 1973), p. 80.

31. John R. Freeman, *Democracy and Markets: The Politics of Mixed Economies* (Ithaca, NY: Cornell University Press, 1989).

32. Hilda Scott, *Working Your Way to the Bottom: The Feminization of Poverty* (London: Pandora Press, 1984), p. viii.

33. Douglas E. Ashford, *Policy and Politics in Britain: The Limits of Consensus* (Philadelphia: Temple University Press, 1981), p. 201.

34. Fiona Williams, *Social Policy: A Critical Introduction* (New York: Blackwell Publishers, 1989).

35. Seymour Lipset, *The First New Nation: The U.S. in Historical and Comparative Perspective* (New York: Basic Books, 1963), p. 339; also see David Roediger, *The Wages of Whiteness* (London: Verso Press, 1991).

36. Fiona Williams, *Social Policy*, p. 35.

37. Fred C. Pampel and John B. Williamson, *Age, Class, Politics and the Welfare State* (London: Cambridge University Press, 1989), p. xv.

38. Kenneth J. Newbeck and Jack L. Roach, "Racism and Poverty Policies," in *Impacts of Racism on White Americans*, eds. Benjamin P. Bowser and Raymond G. Hunt (Beverly Hills, CA: Sage Publications, 1981), p. 156.

39. See Louis Kushnick, "Race and Politics in Europe," Occasional Paper no. 21. (Boston: University of Massachusetts, William Monroe Trotter Institute, 1993).

Conclusion

1. Robin Toner, "Rethinking Welfare," *The New York Times*, July 5, 1992; this was the first article in a series of six titled "Politics of Welfare: Focusing on the Problems."

2. Joe R. Feagin, *Subordinating The Poor: Welfare and American Beliefs* (Englewood Cliffs, NJ: Prentice-Hall, 1975), p. 1.

3. Cited in Barry R. Schiller, *The Economics of Poverty and Discrimination* (Englewood Cliffs, NJ: Prentice-Hall, 1976), p. 39.

4. Cited in Fred Block et al. *The Mean Season: The Attack on the Welfare State* (New York: Pantheon Books, 1987), p. 26.

5. Paul Jacobs, "America's Schizophrenic View of the Poor," in *Poverty: Views from the Left*, eds. Jeremy Lerner and Irving Howe (New York: William Morrow and Co., 1968).

6. David R. Robertson and Dennis R. Judd, *The Development of American Public Policy* (Glenview, IL: Scott, Foresman and Co., 1989), p. 207.

7. Henry George, *Progress and Poverty: An Inquiry into the Cause of Industrial Depressions and of Increase of Want with Increase of Wealth* (1879; reprint, New York: Robert Schalkenback Foundation, 1971).

8. Charles E. Silberman, "Beware the Day They Change Their Minds," *Fortune*, November 1965, pp. 151 and 262.

9. Harold L. Hodgkinson, *The Same Client: The Demographics of Education and Service Delivery Systems* (Washington, DC: Institute for Educational Leadership, Inc./Center for Demographic Policy, 1989), p. 8.

10. Louis A. Ferman, Joyce L. Kornbluh and Alan Haber, eds. *Poverty in America* (Ann Arbor: University of Michigan Press, 1969).

11. William W. Goldsmith and Edward J. Blakely, *Separate Societies: Poverty and Inequality in U.S. Cities* (Philadelphia: Temple University Press, 1992), p. 106.

12. Michael Harrington, "Introduction," in *Poverty in America*, eds. Ferman, et al., p. ix.

13. David McKay, *Domestic Policy and Ideology* (Cambridge, England: Cambridge University Press, 1989).

14. Ann Withorn, "Playing by the Rules: Clinton and Poor People," *Radical America* 24, no. 3 (Spring 1993).

15. M. E. Hawkesworth, *Theoretical Issues in Policy Analysis* (New York: State University of New York Press, 1988); see the chapter, "The Political Cost of Policy Presuppositions: The Case of Workfare."

16. Jane Axinn and Mark J. Stern, *Dependency and Poverty: Old Problems in a New World Order* (Lexington, MA: Lexington Books, 1988).

17. Herbert Gans, "Functions of Poverty," *American Journal of Sociology* 78, no. 2 (September 1972); also see by the same author, *People, Plans and Policies: Essays on Poverty, Racism and Other National Urban Problems* (New York: Columbia University Press, 1991).

18. Gans, "Functions of Poverty," p. 282.

19. Feagin, *Subordinating the Poor*, pps. 120-126.

20. Irene I. Blea, *La Chicana and the Interaction of Race, Class, and Gender* (New York: Praeger, 1972), p. 122.

21. Irene I. Blea, *Toward a Chicano Social Science* (New York: Praeger, 1988), p. 37.

22. Michael B. Katz, *The Undeserving Poor: From the War on Poverty to the War on Welfare* (New York: Pantheon Books, 1989), p. 7.

23. Andrés Torres and Clara E. Rodriguez, "Latino Research and Policy: The Puerto Rican Case," in *Hispanics in the Labor Force*, eds. Edwin Melendez, Clara Rodriguez, and Janis Barry Figueroa (New York: Plenum Press, 1991), p. 261.

24. James Jennings, ed., *Race, Politics, and Economic Development: Community Perspectives* (London: Verso Press, 1992).

25. Thomas B. Edsall, *The New Politics of Inequality* (New York: Penguin Books, 1984), p. 39.

26. Ibid.

27. David G. Gil and Eva A. Gil, *Toward Social and Economic Justice* (Cambridge, MA: Schenkman Publishing, 1985), p. xiii; also see an earlier work by William J. Wilson, *Power, Racism and Privilege.* (New York: The Free Press, 1973), p. 5.

28. Fay L. Cook and Edith J. Barrett, *Support for the American Welfare State* (New York: Columbia University Press, 1992), p. 164.

29. Harrell R. Rodgers, Jr., *Racism and Inequality: The Policy Alternatives* (San Francisco: W. H. Freeman and Co., 1975), p. 187.

30. Douglas Glasgow, *The Black Underclass: Poverty, Unemployment and Entrapment of Ghetto Youth* (New York: Vintage Books, 1980), p. 196.

31. Leslie W. Dunbar, *Minority Report* (New York: Pantheon Books, 1984), p. x; also see the last chapter, "Government for All the People."

32. Gus Hall, *Fighting Racism* (New York: International Publishers, 1985); and Lloyd Hogan, *Afro-Centric Principals of Black Political Economy* (Boston: Routledge and Kegan Paul, 1984).

33. Hogan, *Principles of Black Political Economy*, p. 1.

34. David G. Gil, *Unraveling Social Policy* (Cambridge, MA: Schenkman Publishing, 1981), p. 213.

35. Jacqueline Pope, *Biting the Hand That Feeds Them: Organizing Women on Welfare at the Grassroots* (New York: Praeger, 1989).

36. Jill Quadagno, "Race, Class and Gender in the U.S. Welfare State: Nixon's Failed Family Assistance Plan," *American Sociological Review* 55 (February 1990), p. 16.

37. Ann Withorn, *Serving the People: Social Services and Social Change* (New York: Columbia University Press, 1984), p. 167.

38. James Jennings, "Blacks, Politics, and the Human Service Crisis," in *Race, Politics, and Economic Development: Community Perspectives*, ed. James Jennings (London: Verso Press, 1992), p. 99.

39. Manuel Carballo and Mary Jo Bane, *The State and the Poor in the 1980s* (Westport, CT: Auburn House, 1984), p. 303.

40. Daniel Patrick Moynihan, "Three Problems in Combatting Poverty," in *Poverty in America*, ed. Margaret S. Gordon (San Francisco: Chandler Publishing, 1965), p. 41.

41. Nathan Glazer, "A Sociologist's View of Poverty," in ibid., p. 20.

42. Charles V. Hamilton and Dona C. Hamilton, "The Dual Agenda: Social Policies of Civil Rights Organizations: New Deal to the Present," (Paper delivered at the Annual Meeting of the American Political Science Association, Washington, DC, August 29-September 1, 1991).

43. Ibid., p. 16.

44. Martin Luther King, Jr. "Martin Luther King Defines 'Black Power,'" *New York Times Magazine*, June 11, 1967, p. 26.

45. Ibid., p. 103.

46. David G. Gil and Eva A. Gil, *Toward Social and Economic Justice.* (Cambridge, MA: Schekman Publishing Co., 1985), p. xiii.

INDEX

Abelda, Randy, 51, 177n
abortion for poor women, 112, 187n
Abramovitz, Michael, 177n
Abramovitz, Mimi, 14, 21-22, 98, 117,
    124-25, 171n, 172n, 184n, 187n,
    189n
Accelerated Public Works Act (1962),
    26
Ackerman, Frank, 41, 175n
Agnello, Richard, 93, 183n
Agriculture, Department of:
    estimates of food expenditures, 11-
    12
Aid to Families with Dependent
    Children (AFDC), 14, 20, 26, 28, 34,
    36, 39, 42, 45-47, 49, 51, 52, 75, 76,
    86, 102, 112, 114, 116, 117, 119, 120,
    121-22, 150, 165
Ajanaku, F. I., 105, 186n
Alexander, John R., 124, 188n
Alinsky, Saul, 33, 174n
Allen, Henry, 27, 34, 173n, 174n
Allen, Joyce E., 10, 170n, 180n
Allen, Walter R., 67, 100, 179n, 185n
American Enterprise Institute for
    Public Policy Research, 116
Anderson, Martin, 21, 172n
Andrain, Charles F., 194n
Anti-poverty expenditures, 116, 117,
    119;
    programs, 136, 140
Aponte, Robert, 184n
Applebome, Peter, 133, 190n
Area Redevelopment Act (1961), 26,
    27
Ashford, Douglas E., 154, 194n
Aristophanes, 161
Arkansas Community Organizations
    for Reform Now (ACORN), 135,
    191n
Axinn, Jane, 18, 112, 148, 153, 160-61,
    171n, 187n, 193n, 194n, 196n

Baehler, Karen, 116, 187
Baldwin, James, 55

Bane, Mary Jo, 69, 71, 86, 98, 99, 179n,
    182n, 184n, 197n
Banfield, Edward C., 38, 85-86, 87, 88,
    99, 128-29, 175n, 182n, 185n, 189n
Baran, Paul A., 104, 186n
Barker, Lucius J., 68, 179n
Barrett, Edith J., 24, 120, 164, 172n,
    188n, 196n
Bass, Scott, 73, 180n
Beck, Bertram M., 15, 171n
Beckford, George L., 56, 177n
Berkowitz, Edward D., 20, 21, 172n
Berlin, George, 176n
Bernard, Elaine, 151, 194n
Besharou, Douglas J., 116, 187n
Beskerville, Dawn M., 182n
Bismark, Otto von, 139, 147
Blackwell, James E., 97, 184n
Blakely, Edward J., 79, 90, 134, 160,
    181n, 183n, 191n, 195n
Blank, Rebecca M., 93, 183n
Blea, Irene I., 162, 196n
Blinder, Alan S., 93, 183n
Block, Fred, 110, 186n, 191n, 195n
Bluestone, Barry, 95, 184n
Blumberg, Rhoda Lois, 135, 191n
Boger, John Charles, 75, 173n
Bok, Marcia, 48-49, 134, 176n, 190n
Bonilla-Santiago, Gloria, 134, 190n
Boston Foundation, 144, 193n;
    Persistent Poverty Project, 169n
Bowles, Samuel, 194n
Bowser, Benjamin P., 195n
Brisbane, Robert, 192n
Browning, Robert X., 20, 39-40, 172n,
    175n
Bullock, Charles S., 40, 175n
Bureau of Economic Analysis, 94
Bureau of Labor Statistics, 10, 99, 170n
Burghardt, Steve, 140-41, 192n
Burton, Emory, 62, 178n, 180n
Bush administration, 44-50;
    attitudes toward poverty, 19;
    attitudes toward welfare, 42, 50, 52;

policies and programs, 34, 44, 133, 139, 160
Button, James W., 140, 192n

Campagna, Anthony S., 41, 175n
Carballo, Manuel, 86, 96-97, 166, 182n, 184n, 197n
Carson, Emmett, 186n
Carter administration, 36-38; attitudes toward poverty, 37-38; policies and programs, 34, 36-38, 42
Casey (Annie E.) Foundation, 71
Census Bureau (U.S.), 5, 6, 9, 12, 16,17, 56, 58, 60, 61, 64, 65, 68, 72, 76-77, 94, 100, 170n, 171n, 178n, 180n, 182n, 183n
Center for Constitutional Rights, 123
Center for Law and Social Policy, 122, 188n
Center for Social Policy Studies (George Washington Univ.), 6
Center for the Study of Social Policy, 71, 103
Center on Budget and Policy Priorities, 16, 17, 55, 74, 121, 171n, 177n, 184n, 188n
Chase, Richard X., 101, 185n
child nutrition programs (1971), 34
Clapp, Raymond F., 67, 179n
Clark, Kenneth B., 89, 97, 131, 138, 182n, 190n, 192n
Clinton administration, 4, 50-53; attitudes toward poverty, 19, 160; attitudes toward welfare, 144; policies, 36
Cloward, Richard A., 15, 43, 135, 137, 142, 171n, 176n, 183n, 186n, 191n, 192n
Coalition for Basic Human Needs, 143
Coalition on Human Needs, 142, 192n
Cohen, Marcia B., 143, 192n
Colasanto, Diane, 170n
Colastosti, Camille, 192n
Colby, I. C., 171n
Commission on the Status of Blacks in America, 70
Committee for Research on the Urban

Underclass, 136
Committee on Juvenile Delinquency and Crime (1961), 26
Community Action Programs, 28
Community Mental Health Centers Act (1963), 165
Community Opportunity Act (1991), 49-50
Comprehensive Employment and Training Program Act (CETA, 1973), 34, 35, 36, 40
Congress for a Working America (CFWA), 143
Congressional Budget Office, 117
Connally, Harold X., 82, 181n
Cook, Fay L., 24, 120, 164, 172n, 188n, 196n
Corbett, Thomas, 176n
Cotton, Jeremiah, 67, 179n
Council of Economic Advisors, 11, 38, 41
Covello, Vincent J., 191n
"Coxey's Army," 14, 139-40, 192n
Cross, Theodore, 67, 93-94, 179n, 183n
Cruz, Josè E., 47, 85, 176n, 182n
Curry-White, Brenda, 178n

Danziger, Sheldon H., 28, 44, 103, 117, 173n, 175n, 176n, 177n, 179n, 183n, 185n, 187n
Darity, William A., Jr., 104, 180n, 185n, 186n
Davis, Allen F., 188n
Davis, Mike, 183n
Dawson, Richard E., 25, 173n
Delgado, Gary, 135, 142, 191n
Demonstration Cities and Metropolitan Development Act (1966), 28
Denton, Nancy A., 97, 184n
DeParle, Jason, 10, 133, 169n, 170n, 190n
Derthwick, Martha, 174n
Dolbeare, Kenneth, 174n
Donahue, John, 40, 175n
Downs, Anthony, 37-38, 96, 170n, 175n, 184n
Dreier, Peter, 63, 92, 178n, 183n

Du Bois, W. E. B., 55, 79, 81, 124, 178n, 181n, 188n
Dunbar, Leslie W., 29-30, 164, 173n, 183n, 196n
Duncan, Cynthia M., 4, 169n, 190n
Duster, Troy, 127, 189n

earned income tax credit (1975), 35, 36, 53, 119
Ecklein, Joan, 135, 191n
Economic Opportunity, Office of, 32, 142
Economic Opportunity Act (1964), 28-29, 32
Economic Policy Institute, 90
Economic Recovery Tax Act, 39
Edelman, Murray J., 174n
Edin, Kathryn, 192n
Edsall, Thomas B., 163, 196n
Eggebeen, David J., 72, 180n
Ehrenreich, Barbara, 99, 145, 185n, 186n, 193n
Einhorn, Eric S., 139, 148, 151, 192n, 193n, 194n
Eisenhower administration, 24-25, 27
Ellwood, David T., 76, 109, 117, 118, 180n, 186n, 187n
Engles, Friedrich, 9
enterprise zones, 41, 43, 44, 49, 51-53, 177n
Epstein, Robin, 192n, 193n
Evanson, Elizabeth, 177n
Everhouse, Eric, 187n

Fabricant, Michael B., 140, 192n
Fainstein, Norman, 85, 182n
Fair Labor Standards Act (1938), 21
Falcon, Angelo, 190n
Family Assistance Plan (FAP, 1969), 34, 36, 37
Family Support Act (1988), 42, 45, 46-49, 51
Farley, Reynolds S., 12, 16-17, 67, 100, 170n, 171n, 179n, 185n
Feagin, Joe R., 111, 157, 162, 187n, 195n, 196n

Federal Emergency Relief Administration (1933), 20
Ferman, Louis A., 14, 29, 160, 170n, 173n, 179n, 184n, 195n
Figueroa, Janis Barry, 196n
Food Stamp Act (1964), 28
food stamp program, 12, 16, 33-34, 39, 42, 76, 114, 117, 118, 119, 162, 163
Ford administration, 27, 35-36, 38, 40
Ford Foundation, 26, 44, 142
Fordham Institute for Innovation in Social Policy, 34
Frankel, David M., 7, 17, 18, 70, 71, 72, 74-75, 76, 171n, 179n, 180n, 181n
Franklin, John Hope, 172n
Frase, Mary J., 182n
Frazier, E. Franklin, 89, 98
Freeman, John R., 153, 194n
Frey, William H., 178n
Friedman, Milton, 15, 171n
Froelich, Fran, 133
Fuchs, Victor, 13, 170n
Funiciello, Theresa, 37, 175n
Futrelle, David, 50, 177n

Galbraith, John Kenneth, 12-13, 55, 170n, 177n
Galloway, Lowell E., 88, 182n
Gans, Herbert, 161-62, 196n
Garwood, Alfred N., 179n
Gary, Lawrence E., 13, 170n
Gelb, Joyce, 137, 191n
General Accounting Office, 6, 62, 170n, 178n
George, Henry, 79, 82-83, 95, 124, 158, 181n, 184n, 188n, 195n
George, Herman, Jr., 105, 186n
German Social Democratic Party, 139
Giannaros, Demetrios, 96, 184n
Gil, David G., 163, 165, 167, 196n, 197n
Gil, Eva A., 163, 167, 196n, 197n
Gilbert, Dennis, 92, 183n
Gilbert, Neil, 23, 27, 172n, 173n
Gilder, George, 86, 87, 157, 158, 182n
Ginsberg, Carl, 174n
Gladwin, Thomas, 31, 173n

Glasgow, Douglas G., 131, 164, 190n, 196n
Glazer, Nathan, 2, 151, 167, 169n, 183n, 194n, 197n
Goldberg, Gertrude S., 69, 99, 100, 152-53, 179n, 185n, 193n, 194n
Goldsmith, William W., 79, 90, 134, 160, 181n, 183n, 191n, 195n
Goldwater, Barry S., 42
Gomes, Ralph C., 135, 191n
Gordon, David M., 194n
Gordon, Margaret S., 172n, 197n
Gould, Russell, 51
Grant, Nancy L., 23, 172n
"Gray Areas Project," 26
Great Depression, the, 14, 20, 22, 95, 140, 152
"Green Book, The," 6
Greenstein, Robert, 16, 18, 24, 171n, 172n, 181n
    See also: Center on Budget and Policy Priorities
Greenstone, David, 35, 174n
Griffith, Jeanne E., 182n
Grove, John, 127, 169n, 189n

Haber, Alan, 170n, 179n, 184n, 195n
Hacker, Andrew, 67, 104, 179n, 186n
Haitsma, Marta Van, 66, 126, 178n, 189n
Hall, Gus, 164, 196n
Haller, Mark H., 188n
Hamilton, Charles V., 15, 20, 23, 91, 145-46, 167, 171n, 172n, 183n, 193n, 197n
Hamilton, Dona C., 20, 23, 167, 171n, 172n, 197n
Harrington, Michael, 9, 10, 12, 25, 77-78, 140, 147, 160, 170n, 173n, 181n, 192n, 195n
Harris, Fred, 184n
Harris, Robert, 37, 174n
Hatch, Kathlyn, 169n
Haveman, Robert H., 37, 174n, 177n
Hawkesworth, M. E., 42, 160, 176n, 195n
Head Start Program, 28, 30

Health and Human Services, Department of, 110
health insurance (national), 53, 97
Heclo, Hugh, 33, 153, 174n, 194n
Henry, Charles P., 129, 130, 190n
Heritage Foundation, 15, 16
Hertz, Susan H., 31, 136, 141, 173n, 191n, 192n
Hibbs, Douglas, 175n
Hobbes, Thomas, 86
Hobbs, Frank, 70, 180n
Hobsbawn, E. J., 169n
Hochman, Harold H., 184n
Hodgkinson, Harold L., 195n
Hogan, Lloyd, 164-65, 196n
Hollander, Jacob, 110, 186n
Homeownership and Opportunity for People Everywhere (HOPE), 49
Honratty, Maria J., 149, 194n
Hopkins, Harold: see WPA
Hopkins, Jeanette, 138, 192n
housing, low-income, 38, 118, 119, 145-46
Housing Act (1937), 114-15; (1949), 21; (1954), 24-25
Housing and Urban Development, Department of (HUD), 139, 176n
Housing Law (1968), 167
Howard, Christopher, 120, 188n
Howard, Donald S., 172n
Howe, Irving, 174n, 195n
Humane Society, 157
Hunt, Raymond G., 195n
Hunter, Robert, 9, 10, 128, 170n, 189n

Iglesias, Cesar A., 82, 181n
Immergut, Ellen, 152, 194n
income maintenance, 37, 119, 148
Institute for Puerto Rican Policy, 190n
Institute of Race Relations (London), 6
Institute for Research on Poverty, 125
Institute for the Study of Social Change (Univ. of California), 127

Jackson, M. L., 105, 186n
Jackson, Thomas F., 130, 134, 190n, 191n

Jacob, Herbert, 173n
Jacobs, Paul, 109, 158, 186n, 195n
James, Dorothy B., 22, 62, 111-12, 172n, 178n, 187n
Jamison-White, Leatha, 6
Jaynes, Gerald D., 63, 67, 84, 179n, 180n
Jencks, Christopher, 126, 189n
Jennings, James, 81, 163, 166, 181n, 185n, 188n, 190n, 192n, 193n, 196n, 197n
Jewell, K. Sue, 36, 39, 174n, 175n
Job Corps (1964), 28, 40
Job Training Partnership Act (JTPA), 28, 40, 44
Job Opportunities and Basic Skills (JOBS) program, 46-47
Johnson administration, 27-33, 138, 139, 140; see also: Kerner Commission;
    attitudes toward poverty, 30, 35, 166;
    compared to Roosevelt's "New Deal," 31-33;
    "Great Society," 27, 30, 93, 115, 138, 161;
    "War on Poverty," 27, 40, 115, 130, 138, 166
Joint Center for Political and Economic Studies, 48, 66, 70, 100, 102, 176n, 178n, 185n, 193n, 194n
Jones, Mack H., 129-30, 190n
Judd, Dennis R., 42, 117, 175n, 187n, 195n

Kahl, Joseph A., 92, 183n
Kain, John F., 38, 175n
Kasarda, John D., 6, 182n
Katz, Michael B., 14, 22, 112, 125, 127, 135, 158, 162, 170n, 172n, 184n, 186n, 187n, 189n, 190n, 191n, 196n
Katznelson, Ira, 111, 187n
Kelley, E. W., 172n, 173n
Kelley, Robin D. G., 106, 133, 186n, 190n
Kelman, Steven, 115, 187n
Kemp, Jack, 139, 176n

Kennedy administration, 25-27, 32, 140, 166
Kennedy, Robert F., 139
Kent, Mary M., 179n, 186n
Kerner Commission (National Advisory Commission on Civil Disorders), 31, 75, 173n
Kesselman, Mark, 111, 187n
Keynes, John Maynard, 22, 41, 152, 160, 172n, 194n
Kiang, Peter, 169n
Kilson, Martin, 145, 193n
King, Martin Luther, Jr., 26, 87, 105-106, 140, 167, 186n, 192n, 197n
Kirscheman, Joleen, 184n
Knavitz, Sanford, 173n
Kolko, Gabriel, 10, 95, 170n, 184n
Konechne, Deb, 193n
Kornbluh, Joyce L., 179n, 184n, 195n
Korpi, Walter, 135, 136, 191n
Kremin, Eleanor, 69, 99, 100, 152-53, 179n, 185n, 193n, 194n
Kushnick, Louis V., 6, 155, 195n
Kusmer, Kenneth, 82, 181n

Laffer, Alfred, 41
"Laffer's Curve," 41
Lamb, Curt, 134, 190n
Lampman, Robert J., 9, 27, 50, 170n, 173n, 177n
Larner, Jeremy, 174n
"learnfare," 121-22
Lebeaux, Charles N., 148-49, 193n
Leman, Nicholas, 128, 129, 189n
Lemov, Penelope, 52, 177n
Lerner, Jeremy, 195n
Levitan, Sar A., 6, 28-29, 56, 58, 77, 78, 95, 116, 117, 173n, 177n, 178n, 180n, 181n, 184n, 187n
Levy, Frank, 37, 174n
Lewis, Oscar, 85, 182n
Lichter, Daniel T., 72, 180n
Lieberson, Stanley, 91, 183n
Lindsay, Lawrence B., 41, 175n
Link, Charles, 93, 183n
Lippman, Laura, 70, 180n
Lipset, Seymour, 188n, 194n

Listokin, David, 176n
Lloyd George, David, 27
Logue, John, 139, 148, 151, 192n, 193n, 194n
London, Herbert, 111, 187n
Lowi, Theodore J., 33, 174n, 175n
Luxembourg Income Study, 56, 178n

Maier, Charles S., 194n
Malveaux, Julianne, 99, 127, 185n, 189n
Mandel, Jay R., 81, 83, 181n
Mandell, Betty R., 135, 173n, 191n
Mann, Taynia L., 179n, 186n
Manpower Development and Training Act (1962), 26-27
Manpower Development Research Corporation, 47
Marable, Manning, 89, 104, 183n, 186n
Marris, Peter, 30, 136, 173n, 191n
Marshall, Alfred, 124, 157, 188n
Martin, Linda R., 96, 184n
Martinez, Dierdre, 186n
Marx, Karl, 123
Massachusetts Human Services Coalition, 143
Massey, Douglas S., 97-98, 184n
Matza, David, 123, 188n
McCart, Linda, 46, 176n
McDonald, Dwight, 25, 173n
McFate, Katherine, 49, 67, 177n, 178n, 179n, 185n, 193n
McKay, David, 20, 37, 160, 171n, 174n, 195n
McMahon, William F., 188n
McMurry, D. L., 192n
Mead, Lawrence M., 43, 78, 86-87, 101, 175n, 181n, 182n, 185n
Medicaid, 165;
    eligibility, 12, 23;
    personnel, 162;
    welfare subsidy, 14, 16, 17-18, 24, 28, 39, 112, 114, 119, 120, 187n
Medicare:
    benefits, 20, 23, 24, 28, 113, 117, 141;
    in calculations of income, 16;
    personnel, 162

Melendez, Edwin, 131-32, 190n, 196n
Mellon, Andrew W., 41, 175n
Mill, John Stuart, 19
Miller, S. M., 15, 32, 171n, 174n
Mincy, Ronald B., 96, 184n
minimum wage, 21, 78, 95, 96, 142
Miringoff, Marc L., 34, 174n
Mischel, Lawrence, 7, 17, 18, 70, 71, 72, 74-75, 76, 171n, 179n, 180n, 181n
Mobilization for Youth (MFY), 26
Morone, James A., 32, 173n
Morris, Michael, 45, 48, 176n
Mosley, T. S., 105, 186n
Moynihan, Daniel Patrick, 2, 29, 35, 98, 99, 110, 166, 167, 169n, 173n, 174n, 185n, 187n, 197n
Murray, Charles A., 42, 101, 158, 175n, 185n
Myers, Samuel L., 186n
Myrdal, Gunnar, 123, 188n

National Advisory Commission on Civil Disorders: see Kerner Commission
National Association for the Advancement of Colored People (NAACP), 167
National Conference of Catholic Bishops, 106, 186n
National Council of La Raza, 66, 70, 178n, 179n, 180n, 186n, 190n
National Puerto Rican Coalition, 23, 47
National Urban League, 167
National Welfare Rights Organization (NWRO), 141, 142, 165
Neckerman, Kathryn M., 102, 103, 104, 185n, 186n
Neighborhood Youth Corps, 28
Newbeck, Kenneth J., 154, 195n
Nixon administration:
    attitudes toward poverty, 34-35, 37-38, 42, 157;
    policies and programs, 27, 33-35, 40
Norton, Eleanor Holmes, 181n

O'Hare, William P., 39, 67-68, 118,

175n, 178n, 179n, 186n
Older Americans Act (1965), 28
Omnibus Budget Reconciliation Act
   (OBRA), 38-39, 42
Orloff, Ann S., 179n, 185n
Orshansky, Mollie, 11-12, 55, 170n,
   177n
Ortiz, Julia Teresa, 190n
Ortiz, Vilma, 84, 182n
Osborne, David, 92, 93, 183n
Osofsky, Gilbert, 82, 181n
Ostrogorski, Mosei, 123, 157, 188n
O'Sullivan, Katherine, 137, 191n

Paci, Massimo, 151-52, 194n
Palmer, John L., 180n
Pampel, Fred C., 154, 195n
Pearce, Diana, 98, 99, 184n, 185n
Penna, David, 169n, 188n, 189n
Perez, Sonia M., 70, 72-73, 179n, 180n
Persky, Joseph J., 38, 90, 175n, 183n
Peterson, Paul E., 35, 174n, 182n
Pfeil, Fred, 183n
Piven, Frances Fox, 15, 43, 135, 137,
   142, 171n, 176n, 183n, 186n, 191n,
   192n
Pleck, Elizabeth H., 82, 181n
Plotnick, Robert D., 16, 117, 171n,
   177n, 187n
Polanyi, Karl, 79, 181n
Pollard, Kelvin M., 179n, 186n
Poor Law Commission (1834), 158
"poor laws," 21, 111
poor people:
   dependent upon welfare, 31, 34, 48,
      51, 52, 101-102, 158;
   "flawed character" of, 14, 42, 51, 64,
      78, 80, 82, 85-89, 109-110, 111, 121,
      128, 144, 146, 157, 158, 160;
   proposal for geographical dispersal
      of, 37-38;
   "undeserving," 50, 112, 124, 153-54,
      155, 158; see also Katz, Michael B.
Poor People's March on Washington:
   see King, Martin Luther, Jr.
Poor People's United Fund (1990), 133
Pope, Jacqueline, 142, 165, 192n, 196n

Population Reference Bureau, 63, 118
poverty:
   among African Americans, 19, 29,
      35, 44, 49, 55-82, 84-87, 88, 91, 93-
      94, 100, 105, 112, 123, 125, 130-31,
      140, 144, 145, 158-59, 163, 178n;
   among Asian Americans, 4, 57, 58,
      105, 127, 140, 144;
   among children, 71-73, 100, 121-22,
      144, 149;
   among the elderly, 19, 43, 66, 73-74,
      144, 149, 154;
   among Latinos and Hispanics, 2, 3,
      4, 6, 19, 23, 29, 35, 44, 47, 55-78, 84,
      91, 94, 100, 105, 112, 123, 131, 134,
      144, 159, 162-63, 182n;
   among Native Americans, 62;
   among Puerto Ricans, 81, 82, 85,
      131, 140, 145, 181n, 182n;
   among whites, 3, 55-78, 144, 145,
      178n;
   and civil rights movement, 138, 140,
      166-67;
   and discrimination, 1, 39, 44, 49, 96-
      98, 164;
   and distribution, 162;
   and race, 2, 3, 19, 32, 49, 52, 55-78,
      96-98, 137, 152-55;
   and women, 98-101, 102, 112, 137,
      152-53, 162, 165; see also:
      Goldberg, Gertrude S.; Rodgers,
      Harrell R., Jr.; Kremin, Eleanor
   causes of:
   cultural deprivation, 89;
   demographics, 95-95, 98, 101, 141;
   disintegration of family structure,
      35, 69-71, 81, 86, 98-101, 102-104,
      111;
   ethos, or group attitudes and
      attributes, 81, 85-86, 88, 128;
   "flawed character" of poor people:
      see poor people, "flawed
      character" of ;
   individual's weaknesses, 83-84,
      111, 146, 157;
   low wages, 95-96;
   macro-economics, 90-95;

non-ownership of land, 82-83;
public assistance bureaucracies, 89-90;
racism, 96-98; see also: poverty and discrimination;
"social isolation," 88, 92-93, 95;
systemic, 83, 91, 147-48;
characteristics of, 55-78;
definitions of:
food expenses, 9, 11;
"Fuchs' point," 13;
income, 10, 11, 12, 17, 37, 43, 57, 67-68, 75, 78;
minimum standard of living, 10, 50;
relative criteria, 14, 18, 126;
relative deprivation, 13;
relative vs. absolute, 147;
myths about, 3, 142-43;
demographics of, 6, 9, 55, 57, 69, 71-72, 73-74;
in the Midwest, 59;
in the Northeast, 58-59, 71, 81, 83-84;
in rural areas, 4, 62-63; see also: Duncan, Cynthia;
in the South, 10, 48, 60, 64, 81, 138, 145;
in the West, 60;
effects on wealthy, 1;
estimates of, 16, 43, 62, 63, 66-67, 74, 76-77;
measurements of, 9-18, 55-56, 93, 124-27;
"persistent," 56, 79-107, 134;
solutions to:
education reform, 140, 144;
empowerment, 133-34, 144-45, 155, 164-65, 166;
grassroots organizations, 143-44;
increases in minimum wage, 142;
individual responsibility, 144;
jobs and wages, 142, 145;
militancy, 134, 137;
public education to reduce stereotyping, 144;
redistribution of wealth, 146, 166;
reproductive rights, 145;
universal child care, 145;
U.S. compared to European nations, 7, 56-57, 70, 100-101, 110, 135, 136-37, 139, 147, 149-55
Program for Better Jobs and Income (PBJI), 36
Prosser, William R., 67, 125, 179n, 189n
Public Welfare Amendments (1962), 25-26, 157

Quadagno, Jill, 165, 196n
Quiroz, Julia Teresa, 178n

Ralph, John H., 182n
Reagan, Michael D., 150, 194n
Reagan administration, 38-44, 74;
attitudes toward poverty, 19, 42;
attitudes toward welfare, 39, 41-42, 50, 141;
"New Federalism" of, 38-39, 42, 160;
policies and programs, 24, 28, 34, 160
Rector, Robert, 171n
Reed, Adolph, Jr., 1, 3, 102, 123, 124, 125, 126, 169n, 185n, 188n, 189n
Reed, Wornie L., 180n, 185n
Reilly, Siobhan, 187n
Rein, Martin, 30, 153, 173n, 194n
Rexroat, Cynthia, 176n, 185n
Riis, Jacob, 10
Rivera, Monte, 81, 181n
Rivera-Fournier, Alberto, 172n
Roach, Jack L., 154, 195n
Robertson, David B., 42, 117, 175n, 187n, 195n
Robinson, James A., 25, 173n
Robles, Jennifer Juarez, 66, 179n
Roby, Pamela, 15, 32, 171n, 174n
Rockefeller Foundation, 136, 191n
Rodgers, Harrell R., Jr., 35-36, 39, 46, 47, 69, 110-11, 149, 151, 164, 174n, 176n, 179n, 187n, 193n, 194n, 196n
Rodriguez, Clara E., 130, 131, 163, 190n, 196n

Roedigger, David, 194n
Rolodner, Fernie R., 173n
Romo, Harriet, 66, 178n
Roosevelt administration:
    attitudes toward poverty, 32, 42;
    compared to Johnson's "Great
        Society," 31-33;
    New Deal, 1, 19-24, 31-33, 161, 167;
    policies and programs, 21, 64;
    unemployment during, 20
Roseman, Mark, 91, 183n
Rowntree, B. Seebohm, 9, 109, 110,
    169n
Rubin, Lillian B., 26, 139, 173n, 192n
Ryan, John A., Fr., 10

Saasta, Timothy, 192n
Sagara, Carlton, 169n
Santiago, John, 190n
Sardell, Alice, 137, 191n
Sawhill, Isabel V., 56, 62, 101, 125, 126,
    178n, 180n, 185n, 189n, 193n
Schenk, Christopher, 151, 194n
Schiller, Barry R., 1, 13, 71, 80, 110,
    169n, 170n, 180n, 181n, 195n
Schwantes, Carlos, 192n
Sclar, Elliot, 90, 183n
Scott, Hilda, 153, 194n
Shapiro, Isaac, 56, 77, 78, 95, 117, 177n,
    180n, 181n, 184n, 187n
Shaw, George Bernard, 1
Shephard, George W., Jr., 169n, 188n,
    189n
Sherraden, Michael, 9, 80, 112, 119-20,
    170n, 181n, 187n, 188n
Shriver, Sargeant, 142
Sigelman, Lee, 2, 80, 101, 169n, 181n,
    185n
Silber, John, 115, 129, 187n, 189n
Silberman, Charles, E., 158, 195n
Sills, D. L., 169n
Simms, Margaret C., 10, 170n, 180n
Singh, Vijai P., 93, 183n
Skidmore, Felicity, 16, 117, 171n, 187n
Sklar, Holly, 99, 145, 185n, 193n
Skocpol, Theda, 23, 172n, 179n, 185n
Smelser, Neil, 188n

Smith, Adam, 14, 170n
Smizik, Frank, 177n
Smolensky, Eugene, 187n
Sobol, William J., 186n
social insurance, 20
Social Science Research Council, 6,
    125, 135-36
Social Security Act (1935), 20, 22, 113,
    114
Social Security Administration (SSA),
    23
Social Security benefits, 23, 24, 34, 97,
    113, 117-18, 121, 141, 147-48, 150
Southern Regional Council, 134
Sowell, Thomas, 137, 158, 191n
Sprinkler, Michael, 183n
Starr, Paul, 152, 194n
Starr, Roger, 38, 175n
State and Local Fiscal Assistance Act
    (1972), 34, 35
Stegman, Michael A., 176n
Stern, Mark J., 18, 24, 95, 106, 112, 148,
    160-61, 171n, 172n, 184n, 186n,
    187n, 193n, 196n
Sternlieb, George, 176n
Stevens, Dorothy, 143, 192n
Stoesz, David, 175n
Stollard, Karen, 99, 145, 185n, 193n
Storey, James R., 37, 174n
Subsidized School Lunch Program,
    114
Sugrue, Thomas J., 124, 189n
Suitts, Steve, 134, 138, 191n
Sullivan, Charles, 169n
Sum, Andrew, 176n
Summers, Lawrence H., 117, 187n
Supplemental Security Income (SSI),
    23, 24, 114, 119
supply-side economics, 41
Survivor's Insurance (SI), 112, 113, 117
Suttles, Gerald D., 91, 183n
Sweet, Stephen, 4, 169n
Sweezy, Paul M., 104, 186n
Sylvester, Kathleen, 47, 176n

Tax Equity and Fiscal Responsibility
    Act (1982), 39

Tax Reform Act (1986), 36
Teninty, Ellen, 36, 174n
Tennessee Valley Authority (TVA), 23
Thernstrom, Stephen, 83, 182n
Thomas, Marc, 188n
Thornburgh, Richard,, 177n
Thornton, James, 93, 183n
Tienda, Marta, 131, 190n
Tiernan, Kip, 133
Titmus, Richard M., 117, 148, 187n, 193n
Toner, Robin, 157, 195n
Torres, Andrés, 130, 131, 145, 163, 190n, 193n, 196n
Torres, Esteban, 133
Townsend, Peter, 9, 13, 123, 147-48, 166, 169n, 170n, 193n
Truman administration, 24-25

Udesky, Laurie, 47-48, 176n
"underclass," 3, 6, 66, 85, 93, 94, 101, 104, 105, 112, 122, 123-32, 136, 144, 157, 164, 169n, 179n, 182n; see also: Glasgow, Douglas G.; Katz, Michael B.; Reed, Adolph, Jr.; Wilson, William J.
unemployment
among African Americans, 158;
change from manufacturing to service economy, 160;
during Roosevelt administration, 20;
insurance, 24, 113, 117;
in Massachusetts, 97
Urban Institute, 37, 74
Urban Renewal (Title I, Housing Act [1949]), 21

Valentine, Charles A., 88-89, 182n, 183n
Veterans Non-Service Pensions, 20
Vines, Kenneth, 173n
VISTA (Volunteers in Service to America), 28

Wagner, David, 143, 192n
Warner, Amos G., 110, 186n

Warren, Donald, 178n
Waxman, Chaim Isaac, 32, 80-81, 171n, 174n, 181n
Ways and Means Committee, U.S. House of Representatives, 6
Weaver, Robert C., 172n
Weinberg, Daniel H., 9, 28, 103, 117, 169n, 173n, 177n, 179n, 183n, 185n, 187n
Weir, Margaret, 152, 179n, 185n, 194n
Weiskopf, Thomas, 194n
Weiss, Peter, 123, 188n
Weitz, Judith, 180n
Welch, Susan, 2, 80, 101, 169n, 181n, 185n
welfare:
expenditures as percent of GNP, 22, 27, 28, 117-18;
dependency on, 110, 157;
in the U.S., 109-22;
Welfare Dependency Act (1992), 110
welfare policies:
"means tested" vs. "non-means tested," 113-18;
private sector support for, 150;
public attitudes toward, 1, 14, 24, 109, 110-12, 115, 120-22;
"targeted" groups, 23, 45, 46, 51, 144, 148, 150;
"universalism," 22-23, 45, 49, 113, 144, 148, 150, 151;
U.S. social welfare compared to systems in other countries, 147-55;
welfare state, 40, 148-52
West, Cornel, 89, 183n
West, Guida, 135, 191n, 192n
White, Sammie B., 188n
Wiewel, Wim, 90, 183n
Wilensky, Harold L., 148-49, 193n
Wilhelm, Sidney M., 130, 190n
Wilkins, Roger, 30, 173n, 184n
Williams, Brett, 95, 184n
Williams, Fiona, 137, 154, 191n, 194n, 195n
Williams, Franklin, 169n
Williams, Linda F., 135, 191n
Williams, Robin M., Jr., 63, 67, 84,

179n, 180n

Williamson, John B., 45, 48, 154, 176n, 195n

Wilson, Pete, 51

Wilson, William J., 22, 63, 88, 92, 94, 102, 103, 104, 129, 131, 172n, 178n, 182n, 183n, 184n, 185n, 186n, 189n, 196n

Wiseman, Michael, 3, 169n

Wiseman, Steven, 146, 193n

Withorn, Ann, 134, 135, 160, 165, 190n, 191n, 195n, 196n

Wocquaint, Lois J. O., 184n

Woodson, Robert L., 183n

Woody, Bette, 45-46, 105, 149, 150, 176n, 186n, 193n, 194n

Work Incentive Program (WIN), 28

"workfare," 42, 45, 48, 142

Works Projects Administration (1939): see Works Progress Administration

Works Progress Administration (WPA), 10, 20-21, 166, 170n

Wu, Jiping, 127, 169n, 189n

Zipp, John F., 188n

About the Author

JAMES JENNINGS is a professor of political science and the Director of the William Monroe Trotter Institute at the University of Massachusetts/Boston. He has lectured and published extensively on Black and Latino politics. Among his publications are *Puerto Rican Politics in Urban America* (Greenwood, 1984), and *Blacks, Latinos, and Asians in Urban America* (Praeger, 1994).

ISBN 0-275-94953-2

EAN

9 780275 949532

90000>

HARDCOVER BAR CODE